Gilbeys, Wine and Horses

Portrait of Sir Walter Gilbey Bt by Orchardson presented to him following the subscription of 1,234 people in recognition of his services to horse breeding.

Gilbeys, Wine and Horses

Jane Kidd

The Lutterworth Press

Cambridge

DEDICATED TO
SIR WALTER GILBEY, 1st BART.
AND
SIR HENRY WALTER GILBEY 2nd BART.

The Lutterworth Press
P.O. Box 60
Cambridge
CB1 2NT

British Library Cataloguing in Publication Data:
A catalogue record is available from the British Library.

ISBN 0 7188 2940 9

Copyright © Walter Anthony Gilbey 1997

Printed in Great Britain by
Redwood Books Ltd., Trowbridge, Wiltshire

Contents

Illustrations

The Family Tree on 30 June 1951

Acknowledgements

There are many people whom I would like to thank for their part in the production of this book: John Radcliffe, who initially collated my family archives; Wally Wright and his colleagues at the Bishop's Stortford and District Local History Society, who set up the Gilbey Archives and have provided invaluable help in checking and advising on the book, my long standing colleague and friend, Stanley Lee, whose wise counsel has been of great value as always, and all those who have read and commented on drafts of the book, including my wife, Jenifer, son, Walter Anthony, and daughter Caroline, and my office staff in the Isle of Man, Elaine Hadwin, Rosalind Edwards and Melanie Quayle.

Enormous thanks are due to my cousin Henry Gold for the vast amount of research work he has undertaken with Jack Gold and for his numerous excellent suggestions and ideas. Thanks are also due to my daughter, Sarah Gilbey, who has very efficiently and professionally edited and proofread the manuscript.

I am also most grateful to the Lutterworth Press and particularly Colin Lester, Adrian Brink and Teresine Milnes for publishing and distributing this book and for their excellent printing.

Above all, I deeply appreciate the years of work that my wife's and my long standing friend, Jane Kidd, has put into writing this book. She has fulfilled all the hopes that I had when I suggested that she was the ideal person to write it, due to her great knowledge and love of horses and the similar fate that has befallen her own family business, Beaverbrook Newspapers - her Grandfather was the great Lord Beaverbrook.

Jane and I have arranged that 10% of any profit from the book will go to each of the British Horse Foundation, the Dressage Supporter's Group, the London Harness Horse Parade and the Gilbey Archives.

Finally, I hope the example of my Grandfather will encourage future generations of Walter Gilbeys to ensure that the name of Gilbey once more rises like a phoenix from the ashes.

Walter Anthony Gilbey

Portrait of Sir Walter Gilbey Bt. in his later years by Frank O Salisbury RA., exhibited at the Royal Academy in 1916. (Reproduced by kind permission of Jack Gold.)

Prologue

It was a general holiday in the tiny village of Elsenham in Essex on 2 May 1911. Flags hung from the windows of the thirty odd small cottages that lined the main street and for much of the morning the church bells pealed merrily. All this was in honour of the 80th birthday of 'The guvn'r', that kindly, eccentric, but astute old gentleman, Sir Walter Gilbey.

The press were there to write about it, trying to find out the keys to his success, even down to what diet he used to keep himself healthy for so many years – a large number of onions. They wanted to know more about his past; for this delightful, eccentric epitome of a gentleman had lived right through the Victorian era and witnessed more changes than anyone from a previous generation. When he was born people travelled in carriages pulled by horses or even dogs (banned in London in 1839), yet by 1911 they were flying through the sky in aeroplanes.

So many people wanted to join in congratulating this popular figure that the postman had a busy day carrying bags full of letters and telegrams up the long, immaculately kept drive with wide grass verges to his home at Elsenham Hall. At the drive's end the rather austere red brick turreted house was softened by the presence of literally hundreds of family and friends.

The basis to Sir Walter's success had been his family. Together with two brothers, two brothers-in-law (Golds), two nephews (Blyths) and one cousin (Grinling), he had created the firm of W & A Gilbey and developed it into Britain's leading wine and spirit merchants. As one of the partners, and then its first Chairman, he had an annual income of £100,000, massive in those days, roughly equivalent to in excess of £5 million in the mid 1990s.

Remarkably, that same firm was run by those closely interconnected families long enough for them to enjoy the heady celebrations of a centenary. At the parties in 1957 one of the most talked about achievements during the past hundred years was that not one outsider had joined the Board, not one owned a voting share.

Yet just twenty years later the firm had been merged and taken over three times and not a single member of the family was still involved at Board level. It was the classic case of clogs to clogs in three generations – although clogs is a little extreme, for there are many Gilbeys, Golds, Blyths and Grinlings who still lead sterling lives. But they have lost the firm that had made them all rich and proud to have these names; they are no longer household names, nor have they done deeds which, like their forebears, are worthy of honour by the Queen.

On Sir Walter Gilbey's eightieth birthday the family could be said to be at the pinnacle of their influence, although 'plateau' would be more appropriate, for their heyday had lasted for a number of decades. The warning signs were beginning to accumulate, however. The fortune-makers of the

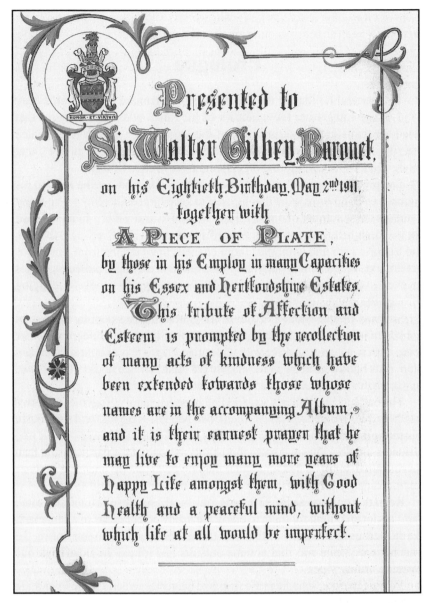

Presented to

Sir Walter Gilbey, Baronet,

on his Eightieth Birthday, May 2nd 1911,
together with
A PIECE OF PLATE,
by those in his Employ in many Capacities
on his Essex and Hertfordshire Estates.
This tribute of Affection and
Esteem is prompted by the recollection
of many acts of kindness which have
been extended towards those whose
names are in the accompanying Album,
and it is their earnest prayer that he
may live to enjoy many more years of
happy Life amongst them, with Good
health and a peaceful mind, without
which life at all would be imperfect.

2. Illuminated Address presented to Sir Walter Gilbey on his 80th Birthday

first generation had been quick to adapt and seize opportunities. The second
and third were born into a life of security and riches. They had more to lose
in taking gambles and were less willing to adjust to changes. They had joined
the 'establishment' and would never take the risks that had made their
forebears rich.

That day at Elsenham three of the original partners joined Sir Walter in
his celebrations. Two, like him, had been honoured for their contributions to
the country: the generous, quick-minded Sir James Blyth and the autocratic
yet considerate Sir Charles Gold; the former honoured for his contributions

to agriculture, the latter for politics (business success in the Victorian era was rarely seen as being a contribution worthy of honours). The third partner present was plain Henry Grinling, a cousin by marriage who did not have the flair of the others, but who had acted as an invaluable statistician in their enterprises.

Four of the original partners were dead: Sir Walter's brothers, Alfred and Henry Parry, his brother-in-law Henry Gold and his nephew Henry Blyth. Their absence had little effect on the numbers, however, as the original partners had produced sixty-five children between them, and by this date many of them had their own sons and daughters. The family of the firm of W. & A. Gilbey was massive and strongly ramified through frequent family parties and from some cousins marrying each other. There was, too, a marked tendency to live in houses along the eight-mile ride between Elsenham and Bishop's Stortford in Hertfordshire, so that an extended family atmosphere prevailed.

The 'family' was notable for its traditionalism and conformity and amongst them Sir Walter alone stood out for his picturesque appearance. He looked like a wicked, ageing 'dandy'; his few remaining locks of grey hair were greased and combed forward and in his right eye he sported a rimless monocle, which, if it had fallen (though it never did) would have been saved by the cord that went around his stiff high collar. There were still enough hairs above his lip to constitute a moustache and these had been carefully groomed into a slightly upturned shape.

His body was so thin and waif-like that his eccentric, expensively tailored clothes were not shown off to their best – the suit and waistcoat were of a russet colour and the shirt was frilled with a small white cambric tie. But these unusual clothes were not the only things to attract attention, for his hands were small, delicate and exquisitely manicured and his feet were extraordinarily tiny.

With this odd appearance it was quite startling to find that when he spoke he was not an outrageous extrovert, nor did he demand attention. His words were measured and very limited, emanating cool, quiet common sense. His manner was genial and unaffected and, although he was a friend of royalty, it was the ordinary person's respect he appeared to seek, both in conversation and with generous schemes to help the impoverished and the welfare of his neighbourhood.

It made him an intriguing character. He had an extraordinary combination of a racy appearance and an ordinary manner, in speech and behaviour.

Although this racy-looking character had plenty of money to spend, it did not go on high living and a fast life. He was a friend of the Prince of Wales, but he did not join the 'champagne' set. Instead Sir Walter concentrated his energies on improving the position of the horse; and yet again surprisingly not the racehorse, but the more common-or-garden carriage and riding horse. He played a major part in the battles to establish societies like the Shire Horse, Hackney Horse and Hunters Improvement, which celebrated their centenaries towards the end of the twentieth century. He started the Whit

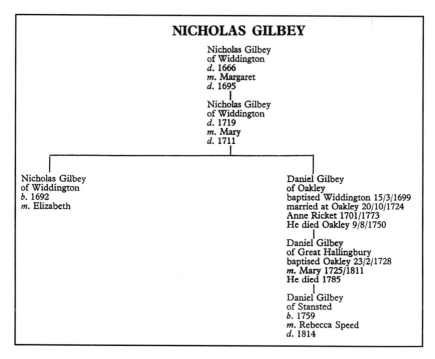

NICHOLAS GILBEY

Nicholas Gilbey
of Widdington
d. 1666
m. Margaret
d. 1695

Nicholas Gilbey
of Widdington
d. 1719
m. Mary
d. 1711

Nicholas Gilbey
of Widdington
b. 1692
m. Elizabeth

Daniel Gilbey
of Oakley
baptised Widdington 15/3/1699
married at Oakley 20/10/1724
Anne Ricket 1701/1773
He died Oakley 9/8/1750

Daniel Gilbey
of Great Hallingbury
baptised Oakley 23/2/1728
m. Mary 1725/1811
He died 1785

Daniel Gilbey
of Stansted
b. 1759
m. Rebecca Speed
d. 1814

A. The beginning, Nicholas Gilbey

Monday Carthorse Parade with the worthy aim of encouraging the horses of London to be kept in good condition. He enabled, too, thousands of pounds to be saved in imports by stimulating home breeding of horses. It was for these efforts that he was awarded a baronetcy and it is these societies that remain his memorials today.

For that special Birthday at Elsenham Hall one of the telegrams received read: 'The Secretaries of the Shire Horse, Hunters, Polo Ponies and Cart Horse Parades Societies, whose present success and influence owe so much to your fostering interest and support, tender respectful congratulations on the occasion of your birthday.'

In the afternoon family, friends, employees and tenants lined up to give him presents while he sat in splendour – with a characteristic touch of eccentricity – in his motor car outside the front door. The inscription on one of the presents, a gold mounted stick presented to him by his friends and neighbours in Elsenham, gives further insight into this extraordinary old man and explains the reason for the local public holiday: 'In recognition of his many kindly acts and never ceasing efforts to better the condition of those amongst whom he has dwelt for thirty-five years.'

A man who dressed so bizarrely, enjoyed eccentric touches and yet behaved so properly, who made himself a fortune by being, as he claimed a 'plodder', yet possessed unusual foresight in seeing where the fortune could be made, and why societies were needed to help the equestrian world, was a man full of contradictions and who stimulated questions as to his origins and upbringing.

I
The Origins

Walter Gilbey was born into a comfortably prosperous family on 2nd May, 1831. They had a big house with bay windows called The Links, which lies in the centre of Windhill in Hertfordshire's quaint old market town of Bishop's Stortford. The space was needed, for there were already six surviving children (two sons had died) and there was a constant flow of visitors to the house. Walter's father, Henry, was a great raconteur, a jovial round-faced figure who was a magnet for social gatherings. Henry's easy manner and enjoyment of company must have been nurtured by his upbringing, for he was the son of the innkeeper Daniel Gilbey, who ran the White Bear at Stansted. The Gilbey family had deep roots in the Bishop's Stortford area, traceable back well before the eighteenth century, when Daniel's father (1728-1785) was the Ranger of Hatfield Forest. Daniel acquired three inns in Stansted, including the White Bear, and was a Parish councillor and church warden.

Henry Gilbey was himself an innkeeper, running the Bell Inn at Stansted when he married Elizabeth Bailey in 1814. Elizabeth's mother, Harriet, was of a distinguished background, her sister Catherine being wife to the 1817 Lord Mayor of London, Christopher Smith.

Legend claims that Harriet had a dashing start to her married life, as she climbed down the ivy on the house where she was staying to run away with the gardener, William Bailey. The facts are that she did marry a gardener and he was called William Bailey, but the elopement remains an allegation, and nobody has verified whether her husband was gardener to Harriet's own family, the Churchs, or to her sister's, the Smiths.

The Stansted parish registers verifies William Bailey's occupation as a gardener when recording that his marriage to Harriet Church produced three sons and two daughters. The only surviving son, James Church Bailey (Walter Gilbey's uncle), made the first known connection with the wine trade, as he was employed, first, by his distinguished uncle in Smith Woodhouse & Co., a wine company, then he became a partner with Sebastian Smith, son of his aunt and uncle, in Smith Bailey & Co.. This company prospered from 1836 until 1842, when the partnership split and James Church Bailey continued running a firm under his own name.

Even more fanciful rumours exist about the origin of the Gilbeys, although possibly only arising because of gossip about Henry's background and attempts to explain Walter's unusual abilities and characteristics. In Henry's lifetime the Prince Regent showed him great kindness, even giving him a pair of horses. The small feet and hands of the Gilbeys, the rather extravagant, colourful tastes of Walter, his love of horses and of Brighton, were all features shared with the Prince Regent, and although probably coincidental, could

3. Henry Gilbey

have been the result of one of the nights the Prince Regent spent at a local inn on his frequent trips to and from Newmarket. There must have been many Royal visits, as Stansted was a convenient place to stay for those travelling between London and Newmarket: between 1788 and 1792 the Prince Regent's horses won for him more than 100 races. Who could say whether it was nine months after one of these visits that Henry was born?

Henry, Walter's father, was the first member of the Gilbeys to show the love of horses that was to become one of the family characteristics. He forsook the indoor life of pub-keeping for the tough and demanding occupation of coachman, taking the reins of a team of four horses to provide a fast means of transportation for those who could afford it. He timed it well, for a boom was on its way. The bodies of coaches were being sprung to make it possible to travel in them for longer distances. In 1818 John Macadam's idea of laying relatively small uniform stones to a depth of six inches as a road foundation was tried out and met with such success that the system spread rapidly to transform British roads from rutty, holey surfaces into smooth roads along which the newly sprung coaches could travel at twice the rate and double the comfort. One further improvement was made to bring about the Golden Age of Coaching (from 1825 to the late 1830s) and that was the reduction of 'stages' the distance each team of horses pulled the coach before a change – to twenty miles and then ten miles. This made it possible for coaches to cover the entire journey travelling at average speeds of about ten miles per hour, as, due to the shorter distances, the horses could be driven faster without exhausting them. Nor was it unusual for young gentlemen to tip the coachmen and urge him to get his horses to gallop at speeds of up to twenty miles per hour.

It seems likely that 'Old Harry Gilbey', as he was affectionately called, would have had plenty of young 'toffs' eager to experience the exhilaration and dangers of galloping a coach along the road, as he ran the route which Cambridge undergraduates took to London.

Starting as coachman to James Roger Bolton, whose father owned the Crown Inn at Hockerill on the Cambridge/Newmarket route, he went into partnership with William Low on the London, Bishop's Stortford, Cambridge, Newmarket route. Then in 1824 he set up on his own to run the coaches from Bishop's Stortford and Saffron Walden, through Epping Forest to the Bull Inn at Aldgate. This was a sixty mile round trip, which was completed in one day, and he frequently took the reins of his team of horses, which drew coaches containing many eminent persons. The coach was the principal means of transport and the only alternative was horseback or on foot.

These were exciting times for the coaching fraternity. Punctuality and speed were crucial in the battle for passengers. Inns at ten mile intervals would have a new team of horses waiting and the changeover was so quick that only the coachman disembarked for a quick thirst quencher, which was much needed to keep up his energy for his responsible and physically demanding task. Passengers knew the dangers of this form of travelling; horses would run away, coaches overturn and head on collisions were not infrequent, due to coachmen losing control of their four straining animals. Those who could drive fast and safely became much respected for their skills. They were usually great personalities with a wealth of anecdotes about occurrences en route. They were popular people and 'Old Harry Gilbey' was particularly famous after a great drive through one of the heaviest snowstorms ever recorded in Britain, on 26 December, 1836. A poem commemorates his feat of getting to London and back to the edge of town, before the coach could move no further and had to be abandoned.

Hold Fast; was the word, as the rugs were withdrawn
  From the backs of a good useful team,
And dull was the light of the lanterns that morn,
  For the falling snow thickened their gleam.
St Michael's proclaimed the hour to be five,
  When Gilbey adjusted the reins,
And prepared for a terrible coarse cold drive
  Long before the commencement of trains.

Chorus:

Then Hurrah for the Road, a good team and good whip,
  The greeting attached to the wayside 'nip',
And in memory drink, though they may have been slow,
  To the Old Stortford Coach days of Gilbey and Low.
The snow had been falling the whole night long;
  The roads were all covered so deep,

That only a team that was plucky and strong
　　Could stick to it where it was steep.
And in places all hands had to shoulder the wheel,
　　Which they did with an earnest good will;
Tis the noble true heart which for others can feel
　　That helps up a difficult hill.

Chorus:

So onward they tugged with a resolute mind,
　　For the cattle a strain and a pull,
Till London was reached a little behind
　　Their time at the famed 'Aldgate Bull'.
There was no better Inn for Sterling good cheer,
　　If you searched the Metropolis through;
So with appetite keen, forgetting past fear,
　　To breakfast, they all buckled to.

Chorus:

When business was done and the clock had struck four,
　　Ann Nelson's they left in good form;
All had faith in their pilot to battle once more
　　With the pitiless withering storm.
So forward they went, but wretchedly slow,
　　The horses were fretting in foam;
'Twas such frightful hard work to get through the snow
　　That they thought they would never reach home.

Chorus:

What a wild dreary night when they reached Buckhurst Hill,
　　To face that long Forest Road,
But there's mostly a way if there's only the will,
　　And pluck always lightens the load.
So they strove with their might, for their hearts were all right,
　　When they found the old coach sticking fast
They all lent a hand when they came to a stand,
　　And through many such dangers they passed.

Chorus:

Thus they tugged and they toiled as true Britons can;
　　What a help was that passenger power;
'Twas a struggle for horses as well as man
　　To keep moving at three miles an hour.
But they never lost nerve, so they pegged on their way
　　Till within a short mile of the town;
And 'The Old Stortford Coach' made a record that day
　　Which won for its Driver renown.

4. Bishops Stortford/London coach

HENRY GILBEY

of this Town many years Coach Proprietor

DIED SEPᴿ 29ᵀᴴ 1842

AGED 52 YEARS

WILLIAM J.C. GILBEY

SON OF THE ABOVE

DIED NOVᴿ 2ᴺᴰ 1847

AGED 20 YEARS

5. Gravestone

Henry Gilbey had a great life in that Golden Age of coaching, with many friends and a good income. He could not believe that this way of life would come to an end.

Although the first 'steam monster' began travelling down the tracks between Stockton and Darlington in 1824, even before the heyday of coaching, there was a lapse of some years before this revolutionary new form of transport was introduced on a wider scale. The next ran in 1830 over the thirty-one miles between Liverpool and Manchester. It was not much faster than the coach, travelling at fourteen miles per hour, but it was much stronger and more economical. Increasing numbers of

HOCKERILL.

6. Red Lion/ye olde Cock Tavern

people used it, opening the way to dramatic changes, with many more tracks being laid. The first major coach route to be superseded by the railway was that from London to Birmingham, in 1838. As railway lines were laid, more coaches found themselves uncompetitive and their business destroyed.

The end to Henry Gilbey's golden era came in 1839, when the Eastern Counties Railway to Chelmsford was opened. Henry had scoffed at the idea of competition from a rival that 'wouldn't even stop to pick up passengers' and he refused to adjust and consider new ways. When he did realise it was a threat, instead of adapting, he led rebellions and presided over a protest meeting at Bishop's Stortford.

There was no way to stop progress, however, and the Northern & Eastern railway reached Harlow in 1841 and Bishop's Stortford a year later. Henry Gilbey's resistance led only to financial disaster and to him being forced out of business. Perhaps the only good feature of this sad ending was that it taught his children the dangers of absolute conservatism and the need to anticipate change and adapt to it.

Even before Henry Gilbey's sad predicament, *The Times* in 1839 explained what was happening to coachmen:

Steam, James Watt and George Stephenson have a great deal to answer for. They will ruin the breed of horses, as they have already ruined innkeepers and the coachmen, many of whom have already been obliged to seek relief at the poor house, or have died in penury or want.

Henry Gilbey had ten surviving children aged between twenty-five and two, when the dwindling income from coaching finally became non-existent. They had all become used to the ease of a comfortable income. The only other way he knew of earning was as an innkeeper, so in 1841 he sold the Links at Bishop's Stortford and returned to being a publican at the Red Lion at Hockerill. However, inns were hit hard too by the end of coaching, so this change did little to keep his family in the manner to which they had been accustomed. The shock of such a sudden change of fortune and the ignominy of a vastly reduced income was too much for Henry and he died only a year later, on 29 September 1842. He was just fifty- two years of age.

The Gilbey family was penniless and young Walter was just eleven years old. His elder sisters hastened into marriage, the eldest, Caroline, having done so at the start of the troubles in 1839, to James Blyth, a provisions merchant in Chelmsford and Norwich. Harriet chose Arthur Nockolds, an auctioneer, in 1843; Emily married Jabez Thomas in 1846; and Julia wed Alfred Ellis, another auctioneer, in 1849. The weddings must have been high spots in what appears to have been a pretty sombre youth. Henry Parry was the only son old enough to provide any income to help the family in their straightened circumstances and he was just 18 at the time of his father's death.

There were still more children, younger than Walter: another brother, Alfred, two years his junior and two more sisters, Charlotte and Fanny, who was the baby of the family, being only two years old when her father died.

Henry Parry Gilbey had had a good start to his life and when circumstances had begun to deteriorate, his great uncle, Christopher Smith, had been instrumental in getting him a coveted place as a scholar at Christ's Hospital. This unique school with a reputation for scholarship took great pride in maintaining traditions. The uniform and ceremonies were then still the same as when it was founded by King Edward VI as a school to educate poor boys and girls. Admission was – and still is – given to bright children of parents in need of assistance, with fees being proportional to income.

Henry Parry was very proud of being a 'Blue', the name given to Christ's Hospital scholars, and was later to become a governor of the school. He left school the year the railways came to the east of England and, at just fifteen, joined the firm Smith, Bailey and Co., the partnership being run by his uncle, James Church Bailey together with Christopher Smith's son. The firm was one of Britain's major shippers of the popular nineteenth century drink of port. Since it was based in Cheapside, London, little was seen of Henry Parry at the family home in Bishop's Stortford.

The eldest Gilbey was a source of pride to his poor widowed mother, but she had nine further children in her care. They depended on such bonuses as were granted to fatherless children from the Drapers Company, which enabled

7. Christopher Smith

Walter to stay at school two years after his father died. As soon as they reached their teens they had to face up to their livelihood depending on their own exertions. Even when Walter was still a schoolboy, most of his free time was spent earning extra pennies, but also gaining useful knowledge in the art of buying and selling, as he helped his brother-in-law, James Blyth, at his shop in Chelmsford.

Walter began his education at a private school, but with the change in circumstances was transferred to the Grammar School in Chelmsford. Neither school brought him much happiness or inspiration. These times were so unhappy that Walter tried to blot them out of his memories and in later life was able to recall little about them. One of his few comments about this time was: 'My schooldays were beastly. I can remember nothing other than always being dragged around by the scruff of the neck.'[1]

Walter was delighted when he was allowed to finish school and start earning a living, although it was less than a pound a week. He was just thirteen when he became an office boy in the Tring Estate Agency run by his cousin, John Gilbey Glenister. A good part of John Gilbey Glenister's work was surveying land for acquisition by the railway companies and Walter would, ironically, have participated in this work for the very business which had ruined his father. He did not find his duties very satisfying until they started to include some driving of carriages and riding to collect information at various estates such as Tring Park. The highlight of his year was to attend the Tring Horse and Cattle Show. (His grandson, Walter Anthony, competes at Tring Horse Show over 150 years later.) The reason he found these visits so stimulating was that they brought him into contact with horses which were, he later said: 'the joy of my life. To this day I cannot understand how as a youngster I did not apprentice myself to a horse dealer or a circus proprietor, or at least in some way become connected with the care and management of horses.'[2]

Apart from these occasional interludes with horses, the work was very dull and tedious to this teenager, who had a touch of flamboyance and a taste for the unusual. He also, however, had a strong sense of duty and great loyalty to his family, who were brought even closer together in their efforts to simply keep existing. One elder brother, William, died when Walter was sixteen, giving him even more responsibility and keeping him tied to a job he disliked almost as much as school.

He stayed there for six years, but at the age of 19 his sense of adventure got the better of him, and, reinforced by the assurance that his mother's position was improving, with fewer children dependent on her, he headed up to London and, with his brother Alfred, stayed with their elder brother, Henry Parry. There he became a clerk to Mr Walmesley in a firm of Parliamentary solicitors, with offices within the House of Lords. Walter's role was rather minor and certainly not political. He was a 'barker', who was supposed to greet those coming into the office, and the political element (with a small 'p') was to decide who was important, 'barking' at those of little consequence, but being very polite to those who, as Walter said: 'might return my bark with a bite'.[3]

For the first time there is a note of excitement, of youthful high spirits, in Walter's recollections. He was stimulated by his surroundings, his place of work and the bustle of the City of Westminster. He roamed the streets of London taking in this colourful atmosphere which was a contrast to what he felt then was: 'the monotonous quiet of the country'.[4] A delightful letter from Walter, to his brother Alfred, who was spending Christmas at Bishop's Stortford, and dated 29 December 1851, indicates his enjoyment of life at that time. It describes a party given the previous evening at 27, Surrey Street, Strand, where his sister Emily Thomas kept a lodging house. The 'Wigmore Street young ladies' – nine of them, mentioned elsewhere in family correspondence at the time – attended with ten other friends and relations: 'what I should term a select party', reported Walter, 'cards till ten, then dancing which lasted till half past twelve, then supper which was served up in fine style – I will just give you an outline – Roast beef, Turkey, etc. etc., plum pudding, mince pies, tarts of all descriptions, custards, etc. etc. After supper, singing, spouting, kissing and lots more amusing tricks too numerous to mention on paper. We kept the game alive merrily until very nearly four o'clock, when they all departed.' Two street musicians had been hired at 5 shillings per head for the evening. One became 'rather in a state of beer' and 'fell ass over head going down stairs'. On his taking final leave 'he insisted on shaking hands with all the Gentlemen which made things look rather small but taking one thing with another the party went off admirably.'

A further assumption that can be made about Walter's time at the House of Lords is that it would have given him the opportunity to observe the manners and bearing of the highest in the land at close quarters. In later life his own courtesy and good manners were often remarked upon. After being shown around Blenheim Palace, when a guest there, his guide described him as 'a great gentleman'. The early example of party-giving described above is a fore runner of his later, much exercised skills in hospitality.

It was a stimulating time to come to London, for this was a period of enormous growth and transition. More and more people were finding work in the cities rather than on the land, so the population was becoming urbanised, both in residence – more than half the population lived in towns by the 50s – and in distribution of power – the landed gentry losing their domination in favour of the more numerous and financially stronger city dwellers.

In the 1840s this transfer to the cities had put pressure on resources, created new unsatisfied demands and led to much hardship. Known as 'the Hungry Forties', this was the period of the potato famine in Ireland, the decade when Walter was also fighting to make ends meet.

In London, many of those who had moved to the city lived in dreadful slums, with as many as four families to a room and little concern for cleanliness. Cholera reached England in 1831, killing 18,000 people. A second cholera outbreak in 1848 killed even more – 54,000. Alongside the devastating effect of so many deaths, basically due to a lack of hygiene, was the growth in a number of working class movements (e.g. the Chartists, Trade Unions and Co-operatives). The working classes were showing their growing power by demanding better conditions and improved 'rights'. Improvements were made, the importance of hygiene was recognised and by the time Walter came to London in 1850, the city was being cleaned up and beginning to smell of prosperity (at least away from the slums).

The free trade era was under way – the Corn Laws had been repealed in 1846, removing duties on imported corn in order to make food cheaper and more available for the city dwellers. The railways were opening up and linking the country, telegraph lines were making quick communication feasible and steam ships were providing a faster and more economical means of bringing in raw materials and taking away manufactured goods.

Walter was in London for the Great Exhibition of 1851, which was a symbol of Britain's growing prosperity. Britain had got so far ahead of her rivals in terms of industrialisation that she had no real competitors in supplying the world with manufactured goods. It was not until the 1870s that both America and Germany came into the picture; America, largely because of her enormous natural resources and Germany because of the sound scientific and technical education given to her people.

The 1850s and 1860s were an ideal era for an ambitious young man to make his fortune and Walter, after the tragedy of his father's last years and a penny pinching upbringing, was soon to prove that he was not one to let these opportunities slip by. His elder brother, Henry Parry, was already showing the way, having moved on from the security of working for his uncle's firm to establish his own wine merchants, Southard Gilbey & Co., in Crutched Friars. Walter and his younger brother Alfred were, for the first time, enjoying the freedom of being able to spend some money.

London had another attraction. More than a quarter of a million horses were housed within its precincts, about the same as Britain's entire equine population 100 years later. The railway did not begin to supersede the horse in the cities until the coming of the Underground in the 1860s. Walter saw that many of those quarter of a million horses were ill treated, ill fed, or at best had such a hard job that their working life was very short. The state of London's horses direly affected him and, when he had the funds in later life, he was to do as much as anybody ever has done to improve the horses' welfare.

Horses were needed everywhere. They pulled the less well to do in omnibuses, with room for twenty-two seated passengers and a conductor who had to hold onto a strap to keep himself steady on his special step. It was a rough ride, as many of the streets and centres, like Regent Circus and Oxford Circus, were cobbled: only the major thoroughfares were macadam. The tram horses had a smoother pull, with the trams themselves running on rails, but the load was heavier as there were even more passengers. The cab horses had the lightest loads, being driven as singles or pairs to the two-wheeled Hansom Cabs and the four wheeled Clarence Cabs, but they had to work six days a week and cover up to forty miles a day. It was a very hard career to pull the ladies and gentlemen around London's rough cobbled streets and few horses could stand more than three or four years of this work. The massive heavy horses that pulled the goods vehicles had a better time. Speed was not so crucial in the collection of refuse, coal and beer as when transporting men and women. By taking their time there was less strain, but theirs was still an unenviable life.

This massive number of horses needed massive numbers of stables and the city was full of yards, which have been converted into the mews houses of today. Walter was a frequent visitor to the horses' stables, the places where they could rest and recover for the next day's work and where horses were hired out for riding. Here he used to talk his way into getting rides. 'It was wonderful how a genuine love for horses will soften a livery stable keeper,' he reflected later.[5]

Life was fun, interesting and stimulating. Walter's narrow, dull, penny

8. *Crimea War, British Hospital at Renkioi*

pinching childhood was behind him and he was breaking out, showing signs of the flamboyance that was to distinguish his outward appearance in later years. In his memoirs he said: 'I was 22 years of age and no end of a dog in my opinion'[6] and like other adventurous minded young Englishmen he wanted to serve his country when England stumbled into war with Russia.

The spirit of patriotism ran high after forty years of peace. The general public wanted the government to help the poor defenceless Turks against the territory-seeking Russians and they feared that if Russia's aggressive tactics were not stopped at an early stage they could be directed against Britain herself. Czar Nicholas I might have had some justification for sending his troops in to protect Christian interests in the disintegrating Turkish Empire, but success would give him a dangerously powerful position in the Mediterranean. Hence, when his troops in 1853 invaded Wallachia and Moldavia (now Romania), Britain and France leapt to the support of the Turkish Sultan and sent their men in to retake these two Danubian provinces. That aim was achieved quickly and with few losses, but the next step was much less well justified and led to unnecessary suffering and loss of prestige. The allies decided to cripple Russian power in the area around Sebastopol, the main Russian naval base on the Black Sea. At first it was thought of as a glamorous and righteous project and young Englishmen clamoured to head off to the Crimea.

Walter was no exception; he concentrated his energies into getting to the war, but realised that if he joined the army it would probably have been over by the time he had sufficient training. Instead, he engineered an introduction to Sir Benjamin Hawes, an official at the War Office, and he used all his tenacity and persistence to inveigle his way to the Crimea: 'We badgered him until he gave us permission to go to the front'.[7] The role he was given was not glamorous. He became a civilian clerk attached to the Pay Department and saw no fighting, being based at the Convalescent Hospital of Renkioi on the Asiatic shores of the Dardanelles. He did see plenty of suffering, however, and hopeless inefficiency.

The voyage out was a nightmare because of the huge numbers accommodated in the ship and the lack of organisation which created chaos whenever there was the slightest problem. Walter's stomach rebelled against the rough seas, making it even harder to bear. The memories of that trip 'I would like to blot out from the tablets of my mind but are ever present in my waking dreams.'[8]

He soon began to realise that, far from being on a chivalrous escapade, he was in the midst of a dreadful bumbling attempt at war. What disillusionment – to have been inspired by patriotism to help his country and then to find that the enemy (Russia) was a much less serious foe than the dreadful inefficiency, which even deteriorated at times into corruption.

In the Crimea, he said: 'there was no such thing as a properly organised Army Medical Staff'.[9] There was a complete breakdown of medical and commissariat arrangements and this induced Mr (afterwards Sir) William Russell, the famous Times correspondent, to write the series of scathing letters that disturbed the English and about which Walter commented: 'to the justifiable severity of which I can add nothing'.[10]

For two years he lived two hundred yards from the waters of the Dardanelles, which at that point, close to Renkioi, were five miles wide. He was some distance from the real war and the field hospitals where Florence Nightingale did so much to improve their horrifying conditions. Walter's responsibilities lay with the convalescent hospital and, although he saw some harrowing cases and endured much hardship, it must have helped him to withstand the appalling conditions knowing that elsewhere everything was so much worse. In that first Crimean winter of 1854-55 cholera, scurvy, dysentery and fever were such common hazards that the numbers of those suffering from them, when added to the wounded, meant there were more troops in the hospitals than outside them.

Walter was at least able to share his experiences, as his younger brother Alfred worked with him. They shared premises, a cubicle in a large wooden hut which housed the medical and nursing staff for the hospital. His cousin, Henry Grinling, had also engineered a job in the Crimea and was based nearby as secretary to Dr. E.A. Parkes, head of the British Civil Hospitals in the East.

Conditions and administration did improve following the arousal of public opinion and the government, largely through Russell's reports in *The Times* and Florence Nightingale's single-minded determination. Then Sebastopol was stormed and taken in September 1855 and the Treaty of Paris brought peace in March 1856.

Walter did not return home until June 1856, so the latter part of his stay began to be mixed with an increasing amount of fun. Walter's accounts in his diary left no descriptions of the hardships, other than that they existed, but there is quite a bit of information about entertainments.

Much of Walter's spare time was spent on his new found passion of cribbage: 'I so enjoyed cribbage that I used to swop my rations of rum with the soldiers for candles, so that I might sit up all night to play my favourite game'.[11] The fortunate result of this was that he won enough money to nurture his other passion – horses. The very first horse he owned was bought with money won at cribbage.

There was time in the afternoon to go for rides and, on occasional expeditions, shooting woodcock and duck. Although they did not have to face the enemy on these expeditions, there was some danger, for he describes in his diaries how one of his mounted companions, a Mr Fox, damaged his foot and had to have a treatment of twelve leeches to make him sound again.

Towards the end of their term in the Crimea they organised a hunt, the first Renkioi Hunt, which took place on 26 January 1856 about two miles from the camp. The trail was paper rather than live quarry and Walter was pleased as he kept second the whole way: 'over hedge and ditch, my little Pluckey never refused a fence, a remarkably jolly afternoon'.[12] Later the hunt took to chasing jackals.

The equestrian activities became more ambitious. Walter wagered half a sovereign in a match and, as his own horse was not fast enough, he procured the ride on his friend Ram's horse. His adversary was another friend, Malcouroumre on his black horse, and the distance of the race was one and a quarter miles between Turrentene and Frenchman's Grave. In a neck and neck finish, Walter was the loser by a mere half a head. He said: 'there was quite a party then'.[13]

The stress of being at war was alleviated quite frequently by parties. On New Year's Day of 1855 there was a ball and Walter remarked that: 'the tickets at £1.13s each were very reasonable for the style the affair was managed in'.[14] There did not even seem to be a shortage of ladies, with some wives, many nurses and local Greek residents.

They often joined in the local social scene. Walter went to a Greek marriage: 'had some wine – saw the dancing – gave the bride a shell – she kissed my hand'. He celebrated the Greek New Year too: 'music – dancing – some very pretty girls dancing', but sadly he goes on to say: 'they were remarkably shy'.[15]

Walter's recollections in his diary are exemplary epistles of Victorian principles and do not expose any emotion. There are no indications of romantic attractions and little colour, just the facts. The frequent mention of ladies shows that he did enjoy their company, although the closest he got to an adventure was when he: 'saw some ladies on the hills – got a glass and found them to be Miss Guisdale and Mrs Newman [lady nurses] waving their handkerchiefs walked up with Mac – [a friend] – took some bacca – sat down and had chat till past five'.[16]

It seems likely he was already romantically attached, for letters received and sent were noted in his diary and included correspondence with Ellen, his future wife. She was the only non-family person mentioned.

Walter grew to love the life and climate of the Crimea. On 13 January 1856, he noted: 'it was as warm as the hottest day in England – bathed at 12.30'. Then the following day: 'Never more surprised in my life to find a deep snow on the ground – bitterly cold – a difference of 36 degrees in twenty four hours'. The snowy day was a freak; for the most part the climate was good enough for bathing, for excursions on horseback and picnics in the beautiful countryside. Walter's stiff-upper-lip, take-it-in-his-stride attitude to the exciting life he was leading only very occasionally broke down to show a trifle of emotion . When a long ride took them to the foot of the high mountain of Athos he wrote: 'the beauty of the evening surpassed all description – the rich glowing tints of the setting sun behind the European mountains'.[17] He must have been a little intoxicated by the freedom and the fun with the horses and the ease of life, especially after his narrow, penniless upbringing. He seriously thought of settling there as a farmer.

A good life it might have been, but Walter had other interests as there was growing evidence that he was good at making money. Not content with his role as a pay clerk, he and his brother Alfred had discovered a market and had imported the goods to satisfy it. Their elder brother, Henry Parry in

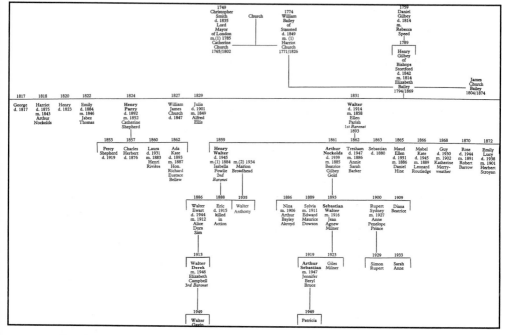

Family Tree – The Gilbeys, part 1

England, received from them requests for wine and second-hand saddles and bridles. Henry Parry arranged their shipment and Alfred and Walter did the selling.

The brothers' enterprising efforts aroused some jealousy and a certain Captain, who was never named but frequently referred to as 'the old devil',[18] demanded that their superior, Major Chads, should report them to General Norkes. The Major avoided the problem the first time it was raised by writing to their cousin's superior Dr. Parkes, but the Captain persisted (in Walter's diaries he then became 'the infernal old devil').[19] The Major was obviously on their side, as were all their colleagues who enjoyed drinking the products of their enterprise. It was suggested that they themselves write to the General explaining the situation. That seemed to have ended the matter, but it also ended their commercial enterprise and the accumulation of their first small profits.

Their entrepreneurial talents were not to be frustrated for long, as on 26 April 1856 they received the first instructions for the breaking up of the camp. On 2nd May, 1856 Walter celebrated his twentieth-fifth birthday and was obviously conscious of time passing without much being achieved, as in reference to his new age, he said: 'I wish it to be thought to be under'.[20]

Another month passed before the break up became official on Friday 13th June and then there were plenty of celebrations at the prospect of returning home. There were the final long rides, including one to Illium Novum (New Troy): 'a long ride – back by 8 galloped all the way back full pace'. There were some good feasts: 'did a couple bottles claret', 'roly poly pudding –

very nice' and there were luxuries: 'had Turkish bath with Rams which occupied two hours'.[21]

Finally, Walter had to sell the horses which had helped him explore the country on rides, expeditions, hunts and races. He was bid £8.10s for two but held out for £9, which he got the next day, though it did include the saddles. He then spent all this capital and a further £8.10s on presents.

The trip home 'was not quite so awful as the first' and it was enlivened, too, by good company. Walter's experiences in the hospital gave him a good means of communication with the medical profession. This helped him on this voyage to start a friendship with the famous surgeon, Sir Thomas Wells, Bart., which lasted until the latter's death in 1897.

Walter returned home with his younger brother, still penniless but much more prepared to recognise and snatch all opportunities that were offered to him. His outlook had been broadened by his close experiences of war and first hand experience of being amongst the Greeks and reminders of their ancient civilisation. He had pursued his passion for riding, had discovered the excitements of gambling on cards and found that he could make money out of the troops' and medical staffs' liking for inexpensive wines. He had discovered the pleasures of balls, owning horses, drinking wine and gambling, and was no longer content to be a clerk. He was ready to gamble with his future and he and Alfred had nothing to lose by doing so, for, as he said in the unpublished manuscript 'In the Days of My Youth': 'We returned to London with the proverbial half crown in our pockets and immediately started to look round for something to do'.

II
The Making of a Fortune

The two young brothers, Walter and Alfred Gilbey, who landed in England in July 1856 had had their ambitions stirred at the right time. The demands for reform, the reforms themselves, the population move from the country to the town and the difficult economic situation had disturbed the 1830s and 1840s, but had paved the way for the boom of the following decades. This was the time to make fortunes: England was the workshop of the world. Her goods were being sold all over the world and the sellers could afford to buy the luxuries that went with success.

Walter recognised the fortuity of timing in his speech at a banquet to honour his baronetcy: 'I do not think I am blessed with genius beyond the genius of my brother townsmen, but there is a time in the affairs of man that if he takes them at the tide he brings them to success'.

The tide they decided to run was a sensible one – the wine trade. This was the trade with which they now had most connections. Their grandfather Daniel Gilbey had kept 'The Old Bell' at Stansted (although the wine served there was likely to have been the 'English wine' of beer). Their great uncle, Henry Parry's benefactor, Christopher Smith, had become a wine merchant back in 1775 and had established his own firm Smith, Bailey & Co. by 1784. It was this same firm that Henry Parry had joined before going on to set up his own business of Southard Gilbey, where he had employed Alfred for a short spell prior to his Crimean adventure.

Walter's and Alfred's brother-in-law, James Blyth, was in the retail grocery business and his son James had entered the wine business at 14 years of age, during the time the uncles were away at the Crimean War.

The choice must have been almost inevitable, with such a clan of wine interests and especially as the two brothers had already enjoyed the sweet taste of profits accrued by selling wine to the troops and medical staff in the Crimea.

What was not so inevitable was the direction they chose for their new firm. They did not focus on the established market for the sweet heavy wines – ports, sherries and madeiras. Nor did they try to compete with those who supplied the rich with their normal beverage of champagne. The Gilbeys were not snobs. Their connections and sympathies were with the ordinary British people and in the Crimea they had found that the ordinary person, the normal working class soldier, liked wine as much as beer. They aimed at the mass market by selling their product at modest prices.

French wines did not come into this category as, since the Methuen Treaty of 1703, a massive duty had been levied on them by the British in an attempt to destroy the French wine trade. In 1857 the duty was still twelve shillings a case, which restricted French wine drinking in England to the rich and the trade to a quarter of a million gallons a year.

On the other hand trade with the Colonies was being promoted. Duties were half those on French wines and Henry Parry suggested Cape wines as the product for the brothers to concentrate on. Their sixteen year old nephew, James Blyth, already had experience in this field, as it was the area in which the wine company that he worked for specialised. He gave further reassurance as to the opportunities.

The selling point of the Cape wine was its cheapness and the Gilbeys aimed to maximise this attraction by having a low profit margin, relying on a big turnover, and standardising the products rather than adjusting to individual idiosyncrasies. They became the pioneers of low priced wines, supplying a new class of wine drinker ready to be encouraged into buying.

The encouragement was another important aspect of the success story, for they spent heavily on advertising, appealing directly to the customer. They advertised in national and local newspapers and in magazines like the *Illustrated London News*. This was Walter's special domain. With his flair for the unusual, his touch of flamboyance and his awareness of people's needs, he had the credentials to be a first class advertising agent.

Henry Parry's sound knowledge and experience of the trade, Alfred's business sense and Walter's flair combined to give the W&A Gilbey partnership one of the most meteoric successes of any business. The first premises were opened, in cellars in Berwick Street, which runs between Oxford Street and Soho, in February 1857. Advertisements were soon placed in newspapers throughout the country, offering Cape Port and Sherry at twenty shillings per dozen, Universal Brandy at thirty shillings and samples for twelve one penny stamps.

Circulars were another means chosen to appeal to the less wealthy public, but a lack of directories made it difficult to find the potential customers to whom to send them. The brothers surmounted this difficulty by sending local postmasters some fifty hand bills each, with the request to address them to leading local people and enclosing stamps and remuneration. This approach was one of the ways that helped W&A Gilbey build up a base of twenty thousand customers within just a few months. The yields from this operation were high as they were free from the restrictions on today's commercial enterprise. Income tax was one per cent and, with no Company Taxation, 99% of the profits could be ploughed back and there were few official regulations.

The first few desperate months of finding the capital, mostly from brother Henry Parry, and living on less than a pound a week, were soon behind them. For two years Walter, true to his Victorian upbringing, 'recognised the principle of economy was of the first importance and my private expenditure did not exceed £200'.[1] The long hours of work continued for much longer than the shortage of money. Walter claims to have been in the office for an average of ten hours every working day and to not have taken a day off for the first ten years of the business.

Help was needed and there was plenty within the family, many of whom had the qualifications to contribute towards the making of a fortune. The first to come in was Henry Gold, who was wooing Walter's sister, Charlotte (he married her in 1858). Walter was likely to have been the match maker and probably introduced them. He had made friends with Henry and his brother Charles during his times as a 'Barker' at the House of Lords when the Gold brothers were clerks in their uncle's firm of law stationers which had printed Parliamentary reports. The two families had suffered unfortunate common experiences, as the Golds had suffered a financial disaster like the Gilbeys. Their grandfather, John (who, with his son Michael, the father of Henry and Charles, was the latest in a line of prosperous ironmongers and manufacturers from Birmingham), had been ruined when a partner defrauded him and he stoically refused to prosecute, as he knew the penalty was transportation.

Henry Gold, an affable, kindly person, was first taken on as a salesman, but it was soon recognised that he had a useful legal bent, developed during his days as a law stationer. He helped to keep the peace both in dealing with legal matters and in calming the more excitable partners.

A few months later Alfred's and Walter's nephew, fourteen year old Henry Blyth, joined them. He had a quick brain and was good at figures, so he took charge of the books and very soon the finances. He proved to be a good organiser – strict, but respected for it, especially as he was so kind-hearted.

Henry Blyth's elder brother, James, saw that his uncles were selling Cape wines more successfully than the company he worked for, so he moved over in 1858. At just seventeen years of age his role was purchasing and he remained the firm's principal buyer until retirement, showing a great flair as a wine taster. In character he was strong minded and very hard working and expected others to be equally thorough.

The Golds and the Gilbeys proved to be exceptionally compatible. Henry Gold's younger brother, Charles, joined the firm in 1858 and one year later, like his brother before him, married a Gilbey girl, this time Walter's youngest sister Fanny.

The Golds were sent off with their newly acquired wives as spearheads to the expansion of the company, Henry opening a branch in Dublin in 1858 and Charles doing the same in Edinburgh in 1859. This quick response to demand for wines from Ireland and Scotland was risky and needed a little of the daredevil spirit for such swift expansion. That the spirit was found went a long way to ensuing the success of W&A Gilbey. This enterprise may be linked to the youth of the administrators. They were all under thirty; the Blyths being in their teens, the Golds in their early twenties and the Gilbeys their late twenties.

They all had a great capacity for hard work, but seem to have found time for courting. The Gold brothers were not the only ones in action in this field. Walter had written to a certain Ellen when in the Crimea and: 'Within a year of starting the firm, I was in position to marry'.[2] Ellen Parish from Bishop's

9. *Ellen Gilbey*

10. *Elizabeth Gilbey*

Stortford, the town where he was born, was the fourth daughter of an inn keeper, John Parish and his wife Marie. Walter and Ellen were married on November 3rd, 1858 at the parish church of St. James, Westminster.

Alfred too joined the trend and married Agnes Crosbie in the same year, 1858. Mrs Elizabeth Gilbey's desperate struggle to bring up her children was over. In one year two sons and a daughter had started their own homes and one year later her last daughter did so. Not only had she lost her responsibilities, but she was also secure and a senior figure amongst a large family which was making itself a great deal of money. She enjoyed the rewards of her struggles in the following decade, before her death in 1869.

Business was expanding so fast that the cellars in Berwick Street were no longer large enough to accommodate it. Premises at 357 Oxford Street were taken on, together with cellars in the Princess Theatre opposite. Even

11. The Stores, Great Titchfield Street

12. Gladstone and Sir Walter Gilbey in a cartoon by A. B.

these were quickly outgrown and in 1860, just three years after starting operations, the cellars, packing and forwarding departments moved to Great Titchfield Street.

W&A Gilbey were making money fast by providing a good product to a new group of consumers, using two novel features in the wine business: keeping the price low and using national advertising. Then the bombshell hit. Cobden, leader of the Free Traders, negotiated a treaty with France, removing duties on almost all goods. The terms were incorporated in Gladstone's famous budget of 1860, turning Britain into a Free Trading nation. Bismarck put it well: 'Free Trade is the weapon of the strongest nation'; and the firm of W&A Gilbey, which had benefited from this economic strength in finding a good market for their products, was now struck down by the country being strong enough to lift more restrictions and establish virtual free trade. The duty on French wines was reduced from twelve shillings to two shillings a dozen. There was no imperial preference on Cape wines, so the French wines were now competitive with them. Cape wines had lost their advantage and W&A Gilbey the source of their profits.

For Walter and Alfred it must have brought back the memories of childhood, when the railway had steamed ahead to drastically reduce their father's income from coaching. His sons had been brought up with the consequences of their father's inflexibility in the face of change, but they were ten years younger when this similar blow struck. Instead of carrying on with the same methods that had led to their astronomical growth and accepting that the advantage had now been cancelled out, they seized the initiative and took such a bold step that it left their competitors standing and turned them into the largest wine merchants in Britain.

REDUCTION OF THE WINE DUTIES.

W. & A. GILBEY, Wine, Spirit, and Liqueur Importers and Distillers, are now doing by far the largest Trade of any other house in the kingdom, their connection exceeding at the present time 16 000 private families and more than 60 of the most important Hospitals, Military Messes, and Public Institutions, beg to offer the following advantages to consumers on the reduced duties lately fixed by the Chancellor of the Exchequer.

WINES FROM THE CAPE OF GOOD HOPE.

PORT, SHERRY, MADEIRA, MARSALA, all first growths, 20s. per dozen, £3 6s 6d. per 7-gallon cask, £6 11s 3d. per 14-gallon cask, and £12 19s. per quarter cask of 28 gallons.

Also first growths with age 24s. per dozen, £4 0s 6d. per 7 gallon cask, £7 19s. 3d. per 14 gallon cask, £15 15s., per 28 gallon cask.

They are pure, delicate, wholesome, and in every way suitable for either dinner or dessert.

The exclusive use of these Wines in most of the important institutions, of which a List can be had, is a sure proof of their restorative qualities.

The Custom House returns for 1859 show that W. & A. G. paid duty on the unprecedented quantity of 73,434 gallons of these Wines alone in that year.

WINES FROM FRANCE AT THE REDUCED DUTIES.

CLARETS, VIN ORDINAIRE, 18s. and 24s. per dozen; and White Wines CHABLIS and SAUTERNE, 18s. and 24s. per dozen.

These, our leading importations, are superior to those generally drank in this country, and together with our other high-class French Wines, of which full particulars are detailed in our Prices Current, are all shipped to us under the superintendence of one of the leading Bordeaux Houses.

CHAMPAGNE AT THE REDUCED DUTY.

CHAMPAGNE 33s per dozen Quarts, and 18s. per dozen Pints.

A most superior sparkling Wine. Since the reduction of the duties, we have made a large contract to have the above Wines shipped direct from the Epernay vineyards. We consider it as good as any gentleman can wish to have on his table.

WINES FROM MARSALA AT THE REDUCED DUTIES.

MARSALA 20s. per dozen, £3 6s 6d. per 7-gallon cask, and £6 11s. 3d. per 14-gallon cask, and £10 3s. 6d. per quarter cask of 22 gallons.

This is Ingham, Stephens, & Co.'s superior old Bronte Wine, and is considered by many superior to the finest Sherries.

WINES FROM SPAIN AT THE REDUCED DUTIES.

SHERRIES, Pale and Golden, 26s. per dozen, £4 7s. 6d. per cask of 7 gallons, £8 13s 3d. per cask of 14 gallons, and £17 3s. per cask of 28 gallons.

The almost total disappearance of the Vine Disease, combined with the reduction of the duties enables us to import an extremely good Dinner Wine at this price.

WINES FROM PORTUGAL AT THE REDUCED DUTIES.

Fine old PORT from the wood, 8 years old, 28s. per dozen, £5 1s. 6d. per cask of 7 gallons, £10 1s. 3d. per cask of 14 gallons, and £19 19s per cask of 28 gallons.

This, our leading article from Oporto, is the old school of mature silky Port from the wood with body and bouquet. This is more palatable and wholesome than those extremely high-priced old Bottled Wines, which have nothing left to recommend them but vegetable decay.

Other Ports of various ages, both duty paid and in the docks.

FOREIGN AND BRITISH SPIRITS AT THE REDUCED DUTIES.

BRANDY, the finest Cognac,	..	..	20s. per gallon.
Do. very old	..	..	24s. "
RUM, finest Jamaica,	..	..	14s. "
WHISKY, Pure Old Scotch,	..	..	16s. "
Do. Pure Old Irish,	..	..	16s. "
GIN, excellent Household,	..	..	9s. "
HOLLANDS, Geneva or Schiedam, "the Silver Stream," as imported,			12s. "
Do. do. in the original green Cases and square Bottles as imported,			28s. per dozen.

In consequence of the universal consumption of Spirits, we have devoted especial care and attention to this branch of the trade, in selecting the only of a pure and genuine high character, and are reserved to maintain the reputation we enjoy throughout the United Kingdom, as purveyors of the finest old Spirits that can be had.

A dozen full-sized bottles of any of the above Wines at the quoted prices, or for 5s. in stamps a dozen samples of nearly all of the above can be had, or any two samples for 12 stamps, sent securely packed and labelled.

A detailed Price List of our Wines, Spirits, and Liqueurs sent on application.

In Scotland Cheques to be crossed to our bankers, the BANK OF SCOTLAND, and Post Office Orders made payable to the General Post Office, EDINBURGH; in England, the BANK OF ENGLAND, and General Post Office, LONDON; in Ireland the BANK OF IRELAND, and General Post Office, DUBLIN.

W. & A. GILBEY, 12 St. Andrew's Square, EDINBURGH
357 Oxford Street, LONDON.
31 Upper Sackville Street, DUBLIN.

AGENT FOR GLASGOW,
MR. A. R. BARLAS, 98 QUEEN STREET.

13. Extract from the Glasgow Advertiser, 12 May 1860

Other firms saw the removal of duties as a great way of increasing their mark-up. The established companies did not believe a reduction in price would increase sales, as they thought the taste for claret – nicknamed after the budget 'Gladstone's claret' – was confined to the well to do.

The young Gilbeys, Golds and Blyths saw otherwise. They switched from buying the table wines of South Africa to the clarets of France, but slashed prices, using the same technique of low mark-up and low selling price which had contributed to the firm's original success. James Blyth, who before the Budget had been scheduled to sail to South Africa to superintend the shipping of their increasing volumes of Cape wine, was re-routed. France was now where they would purchase wines which they were to aim at the ordinary British people.

Their original success, they now knew, was due largely to investing in advertising and this they did once again to sell to the less well-off the wines which had been associated solely with the well to do. The 80% reduction in duty was passed on to the customer and the resultant increase in sales made the partnership very rich. In the November *Monthly Advertiser* W&A Gilbey offered red and white Bordeaux wines at twelve shillings, twenty-four shillings and upwards per dozen, Port at thirty shillings, as well as Cape Port and Sherry at twenty shillings a dozen. Brandy was sixteen shillings and sixpence per gallon.

In that same earth-shattering budget, Gladstone introduced 'off-licences'. These could be granted to retailers (usually grocers), enabling them to sell alcohol in small quantities, and ended the previous restrictions confining the selling to wine merchants, hotel keepers and publicans. Gladstone recognised that

14A. Edinburgh Offices

14B. Dublin Offices

many persons of modest means wanted to buy single bottles to take home and drink, especially as alcohol was thought to have many beneficial effects as a stimulant and in convalescence. He wanted to put it at the disposal of the less well-to-do. The availability of alcohol in grocery shops led to another well used nickname – 'Grocer's Port'. Gladstone's Claret and Grocer's Port were the new sources of W&A Gilbey profits. They had turned an apparent disaster to their advantage by adjusting to the new circumstances rather than reeling under the blow. Gladstone had helped them make their fortune even greater.

The introduction of off licences meant that the wine merchants had competitors for the retailing they had previously done on their own premises and W&A Gilbey turned yet another apparent disadvantage to their advantage with their most original concept, a network of agents. Each held an off licence and was given the monopoly of a specific territory, as long as they agreed to purchase all their wines and spirits from W&A Gilbey. This relieved the firm of direct selling to individuals, which reduced their bookkeeping and overheads. W&A Gilbey took great care, however, to appoint the right type of agent who could satisfy their individual customers and they managed this so well that it soon came to be seen as an honour to be appointed a W&A Gilbey agent. These agents were looked up to as persons of some importance in the area where they held the monopoly of W&A Gilbey products.

The first three agents were appointed in 1861, in Reading, Torquay and Wolverhampton. Soon they were all over the country, including Scotland and Ireland, where they reported to the new W&A Gilbey regional headquarters at Edinburgh and Dublin. Many station masters became W&A Gilbey agents, as they had good storage and delivery facilities and excellent opportunities to meet customers. Thus the Gilbey brothers were making use of that very innovation, the railway, that had led to the death of their father. The station masters' agencies flourished, but the railway companies did not approve and eventually banned the practice, leaving the grocers to be the most numerous agents.

The sales operation was becoming much larger-scale, but the agent's method of payment still remained rather archaic. Few had bank accounts. They had to pay in notes and gold, so those within reach of headquarters would bring in the cash personally, which most enjoyed doing as they were treated to an especially hospitable welcome. To avoid theft those further afield would cut five pound notes in two, sending one half in the first post and the second the next day. At headquarters there were special clerks whose job it was to identify the two halves and stick them together again with stamp paper.

The money produced in this way led to even bigger profits and rapid expansion, but the major innovations were behind them and the young partners now set about consolidating this successful formula. No doubt further adventurous schemes were suggested by some of the young partners, but they enjoyed the benefits of a strong calming influence in Henry Parry Gilbey. Seven years older than Walter, he had to bear responsibility from a very young age as he was the head of a fatherless family and he had never enjoyed the broadening effects of an adventure to the Crimea. Henry Parry had always been the partners' father figure. Mature and down to earth, this genial counsellor was able to dampen any outrageous schemes dreamed up by his two younger brothers, who might otherwise have become intoxicated with their success. It was his capital that had started them off, it was his advice that helped to keep the firm running smoothly and it was his contacts that provided them with many opportunities. He made daily visits, calling in

15. Henry Parry Gilbey

on his walk from his house in Brunswick Square to work at his own company. In a typically cautious Victorian manner, he took a long time to make the logical step of joining his younger brothers, brothers-in-law and nephews. It was only at the age of forty-two that he became a partner in W&A Gilbey.

Alfred Carver, who like his son and grandson after him worked for W&A Gilbey his entire life, described Henry Parry in his memoirs, as: 'the guiding spirit of his brothers Walter and Alfred in starting, and was in many ways a steadying influence on the eager spirits organising the undertaking'.

Henry Parry's appearance added to his authority, as his dress was sombre and in keeping with the fashions of the day for a businessman. He wore a frock or morning coat, with a top hat and a black tie. He had a beard, but one which was very neat, and his moustache was carefully waxed. The

16. The Original Partners in the Pantheon: Standing – Charles Gold, Henry Grinling, Walter Gilbey, Henry Gold. Sitting – Henry Parry Gilbey, James Blyth, Henry Blyth, C. Longmead (temp.), Alfred Gilbey.

17. The Pantheon, Oxford Street

effect was distinguished, unostentatious, and in contrast to his brother Walter.

In 1865 Henry Grinling, a cousin by marriage, became the last member of the 'clan', apart from Henry Parry, to join the firm and become a partner. Alfred and Walter had seen quite a bit of him during their Crimean adventure. On returning to England he went into the War Office, so his training and experience were those of a civil servant, which was very useful to W&A Gilbey. He was meticulous and good at statistics, all of which served him well when he was made the chief of the huge warehouses which the firm opened at Camden Town. He was said to keep them in perfect order and was able to reel off minute detail about the stocks whenever required at a Board meeting.

No further families joined the Partnership of W&A Gilbey. The eight founding members might have been linked by close family ties, but their characters were distinctive.

Of the Gilbeys, Henry Parry was the predictable and distinguished personality, whereas Alfred was rather more relaxed about his appearance, although he did put much effort into accumulating business data and getting his facts right. He spent hours preparing reports on his various business trips and labouring over the writing which did not come easily to him. Yet he had a certain vivacity and a good sense of humour. He had that Victorian conscience which made him feel that making money gave him special social responsibility towards the community and he was a philanthropist. Alfred's great contribution towards the success story was his business brain, which helped the company recognise bargains and make money out of them.

Alfred's brother Walter was the odd one out among the Gilbeys and, indeed, among all the families. In the midst of this modest, upright, reactionary and conformist family he was the eccentric. At work he wore a fawn coloured coat and waistcoat, frilled shirt and leather trousers which looked much like riding breeches. He had great judgement, however, and what he said was never as outrageous as might have been expected from his appearance. All respected him for his honesty and tenacity. Walter said: 'First amongst the qualities that makes for success in life I would place the sound practical common sense that recognises opportunity; then courage to take advantage of the opportunity and tenacity of purpose to follow it up'.[3]

Walter was the one with foresight and it was unlikely that it was just his seniority in years (Henry Parry was not then a member) that made him into the first chairman.

Both the Blyth brothers had good brains, helping them to make valuable contributions in those early years; Alfred Carver remarked in his memoirs: 'I owed a great deal to Henry Blyth for his coaching me in my duties as understudy to the Chief Clerk,' but that, after giving more than thirty years to the business, 'he took more leisure and pursued his love of racing to its extreme limit, causing me a great deal of anxiety'. James Blyth was the more powerful brother and Carver said: 'many of the visitors expressed the opinion that he was the tough one to deal with'.

Carver said about Henry Gold: 'he acted as an excellent foil to the excitable and energetic partners'. He was always calm and easy going and did an excellent job in charge of agents' correspondence, licences and general administration. His brother, Charles, was a little more arrogant in appearance and quite autocratic with the staff.

These were the partners who had seized opportunities, turned changes to their advantage, defied their rather narrow, modest Victorian upbringings and made a fortune. At first they had been audacious and adventurous. They had nothing to lose in those early years by making some daring manoeuvres, as they had no capital before they started. Soon they had plenty to lose and their decisions became a little more cautious and predictable. They settled down to consolidate and expand the business, though they still had some audacious moves ahead of them.

Ten years after their foundation they made another spectacular and highly original decision – W&A Gilbey bought the Pantheon premises. They paid £67,000 for this palatial building at 35 Oxford Street, which in the 1990s, considerably altered, houses Marks and Spencer.

It was great publicity. The Pantheon's bizarre history made it a most unlikely headquarters for a fast-expanding Victorian wine merchants.

The Pantheon had been built as an entertainment house. The original building was considered one of the largest and finest of houses in London when it was finished in 1772. Its designer was the renowned architect James Wyatt, but after being gutted by a fire was reopened as a theatre, before being turned into a bazaar and fine art gallery. Horace Walpole wrote after a visit:

It amazed me. The pillars are of artificial giallo-antico. The ceilings, even of the passages, are of the most beautiful stuccos in the best taste

18. Interior of the Pantheon

of the grotesque. The ceilings of the ballroom and the panels are painted like Raphael's loggias in the Vatican. A dome like the Roman Pantheon, glazed. Monsieur de Guisnes [the Ambassador who accompanied Walpole] said to me 'Ce n'est qu'a Londres qu'on peut faire cela.'

The opening caused quite a stir and a newspaper report of 1772 said:

On Monday evening the Pantheon, which for some time past had raised the expectations and engrossed the conversation of the polite world, was for the first time opened. There were present upwards of seventeen hundred of the first people of this kingdom; the whole building is composed of a suite of fourteen rooms, all of which are adapted to particular uses; and each affording a striking instance of the elegance and splendour of these times. Imagination cannot well surpass the magnificence of the apartments, the boldness of the paintings, or the disposition of the lights, which are reflected from gilt vases, suspended by gilt chains. Beside a great number of splendid ornaments that decorate the rotundas, or great room, there are a number of statues, in niches below the dome, representing most of the Heathen Gods and Goddesses, supposed to be in the ancient Pantheon of Rome. To these are added three more of white porphyry, the two first representing the present King and Queen, the last Britannia.[4]

As a place of entertainment in the 1770s it was very exclusive; subscribers had to be recommended by peeresses and pay six guineas. Their entertainment in the evening was balls, concerts and masquerades and, by day, exhibitions. Its success was limited until the Prince of Wales (later Prince Regent and George IV) found it a great place to enjoy himself and, curiously, all in front of the public who were allowed to watch from the gallery.

For a short time the Pantheon was the centre for the young society people of London, then it was gutted by fire, leaving only its ostentatious Wyatt walls. The Prince Regent was actually presented with a petition, asking him to stop the Pantheon from being converted by a Colonel Greville, not into an English Opera house, as was originally thought, but a 'baby theatre'. The Colonel was advertising for fifteen year old girls and banning adult performers, to the consternation of his financial backers, who asked the Prince Regent to 'interpose his high authority'.[5] It was reconstructed as a theatre, but the rebuilding took too long to retain the support of its original smart set and it never regained the prestige of its early years. By the time its most famous patron had come to the throne, it had deteriorated into a second rate music hall.

It seems the Prince Regent was able to do little to stop this extraordinary palatial building deteriorating from an opera house into a run down music hall. In 1832 it was sold for £13,000. Refitted as a fine art gallery and bazaar, it lost its notoriety, but remained a place of much interest with its flamboyant history and architecture.

It was this building, once the scene of such Regency high living, that W&A Gilbey took over as their headquarters. It was another unconventional move, but backed by sound common sense. One just wonders whether there was another reason for its purchase – the earlier associations of the Gilbey family with the Prince Regent might have meant that a hint of sentimentality was added to the cool, but audacious business decision.

The purchase certainly brought the firm into the public eye, made it a talking point and raised them above the level of ordinary wine merchants. Imagine the excitement of having a headquarters where the private rooms for the directors were converted boxes and the board meetings were held on a stage with Corinthian pillars and a lofty domed roof. There were benefits to the family – most of the partners now had country homes and the Pantheon became their London base, a place to stay, in small bedrooms looking out onto Oxford Street, or just to meet and enjoy the daily lunches which were provided in either the staff or partners' dining rooms. It was a collection centre for the fast growing family. Emily, sister to Alfred and Walter, was given a role as a housekeeper. She used to organise the staff and partners' lunches and these were one of the features which helped to make the employees, as well as the partners, feel part of an extended family.

The partners' lunches became a useful means of entertainment to various notables, friends, family and agents. Although the office building was unsusal, the menu was very traditional and apparently hardly varied, almost invariably consisting of fried sole with Surrey capons and rice pudding or strawberries.

The main office on the first floor, formed by building a gallery floor across the centre of the original great hall, was huge, housing one hundred or more clerks at their tall desks with high stools. There was such an intense air of concentration that anyone entering through the doors from Oxford Street and disturbing the quiet was greeted by an atmosphere which emanated: 'Don't stop me, time is money'.

To begin with the clerks would be at work on their ledgers and invoices laboriously writing them out by hand. Then in 1889 typewriters were introduced and their noisy clatter helped to break the earlier silence; but there were not too many of them. W&A Gilbey did not advocate a mass conversion to this instrument of progress. The innovativeness of the firm had slowed down, and only letters were typewritten. Up until the outbreak of World War I invoices were written by hand, with a ledger clerk supervising a journal clerk and an invoicing clerk.

W&A Gilbey were, however, quick to see the potential and make use of another invention – the telephone. They installed an early version of it, the Wheatstone Transmitter, in 1870, connecting their headquarters at the Pantheon with their warehouses in Camden. The instrument at each terminal consisted of a circular disc, with a key for each letter of the alphabet around the outside rim. The message was sent by turning a handle at the same time as pressing the keys to spell out the messages, relayed via a private wire to a similar instrument at the other end. In 1877 came a voice telephone, which must have been one of the first in Britain, installed by a private company called the Telephone Co. (later the United Telephone Co., which merged in 1894 into the National Telephone Company).

Probably the most revolutionary technological development of the century, electricity, was at first too expensive. In 1884 W&A Gilbey turned down an estimate of £200 p.a. for lighting one of the sheds at Camden. But in December 1887 they succumbed to progress and the quaint gas system at the Pantheon was replaced.

For twenty years each desk had used a gas standard and the domed roof had two starlights which were lit by a rather precarious process each working evening. They were very high and it took a very long pole with a taper on its end to light them. Carver said:

> The big end of the pole was steadied against a desk and raised to an upright position and balanced, and the starlights were lit up. This operation was a daily source of delight to the staff who watched every moment, in case the pole should fall.'

The heating of this huge hall was difficult and apparently not very effective. A big stove in the middle of the office had been made for some other purpose to the order of Sir Robert Peel, but he had died before it was completed and it was sold to W&A Gilbey. There were two fireplaces with downdraughts created by lighting fires in the basement. Occasionally, when the wind was in the east, the down draught was stifled and the office would fill with smoke. The workers then had to choose between smarting eyes or shivering in the cold. Apparently the latter was the most popular choice.

Beneath the office were the printing works, a massive set-up sufficient to print a major newspaper and including presses, cutting machines and typecasting machines to print the stationery and those circulars which were such a vital part of the W&A Gilbey boom.

The cellars were below the printing rooms and had their entrance in Poland Street. They were used for storage of vintage ports and clarets, until it was decided they were too dry and the old wines did better in storage at Camden. Between the printing rooms and the office was a fine lofty chamber where another crucial aspect of W&A Gilbey policy was fulfilled. Cork cutting was done here and on every cork was placed an impression of a red seal, which became famous all over the world as a symbol of the W&A Gilbey product.

W&A Gilbey made maximum use of the Pantheon's space, enabling them to cut out, wherever possible, dependency on other firms and middle men for such tasks as printing and cork cutting. Perhaps more importantly, it was unique to provide such an unusual base for work and it became a source of pride to both partners and employees. This pride was promoted and W&A Gilbey workers were made to feel part of an extended family. Alongside this, there was security, assistance being given in times of trouble to employees and their dependants, and promotions like the Pantheon Savings Bank, in which the employees could invest their savings. The 10,000 employees of the firm were part of an operation in which conservatism, loyalty and predictability flourished, but to which were added occasional dashes of flamboyance and ostentatiousness. This contrasting mixture of reliability with the unusual was the special feature of W&A Gilbey and its chairman, Walter Gilbey.

III
Expanding the Business

The story of W&A Gilbey mirrors that of the British Nation. They had lived in poverty through the 'Hungry Forties', made their fortune in the 1850s and 1860s and then enjoyed a steadier expansion through to the end of the century. The 50s and 60s were the decades of opportunity, as Britain was on top of the world; economically, as a result of her manufacturing, and politically, from her leadership of a great Empire. These heady days were followed by a period of steadier growth, when rivals began to appear. The German Empire, formed by a series of amalgamations in the 1860s and 1870s, developed a stronger technical base than Britain. Then the USA opened up her prairies, modernised her farming and, with swifter and easier transportation in the growing armada of steamships, her grain became competitive with Britain's domestic production. Unlike the rest of Europe, Britain let the goods in, free from tariffs, and the result was a devastating agricultural depression, with British grain farmers and their employees being the major losers of the late Victorian era. Generally, however, there was steady expansion of the economy, prosperity abounded, and that touch of complacency which was to blight the British in the twentieth century began to replace the earlier eagerness to be opportunistic and work long hours.

The partners in W&A Gilbey no longer worked the ten-hour days of the early years and they took good holidays. One after another they had acquired country homes and turned to other activities in their increasing hours of leisure. Business was considered rather vulgar throughout the Victorian Era: no businessmen were honoured for making a fortune, as it was the way they spent it that brought them their titles. Respectability, a much coveted description in Victorian times, came from helping politicians and philanthropic efforts. Money was helpful, to assist in politics or to become a philanthropist, and the growth of W&A Gilbey ensured there was plenty of this for the family. The company could simply invest and expand in step with Britain's booming economy. They could build up their capital and use it to take control of a larger and larger share of the drink trade. By the turn of the century W&A Gilbey was the largest distributing company in the UK, no longer run by daring young men, but by a clan who had become part of the establishment.

Capital was relatively easy to build up as the tax was a mere two pence in the pound: when it rose to 8 pence in 1888 there was a public outcry. There were still few other restrictions on industry and profits could be ploughed back to help businesses expand. By 1895 1,044,982 gallons, being one fourteenth of the wine consumed in the UK, was supplied by agents of W&A Gilbey. They diversified, making a bigger and bigger impact in the spirit trade too, and in that same year sold 1,074,584 gallons, one thirty-fifth of the

CLARETS FROM FRANCE

DISTINGUISHING SEAL	DESCRIPTION	PRICES FOR CASH ONLY Bottles 1s. per dozen extra (returnable)	
		Dozen	Bottle

SUPERIOR BEVERAGE CLARETS.—W & A Gilbey guarantee that all the undermentioned Clarets are pure French Wines, shipped by them direct from France. These Wines have been well matured both in cask and bottle, and at the present moment it is almost impossible to buy Clarets of a similar quality at the same prices either in France or England.

		Dozen	Bottle
"Castle A CLARET"	This pure Bordeaux Wine, for use by itself or with water, will be found far superior to the Vin Ordinaire sold on the Continent *6 months in bottle*	12/	1/
"Castle B CLARET"	A Wine of the Médoc growth. It possesses the body, flavour and all the vinous characteristics required in a good dinner Claret *12 months in bottle*	15/	1/3
"Castle C CLARET"	A superior Wine of the Médoc growth. It has full body, fine aroma, and all the characteristics of an excellent Claret *18 months in bottle*	18/	1/6
"Castle D CLARET"	A high-class Wine of the Médoc growth. It will be found of excellent quality, and suitable for a dinner or dessert Wine *2 years in bottle*	24/	2/

The above four Clarets supplied in half bottles at 6d. per dozen half bottles extra.

CHÂTEAU LOUDENNE Vintage 1881	Fine Claret of the 1881 Vintage, with full body and extremely fine aroma	24/	2/

SUPERIOR DINNER AND DESSERT CLARETS.—All the Wines under this heading were purchased direct from the Proprietors, and either bottled at the various estates where grown, or under W & A Gilbey's personal supervision. They are excellent specimens of Médoc Wines.

"Castle E CLARET"	The produce of one of the best districts in the Médoc. It has high character, and is a fine after-dinner Wine, having the advantage of age in bottle *Old in bottle*	30/	2/6
"Castle F CLARET"	The produce of one of the superior classified growths. It is a most delicate Wine, having full flavour and fine bouquet, and has been carefully matured in bottle *Old in bottle*	36/	3/
"Castle G CLARET"	The produce of one of the favourite classified growths. It has been selected as a remarkably fine after-dinner Wine *Old in bottle*	42/	3/6

HIGHEST CLASS CLARETS.—The following Wines are all of the Vintage 1875, the most renowned Vintage of recent years in France. They are now in perfect order for consumption.

"Castle H CLARET" Vintage 1875	The produce of one of the most favoured estates in the Médoc *Old in bottle*	54/	4/6
"Castle I CLARET" Vintage 1875	It has been selected as combining all the qualities sought for by connoisseurs in Clarets *Old in bottle*	66/	5/6
"Castle J CLARET" Vintage 1875	Selected as being the choicest Bordeaux production of recent years *Old in bottle*	84/	7/

SOLD BY W & A GILBEY'S 2,400 AGENTS THROUGHOUT THE UNITED KINGDOM AT THE ABOVE PRICES.

For Shipment Abroad—The above Wines can be supplied, free of duty, from W & A Gilbey's Excise Bonded Warehouse. For particulars see Special Export List.

19. W&A Gilbey list

total volume of spirits sold in the UK. W&A Gilbey boasted 320 varieties of wine and spirits in their 1895 catalogue: only beer was not covered. This range provided another advantage for the 2,760 W&A Gilbey agents, as they could fulfil most of their customers needs.[1]

W&A Gilbey would have probably done well if the partners had sat back and made no changes, but that spirit of adventure which had made them their fortunes in such a short time was still alive and they made occasional audacious manoeuvres which proved yet again the vigour of that first generation.

A typical incident for W&A Gilbey occurred in 1873, when the firm discovered another means of drastically reducing current prices and creating a big market. Alfred Gilbey and James Blyth were the firms' purchasers in France, and on one of their trips they discovered that the white sparkling wines of Saumur were being sold in England as champagne, at the price of champagne, which meant there was a huge mark-up. W&A Gilbey decided that it was both more honest and just as profitable to sell large amounts at lower prices.

They boldly put a whole page advertisement in the Daily Mail, calling their goods sparkling wines, not champagne, and charging the very low price of 25/- and 30/- per dozen. The timing was good as it was just before Christmas and there were many customers for 2/6d bottles of wine that looked and tasted like champagne. 2,000 dozen were sold within a fortnight.

One of their most audacious moves was in 1879, when the dreaded phylloxera was sweeping across Europe. Phylloxera is a tiny insect which destroys the roots of vines. Nobody could halt its slow, devastating progression across Europe in the last 30 years of the nineteenth century. This plant-louse was killing vines wherever it spread and wine was not the only product to suffer, as the Cognac region was badly hit too. As brandy and soda was the staple drink of that generation, the far-sighted could see prices were likely to soar. W&A Gilbey leapt into action, collecting all their capital reserves and even, it is alleged, borrowing, in order to make use of their extensive contacts in France to buy up all the Cognac they could get their hands on. They purchased almost a million pounds' worth and added considerably to their fortune when the price of brandy rose, as it became scarce.

Once again W&A Gilbey had turned a potential problem to their advantage. This time their bold manoeuvring had to be supported by massive investments, but it paid off and their financial rewards were immense.

The use of low mark-ups on alcohol and clever advertising were the basis of the W&A Gilbey success, but another useful and more controversial selling mechanism was the claim that alcohol had medicinal value. The first to be given this marketable promotion was a higher quality Saumur than the champagne substitute, which they named 'Brut Saumur'.

This was put on the market in 1880 and sold as a pure, light and moderately stimulating wine, making it especially suitable for invalids, with its peculiar dryness and tonic qualities. Support for these credentials came from a committee of the House of Lords who, in 1879, had considered the value of stimulants from a physiological and medical point of view. In a letter distributed at large they said:

> The Committee states that it does not appear that there is any theory as
> to the physiological properties, or as to the dietetic or medical value of
> Alcohol, which would warrant it being adopted as a basis for legislation,
> but from a medical standpoint wine should possess exceptional hygienic
> qualities necessary to recommend it to the infirm and convalescent.

W&A Gilbey considered that Brut Saumur qualified under these terms and sold it as such, at less than 3/- a bottle. Demand grew and in their brochure on Wine Growers they said: 'The great demand during recent years for Tonic Wines has caused special attention to be paid to the shipping of wines for consumption by invalids.' The best for invalids they said was: 'Dry champagne specially selected as suitable for consumption in the sick room where a sparkling wine is recommended for stimulating purposes'.

Brut Saumur was the first of many drinks that W&A Gilbey promoted as being good for the drinker. Not all members of the population agreed with them and there was much controversy over the issue. There could be little doubt that drunkenness and the money spent on drink by the less well off was the cause of much crime and the ruin of families, especially in the city slums.

Various attempts had been made to curtail drinking. In the 1850s the 'Blue Ribbon Army' flourished. It was so named because their members

20. Advertisement for Invalid Port

wore blue ribbons as a sign of having taken an oath of total abstinence. Later the Temperance Party became the main source of anti-drink campaigns. Their lobbying met with some success amongst the Liberals and legislative proposals were put forward to suppress the 'drink traffic', as Lloyd George was to name it, but an element of fanaticism damaged the cause of the campaigners and helped the well organised drink interests to ensure that their livelihood was not destroyed through legislation.

Despite these counter arguments plenty of evidence was produced to support claims by W&A Gilbey and others of the beneficial effects of drink. So confusing was the debate over the effects of alcohol on health that, despite the campaigners, W&A Gilbey were able to continue using its alleged benefits not just to contest anti-drink campaigns but as a positive selling mechanism. Port was given a medicinal value. W&A Gilbey had a reputation for honesty and the key for them as to whether alcohol was good or bad was the quantity consumed, as illustrated by their 1869 Catalogue on wines:

In order to arrive at the true value of Port wine as a stimulant, the quantity taken should first be carefully considered. There can be no doubt that Port is a most valuable wine, but on account of its strength the free use of it should never be advised, except in cases of extreme prostration and debility. As regards Port wine medicinally however, it is now pretty generally admitted that it strengthens the muscular system, assists circulation and the digestive powers and is one of the greatest restoratives in cases of depression from disease and sickness.

With so many extraordinary effects it is not surprising that in 1889 the idea occurred to them to sell an Invalid Port. At first it was sold with moderate claims, as 'suitable for general use and nutritious for invalids'. It was not until 1912, in a now famous advertising campaign, that it became a household name and one of W&A Gilbey' best sellers.

The **PORT** *of* **KINGS**

— and the port of the people

GILBEY'S
Invalid
PORT

21. Advertisement for Invalid Port, 1929.

Port was classified as a strong wine and in those quaint, but clever, W&A Gilbey Catalogues was recommended to be used in different circumstances to the light wines. In their 'Brochure on Wine Growers' they said: 'To the young, healthy and, particularly, the sedentary part of the community, the light wines are especially suitable, being grateful and beneficial to the palate and health and promoting purity of the blood; while for those more actively employed or requiring a greater and more concentrated amount of stimulant, also in cases of exhaustion, whether from over-exertion or from physical weakness and debility, recourse may be had to the stronger wines of countries such as Spain or Portugal.'

'Brandy was another product that was sold with medicinal value, although W&A Gilbey never gave it an Invalid tag like Port. In the same brochure they say: 'The Distillation of Brandy in France can be traced back as far as the year 1343, when it was regarded as a medicine only, of marvellous strengthening and life giving powers, hence the term 'Eau de Vie'.'

The case for the medicinal value of alcohol might cause amusement in some quarters today, with doubts about its benefits growing through the twentieth century.

Personal Buying

Another major selling mechanism was cheapness and once again W&A Gilbey used this device in occasional startling policies. They sought out wines from places few other companies ventured – in the Canaries, Australia, California and, in 1887, they found Hungarian wines and were able to sell them at just 1/- a bottle. One wonders about the taste as in the circular letter announcing this it was said: 'If mixed with water they will be found wholesome and invigorating and as beverages cannot be surpassed even by Beer'. Beer of course was Britain's national drink, but W&A Gilbey had been leading a change of drinking habits by putting wines on the market at affordable prices and by 1875 had sold six times more than any other company. Doing their own buying was one of the ways they used to keep costs low and this meant plenty of travelling for the two great adventurers, Alfred Gilbey and James Blyth, who took off on long trips to the Continent.

James Blyth was a linguist, having spent part of his youth in Holland, and was renowned as a wine taster. Alfred had developed his travel bug when in the Crimea. The purpose of these Continental trips was to cut out the costs of the British importers and agents, to find ways of reducing transport costs and to seek out the best sources of supply. Their market was the British beer drinker, whom they wanted to convert to wine drinking, so they did not go to the famous vineyards, but searched for new and inexpensive wines. They built up good relations with the growers themselves, became experts about wines in not just France, but also Hungary, Italy, Spain and Germany. They were able to seek out bargains, find titillating information that interested buyers and built up such a good relationship with the producers that business connections were cemented for generations.

The families' personal contacts were made even stronger when some of the next generation started marrying foreign ladies. Three of Alfred Gilbey's sons married Spanish girls, thus starting a Roman Catholic wing to the family, although as Alfred produced 11 children himself there might have been some Catholic principles in his own make-up! Marriages, as well as business trips, thus helped to cement ties with the Spanish wine trade. Alfred's son, Newman, married the niece of Manolo Gonzalez, Marquès de Torre Soto and this link with the Gonzalez family was further reinforced in the next generation with the marriage of two Gonzalez boys to two daughters of William Gilbey.

There are meticulous records of many of the trips, as James Blyth was a conscientious recorder. Some of these were more like grand European Tours,

22. Archway to Chateau Loudenne

as the partners had a knack of finding ways of combining business with pleasure. An example was in 1867, when six of them – Mr and Mrs Alfred Gilbey, Mr and Mrs Walter Gilbey, James Blyth and an office representative – visited Paris, Strasbourg, Baden, Mainz, Wiesbaden, Koblenz, Cologne and Brussels between April 30th and May 29th. They saw castles and exhibitions and 'took the water' in the baths, travelling mostly by train and eating well at breakfast, lunch and dinner, judging by the amounts spent.

Chateau Loudenne

The adventurism of the firm led to it becoming, in 1875, the first British firm to buy a French vineyard with its own chateau. They chose Bordeaux, the area which had for a hundred years or more produced the clarets that were the most popular wines in Britain. These were termed the 'natural' wines as their quality depended on the growing (the frosts, the heat and the soil) and not the making. The grapes of Bordeaux have sufficient fruit sugar in them to need no additions to the fermentation process. No spirit is added and the grapes are simply placed in a vat, allowing them to ferment before the juice is drawn off into casks and stored for the time needed for the wine to complete fermentation.

W&A Gilbey selected a small, unpretentious chateau which lay in the heart of the Medoc district, on the banks of the River Gironde.

They paid £28,000 for this rather run-down vineyard of 470 acres at Chateau Loudenne. Only 60 acres were planted with vines, but they set to work to show what W&A Gilbey initiative and money could do. They found a top class Estate Manager in 65 year old Edouard Brown, a retired bureaucrat with many family connections amongst the Bordeaux merchants. He supervised projects which ended up costing twice as much as the price they paid for the Vineyard. These included the building of a massive new chais for storage of the equivalent of one and a half million bottles of wine in casks, the purchase of a new wine press and the bringing of 125 more acres under cultivation. They even sent out two Essex men to put in a drainage system and a new harbour was constructed with a tramway running directly to the chais, to help shipment to London. Cottages were built for the workers and stables for the horses. But probably the action that captured most attention in Britain was when Walter Gilbey's cherished Shire horses were sent off to replace the French oxen. The first draught went out in 1880 and by 1889 there were 10 Shires and 7 light draught animals at Loudenne. As a means of publicity it was a huge success, especially as it was immediately claimed that with their extra speed they did twice as much work. It was noted in the diaries of the Loudenne: 'each horse takes the place of two bullocks and performs the work quicker, compelling the ploughman to be more active in his work.'[2] Speed, however, is not always the answer, and the slower oxen did less damage to the vines, so the Shires never entirely won over the workforce at Loudenne. In 1891 four pairs of working bullocks were bought, as they were found indispensable to work in the vineyards on the hills.

Many other innovative ideas were tried out. Cattle were used to help freshen up and fertilise the land. Special wells were bored to try to get water directly from the Pyrenees, as it was famed for its special qualities. The end result of all this work and investment was that by 1887 the output had increased fivefold, despite the disastrous early years when phylloxera swept across Europe to cause damage estimated at an incredible total of £220,000,000, in the year of 1882 alone. Phylloxera hit Loudenne four years after W&A Gilbey bought the estate in 1879. Combating it was expensive

23. Drawing of an aerial view of the Loudenne Estate

FILLING · THE · HOTTE

HOMEWARD ·

BRINGING · GRAPES · TO · THE · PRESS·HOUSE

GENERAL·VIEW
·OF·THE·
·VINEYARDS·

24a. Vintage at Chateau Loudenne

as, although temporary relief could be provided by application of sulpha-carbonate of potassium, the only permanent cure was to import American roots, which were immune to the disease, and then graft the vines onto them.

Nor was phylloxera the only problem. There were bouts of Anthracmose, a vegetable parasite that attacked vines, and Mildew, which had devastating effects on the Loudenne vintages in the early 1880s. Fortunately, a Mildew preventative was found towards the end of the decade – this was a mixture of sulphate of copper, 'fat' lime and water.

The purpose of buying Loudenne was to give W&A Gilbey their own supply of wine. Another important benefit was its use as a port. The estate could never produce enough wine to meet W&A Gilbey' vast needs, but it could be used as a depot for wines purchased in surrounding areas. Taking the French on in their own country earned the firm useful prestige in Britain and gave members of the company the opportunity of overseas trips, which was an appreciated perk generating even more loyalty.

Most of the Directors paid a visit to the Chateau twice a year (James Blyth went there 74 times in 39 years): in the spring, for the flowering of the vines, and in the autumn, for the vintage of the grapes. There was a certain routine to these visits. The typical means of transport was by ferry across the Channel, then onto the train to reach Paris, where the contingent arrived in time for a bath and breakfast. A nine-hour trip on the train to Bordeaux followed, before catching the steamer for the last 25 miles down the Gironde to the Chateau.

Accounts of these trips are recorded in various diaries and the reports, as was the wont of the Victorians, are full of talk about the weather. Although Walter Gilbey's included details about the agricultural activities, others elaborated on the wine and the dancing.

Traditionally the vintage lasted a little over a week, with extra labour being recruited and the cottages around the estate being used for sleeping. To give some idea of the quantities involved, Nicholas Faith, in his excellent book *Victorian Vineyard*, writes: 'During the 1900 vintage the harvesters consumed 15 hundred weight of meat, 20 hundred weight of cod fish and 876 loaves.' It was back-breaking work from five in the morning until six in the evening, the women having to bend low to pluck the grapes for hours on end. The harvested fruit was then carried away by men and loaded into carts which the oxen or horses pulled to the vats. This hard work earned the men 1/-3d a day in 1890 with food and lodging and the women half that. There were plenty of songs when all the grapes were plucked and there was the great Vintage Ball when the house party of twenty or more from England joined in the celebrations with the workers. A fiddle and accordion were the

24b. Directors and Managers at Loudenne (1897).
Newman Gilbey (director), S. Hucks, Alfred Gilbey (director), Paul Aubert.

VINS ET SPIRITUEUX

Fac-simile de la Medaille d'Or décerné par M. le Ministre de l'Agriculture pour la Viticulture des vignobles du Château Loudenne

25. Wine label

traditional music and provided lively melodies to which the couples could either whirl around on the dance floor or listen, seated in the surrounding chairs.

The invasion of France by British people, ideas and horses must have aroused some hostility, but also admiration and the Loudenne vineyard did, in 1888, win a much heralded accolade. The French Ministry of Agriculture awarded it the Gold Medal for the best cultivated and managed vineyard in the Gironde. As the press reported: 'Messrs Gilbey appear not only to have overmastered the jealousy of our lively neighbours, among whom the cultivation of the grape is a vast industry, but to have won their admiration.'[3]

For the first time in the history of the French vineyard the 'Blue Ribbon' had been carried off by an English firm. W&A Gilbey, with their flair for public relations, made sure that this was used to enhance their public image.

The company went on to receive further glories, as in 1900 Loudenne won another Gold Medal at the Paris Exhibition and, in 1901, the Gold medal and Diploma from the Agricultural Society of the Medoc. These were the rewards for enterprise and effort, since it was generally recognised W&A Gilbey had turned Loudenne into a model vineyard.

Sadly, the joint director who played such a great part in the purchase of Loudenne was dead by the time the vineyard received such honours. Alfred Gilbey was just 46 years old when he died in 1879, leaving eleven children, the eldest of whom, Alfred, was only twenty. He had caught a chill and, without penicillin, it soon turned into lethal pneumonia. Reverend Hewett, preaching a sermon in his memory, said:

> He had a simple love of doing good, a deep sense of responsibility attaching to wealth, an unselfish and almost childlike longing that as many as possible should share and have reason to rejoice with him the main successful results of his laborious commercial life.

Exports

Alfred Gilbey was a promoter of foreign trips to make personal contacts, but he was not alive to see this policy extended into exporting. In the 1870s there had been some exports to the British Raj in India, with W&A Gilbey being the first to send bottles of wine to Calcutta, Madras and Bombay, but it was not until 1885 that Fred Collins, head of the advertising department at the Pantheon, took another leap forward for W&A Gilbey. He was sent to Australia, partly for his health, but he brought back so many orders and exciting ideas about expansion that it was decided to give him a post in Melbourne, from which he could cover Australia, Tasmania and New Zealand.

W&A Gilbey sales to the Antipodes flourished, giving confidence for further export expansion. In 1887 they appointed F. N. Bungey as traveller to the West Indies, then Stanley Hill to South Africa, Bruce Douglas to South America and Charles Douglas to Canada. The W&A Gilbey network spread around the world and agents were appointed in all corners of it.

The move into Gin

The first spirit that W&A Gilbey started to produce themselves was gin. This was a bold move, as of all the spirits it was the one with the most damaging reputation. The notorious gin era in the first half of the eighteenth century had led to this drink being spurned generally. That era had started with lower duties on gin being introduced to give grain producers another market, an aim which succeeded as the poor could then afford gin and bought it rather than beer. The demand for gin grew, but so did alcoholism. Drowning the sorrows of poverty in gin was more dangerous than beer and the huge increase in the death rate was blamed on gin being used to dull the senses – between 1740 and 1742 there were twice as many burials as baptisms in London. The Government took steps to reduce gin drinking in 1751, placing a high tax on spirits and banning retailing by shippers and distillers. The results were dramatic in terms of the decline in the death rate and gin got the blame for those horrific decades for the poor.

By the late nineteenth century, however, views were changing. With the reasoning of hindsight and clever marketing, which claimed the cause for these deaths was not the gin itself, but the inability of the persons who drank it to take it in reasonable quantities, a market for gin was again opening up.

Walter Gilbey, writing on the subject of spirits generally in 1869, said:

It is the misfortune of this country, differing in that respect from most other countries, that strong drinks, chiefly it may be believed from want of knowledge, are as a rule consumed at greater strengths than is necessary either to give pleasure or to satisfy thirst. To this practice may no doubt be attributed much of the insobriety of which, at times, we hear such loud and general complaints.

He goes on to say:

It may be taken as a very good rule that, except when consumed under medical advice, spirits should flavour water only, instead of being used

26. The Gin Distillery, Camden Town

in larger quantity, as is too often the case. When spirits are consumed in a moderate way they are an exceedingly economical beverage and, at the same time, are both satisfying and refreshing in a high degree. For medicinal purposes spirits are highly valuable if used at proper times and in proper quantities, although spirits, like drugs, are of course highly injurious if taken in ten or twenty times the proportion that a physician or medical man would recommend.

With arguments like these it can be understood how gin was reinstated as an acceptable liquor. Its value to W&A Gilbey was that it was comparatively simple to produce and, unlike brandy and whisky, was not dependent on specific local products. Its plain spirit was obtained from unmalted barley and rectified to a pure spirit of neutral character so that all tastes unique to this spirit were removed. The flavour of certain plants, particularly juniper, was then added to the pure alcohol, which was then re-distilled. As each manufacturer had his own recipe, gin unlike most spirits, could be produced anywhere; there was another advantage, gin did not need to be matured with the resultant locking up of large sums of capital.

W&A Gilbey decided that they would distil gin at Camden Town, where they built their own distillery in 1879. They hit upon a recipe which made their gin famous, leading to it becoming their first major export in the 1880s and later to it being manufactured around the world under their name.

Creating a base for their London gin distillery was part of the huge W&A Gilbey expansion. The Pantheon was not large enough for their business and warehouses, so cellars were rented from the London and North Western Railway, at the Chalk Farm Goods Yard in Camden Town. There they used

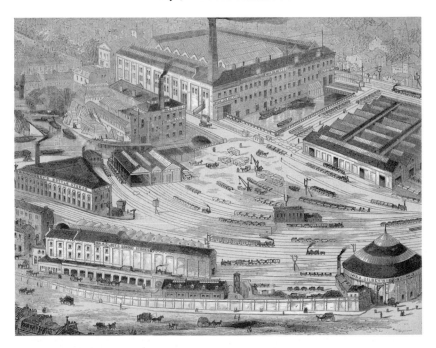

27. A view of some of W &A Gilbey's warehouses at Camden Town with the Roundhouse in the foreground.

the old engine turntable building, known as the Round House, for storing casks of spirits and there was housing, too, for the bottling and forwarding departments, as well as that first distillery and, later on, the export department and bonded stores. This was an area which could be extended as business took off and by 1914 the W&A Gilbey Camden Town premises covered a staggering 20 acres of floor space. There was even a special train, The Gilbey's Special, leaving daily for the London Docks, full of their drinks for export around the world.

Their own distillery cut costs, but they found more controversial ways of reducing the prices of their bottles to attract the less well off. They watered down the spirits to 50% under proof and sold them at a mere 18/- to 20/- a dozen. This was such a questionable circumnavigation of the law, which stated that brandy, whisky and rum had to be 25 degrees and gin 35 degrees under proof, that it caused them to be taken to court. One of their agents was prosecuted at Marylebone Police Court. The magistrate, however, could not dispute W&A Gilbey's honesty, as it was always clearly labelled as 50% under proof and with prices appropriate to this low strength. The case was dismissed and W&A Gilbey continued to offer spirits in up to six strengths, from proof to 52% under proof, but always clearly labelled as such.

Whisky

It was wine that was the basis of the W&A Gilbey success, and it is gin for which they are best known today, but it was whisky that became their big

28. The Whisky Distillery, Strathmill

seller in the last quarter of the century and the beginning of the next. They had stimulated the market for wine by finding ways of putting it on the market at much lower prices and then advertising it extensively. By the time Scotch became an important drink in England the partners lacked the great energy of youth, so they did not create the demand, but they were still astute enough to pick up the trends and see the way popular tastes were moving.

When the business started it was Irish Whiskey which was the most popular drink and in 1858 Henry Gold opened a W&A Gilbey office in Dublin, from which they could organise the supplies. The policy was to buy huge amounts of new whiskey, principally from John Jameson & Sons. The whiskey was then sent to their own warehouses to mature and be sold under the label of Castle Grand JJ; Castle became the emblem that was used on many of the W&A Gilbey spirits. In 1875 the sales of Scotch were a mere 38,000 dozen bottles, which was less than half of that of Ireland's 83,000. But the Scottish people began to realise that there was a market which could bring them better yields than their agricultural products and they turned more and more towards producing the spirit. W&A Gilbey, with their office in Edinburgh since 1859, became big buyers from the various local distilleries, keeping the drink in bonded warehouses in Scotland until needed in London.

Ireland was probably where whiskey was originally produced, being first recorded there in the twelfth century. When Henry II invaded it was noted that the inhabitants made Usquebaugh, or water of life, and it soon became known as Aqua Vitae, the same name as for brandy. According to Walter Gilbey in his book Notes on Alcohol, Aqua Vitae (whisky) was used as a powerful medical agent. He quotes a book of 1692 which says of the interest of Aqua Vitae: 'Tis an excellent Carminative, for two or three spoonfuls being drunk will expell wind in the bowels or any other part of the body.'

Scotland acquired the techniques of making their own whisky and it is mentioned in the Scottish Exchequer Rolls for 1494, where Friar John Cov was issued eight bottles of malt to make Aqua Vitae. The barley combined with the Highland water that ran over the heather-covered hills and was dried in the kiln full of peat from the surrounding areas. The whisky thus produced had a distinct flavour and nothing similar could be made elsewhere – Scotland had a great product.

Before W&A Gilbey arrived on the scene most of the whisky, whether Irish or Scotch, was sold in bulk to the publicans, who watered it down as they required. W&A Gilbey applied the principles of standardised quality and minimum prices that had helped them so much in the wine market. They produced bottles under their own label and sold them to their agents.

With brandy prices soaring after the phylloxera scourge, whisky being thought of as good for the drinker and prosperity increasing general demand, whisky became the boom drink and it was Scotch, rather than Irish, that enjoyed the greatest growth. W&A Gilbey realised that the whisky boom was swinging Scotland's way and in 1887 made their first major investment into Scotch whisky, buying the Glen Spey-Glenlivet distillery for £11,000. The owner, James Stuart, had converted it from a mill for cereals just two years earlier. Many more grain farmers followed suit as the demand for whisky took off.

W&A Gilbey sold their product from Glen Spey as Castle Grand, charging 3/6d a bottle. As the boom continued so they invested further and in 1895 bought Strathmill Genisla-Glenlivet distillery for £9,500. Like Glen Spey, it had only taken to whisky production a few years before, as prior to 1891 it was a mill for oats and was only converted when the value of its location in the golden triangle of malt whisky production was realised.

The boom did not last. Home demand dipped at the turn of the century, but W&A Gilbey, with their well-developed network of agents around the world, used this slackening of the home trade to promote exports. They were even bold enough to expand further, in 1904 buying another Highland malt pot still distillery at Knockando. They paid little for it – just £500 – as it had not been used since the boom's end in 1900.

Use of Advertising

Developing their own sources of supply, at Camden for the gin, Loudenne for the wine and at Glen Spey, Strathmill and Knockando for the whisky, helped to keep W&A Gilbey prices down and, to make this an effective selling weapon, they also used clever marketing. Products were standardised and sold under the famous red seal, which was recognised as a symbol of reliable quality.

From early times, the firm employed the trade mark, still used, of a dragon within a tower. This was the crest of the Gilby or Gilbie family from Lincolnshire and in later life Walter Gilbey sought the help of a herald from the College of Arms to try to trace a connection between his family and what he thought might be his Lincolnshire forebears. The tracing of a link seems not to have been possible, however. In the end the Gilbey's personal family crest, when registered at the College of Arms, was differentiated from that of

29. Sir Walter Gilbey's bookplate.

the earlier Gilbys by the addition of a fleur-dy-lys over the tower door (referring to the family's proprietary interests in France) and Prince of Wales' feathers on each side of the tower (to record Sir Walter's friendship with the Prince of Wales).

Having developed the agency system W&A Gilbey relied on their agents to make direct sales, but they did give them plenty of assistance. They supplied handbills, circulars, statements on the state of the wine trade, together with extraordinarily informative and extensive price lists. These were so full of details about how and where the drink was made and its particular features, that they were more like books. Many of the agents were grocers and it became common practice to put the handbills in their windows. The red seal adorning the bills became a familiar sight all over Britain. W&A Gilbey focused onto this style of advertising and only used some small advertisements in the press.

This policy continued until 1912, when W&A Gilbey experimented with a nation-wide advertising campaign for Invalid Port. It met with such success that it became more important than the agency system, which had been one of the bulwarks of W&A Gilbey development. From that date on they focused on advertising campaigns and used such top-class artists and copy writers that their work became famous.

Some examples of their slogans are: 'The sun never sets on Gilbey's Gin' and the puzzle 'Gee I'LL BE Y's Be wise too' For whisky there was a Spey Royal poster with the phrase: 'Worth Hunting for', and, of course, a picture of a horse.

Imaginative advertising, from the bills in grocers' windows to cartoons, puzzles and gimmicks, enabled W&A Gilbey to hold their household name and ensure the use of their drinks all over the world.

W&A Gilbey were able to carry out a huge expansion through those boom years at the end of the Victorian Era in Britain. They were not content simply to be prudent and enjoy the extraordinary benefits accruing to the British at that time. W&A Gilbey maximised the opportunities. They were quick to adapt and were even opportunistic, as we have seen in their massive investment in brandy during the phylloxera outbreak. They were quick to see a new market developing and did not confine themselves to their initial money maker, wine. They saw the potential for whisky and gin and became the largest British shipper of these two drinks. In every field they were looking for means of putting their products on the market at the lowest possible price so that they could attract customers amongst those who had not been able to afford wines and spirits in the past.

The key to W&A Gilbey' success was that they had found a new market. Previously, the rich had drunk champagne and claret, while the poor had drowned their misery in gin and beer, but the middle class had drunk very little alcohol. The middle class prospered in the Victorian Era and were vulnerable to marketing that lured them into purchasing cheaper wine and spirits, especially when sold as being good for health. W&A Gilbey benefited from the middle class's growing prosperity. The company thus enjoyed a huge growth through the Victorian Era.

The company's sensitivity, reliability, cost cutting and dependence on large turnover rather than big mark- ups, ensured that the base established in those first early years was expanded into a massive business.

IV
Keeping Ahead

'Once you have got ahead by perseverance, you can keep ahead and are safe'[1] was a theory Sir Walter expounded in his middle age, but must have regretted in his later life. He should have kept to his motto 'my greatest joy in life is overcoming difficulties', for at the end of the nineteenth and beginning of the twentieth century W&A Gilbey found they were far from safe.

At a time when many of the founder members of the Board must have been keen to consolidate the business in order to have the time to pursue the other activities that their income now allowed, they had to tackle a series of major disturbances. Weaknesses in W&A Gilbey's financial structure were exposed by deaths in the family, losses in Loudenne required major rationalisation, growing hostility towards alcohol affected government attitudes, the constitution of W&A Gilbey's whisky was challenged by a Royal Commission and the Chairman, Sir Walter Gilbey, and the Board became embroiled in a major dispute.

Deaths in the Family

The first serious disturbance to the family came with the sudden death of Henry Parry Gilbey in 1892.

At 68 years of age he was on his way to London by express train from Bishop's Stortford to St. Pancras. The Essex contingent of partners had their own private coach, which was attached to the train for their journeys to London. Henry Parry was in good spirits, keeping his travelling companions, Walter Gilbey, Henry and James Blyth and Charles Gold, amused, when he was suddenly paralysed by a stroke. He died in hospital, leaving a widow who only outlived him by a year, a son, who was in poor health, and two daughters.

Henry Parry Gilbey had been the guiding light of the firm, directing the energies of his two younger brothers and steering them into the sector of the wine trade that was to prove so profitable. He was recognised as the calming influence on their youthful exuberance. Work was his inspiration and he never developed the outside hobbies that so many of the directors did. He was modest and never spent ostentatiously, living a simple life in The Cottage, Stansted (which was larger than its name implied, being a substantial house, though not, by any means, a mansion). He did amass a fortune of £450,000, but most of his spending was on those in difficulties.

He was so well liked in his neighbourhood that the local paper, the *Herts and Essex Observer*, printed on his death: 'It is long since Bishop's Stortford and the neighbourhood has been plunged into such a general state of mourning as it has this week through the death of Henry Parry Gilbey.' In his lifetime, Henry had provided the Stansted Working Men's Club and had been a supporter of the Bishop's Stortford Working Men's Club; he had donated one quarter of the cost of restoring the parish church in Stansted; he had provided for the construction of the first public sewer in the village; and he had presented (with his brother Walter) the cast-iron fountain in the village centre.

His will became a source of problems. Firstly, his daughter Laura's husband, Henri Riviere, who represented a Cognac firm, contested it, claiming that his account had not been credited with the proper share of the profits. Alfred Carver states in his memoirs: 'I had to attend the Court with books to prove he had signed the balance sheets in the books every quarter for many years'. This evidence meant Henri Riviere was not successful, but he created such problems that it took 40 years to wind up the will.

Even more serious was the effect on the company, as the government had just introduced death duties for the first time and W&A Gilbey, as a partnership, had to find a large sum to meet them. This difficulty had to be avoided in the future, so it precipitated the formation of a private limited liability company, which was registered in 1893 with a share capital of £1,440,000. To safeguard the family concept severe restrictions were placed on ownership. The shares that were not available on the open market could only be held by a director or a direct male descendant of the original holder.

The first directors of the company were all family, as they were to be for a further 60 years. There were six of the original partners: Walter Gilbey, Sir James Blyth, Henry Arthur Blyth, Henry Gold, Charles Gold and Henry Grinling. The next generation were also joining the Board and, in 1893, these were; the sons of Alfred (who had died in 1879) – Alfred, William Crosbie, and Newman Gilbey; the sons of Walter Gilbey – Henry Walter and Arthur Nockolds; a son of Henry Gold – Alfred; of James Blyth – Herbert William; a son of Charles Gold – Arthur; of Henry Grinling – Gibbons; and of Henry Blyth – Arthur.

Three of the original directors died soon after, causing further sadness and disturbances. The first, in 1900, was Henry Gold, who had made his home at Cookham near Maidenhead. Within the company he had been the legal expert and outside it he was a JP and a Deputy Lieutenant, becoming, in 1897, the High Sheriff of Berkshire. He had left eight surviving children and it was Alfred (Argo) Gold who represented them in the company. The girls made a contribution too, as three of his daughters made useful business connections, one marrying Walter Watney, the second marrying her first cousin, Arthur Gilbey, and the third, Arthur Watney. Walter Watney's brother, Ernest, married Charles Gold's daughter. Although of the same family as the brewers, the Watneys had other occupations which were of benefit to the company. Walter and Ernest were sons of John Watney, proprietor of a major spirit distillery, which supplied spirit for gin making to W&A Gilbey. Arthur Watney was a partner in a City surveying firm, Daniel Watney, which became surveyors to W&A Gilbey. The extended family concept brought with it self-sufficiency, which applied not only to social, but also to business relationships.

Henry Gold's death was closely followed in 1901 by that of Henry Blyth, who had, like most of the partners, lived in Essex, at Stansted House. He had been the meticulous bookkeeper and had been in charge of the accounts until the formation of the private company. Then, lacking the qualifications to apply the new standards, he devoted more time to his hobby, one that he shared with many of the directors – horse racing. He had also been one of the best shots in the country, particularly of driven partridges.

In that same year, 1901, the first of the second generation died. This was Charles Gold's son, Arthur. The twentieth century had started sadly for W&A Gilbey and more serious matters were to come. W&A Gilbey had to face the fact that one of their important investments – Chateau Loudenne – was not a financial success.

Loudenne losses

Loudenne might have brought them prestige, but it was not a healthy investment financially. Sales of French wines peaked in the 1870s and then, when W&A Gilbey bought Loudenne, prices gradually declined. W&A Gilbey' sales of claret had fallen by one fifth by the start of the twentieth century. Small profits had been made at the end of the 1880s but most years there were deficits. More of the Board Members became disgruntled, especially those who did not take the trips to the Vintages. There must have been some resentment at the considerable amount of capital invested in the operations. Rigorous attempts were made to reduce expenses at Loudenne and in June 1904 the Board asked that the property be divided into three departments: the Vineyards, the Chais and the Estate. The latter included everything outside the vineyards and the chais; it was the area that covered all those wonderful visits and much of the development of the model estate – these were the luxuries and it was the area which the Board decided could be subjected to the most drastic reductions. These were the instructions that were given to their agent at Loudenne, a young Englishman called Sam Hucks. He was a member of a family which served the company well over several generations. Sam Hucks had the assistance of local expertise, as Monsieur Gombeau's special area was the chais and Monsieur Bayle looked after the vineyards.

It is never easy to drastically cut expenses, as Sam Hucks was asked to do by the Board, and probably even more difficult to manage it when a foreigner. It was no surprise that there were personality clashes and Sam Hucks actually sacked Monsieur Bayle in January of 1905. When the Board of W&A Gilbey asked him for an explanation he claimed it was because of Bayle's extravagance in the treatment of the vineyard. The Board decided he had been precipitate in discharging Bayle and wanted him reinstated. This left Sam Hucks with little option but to resign and that must have been what the Board wanted. Loudenne was left to be run by their French managers and they were to focus just on the chais and the vineyards. In addition, any vineyards not considered commercially viable were uprooted and these included those carefully-drained low lying vineyards. With such events, Loudenne could only be judged as a success in terms of its use as an advertising medium and not on financial grounds.

Anti-Drink Campaigns

W&A Gilbey lost an important assistant to the drink trade when Gladstone retired from the Government. He had stood up to the opponents of alcohol, who were continually lobbying the government to restrict or ban its consumption. There were numerous enquiries throughout the Victorian era to assess the validity of their case.

The end of the Government's liberal attitude towards liquor came with the introduction of a Licensing bill in 1880. This first time they were unsuccessful, as organised opposition from the trade, including the off licence trade, led to its withdrawal. Nevertheless, lobbying from the temperance societies continued and in 1897 a Royal Commission to study liquor licensing laws was set up.

Some idea of the strength and views of those against alcohol can be gathered from the report of the meeting of the Grand Lodge of the Independent Order of Good Templars, in which it was reported that there were 712 societies and 46,402 members pledged against alcohol, tobacco, gambling and profane language.

In an 1897 edition of the Alliance News describing the work of that Royal Commission it said:

> The complicity in numerous instances of the trade with the Watch Committee, the police and the legal advisers of the bench has been shown up, clearly proving that, in addition to the gross forms of evil publicly generated by the liquor traffic, its subtle influence has been shamelessly employed to poison the courts of justice and to paralyse the action of those responsible for the enforcement of law and order.

The Royal Commission produced much media interest and additional agitation from posters, like this example which was aimed at Licenced Victuallers:

> Who have reduced hundreds in the Trade to a state of abject slavery and compelled them to sign agreements of an atrocious and one sided nature; and last, whom, to the everlasting disgrace of a corrupt or incompetent Licensing Authority, are being privileged openly to plunder, poison and impose upon the British public and to feed and to fatten on the most gross and scandalous monopoly which ever existed?
>
> Is there but one answer?
> Monopolist Brewers and Spirituous Liquor Dealers
> alias
> Public House Grabbers

It was strong stuff. On the one hand there was the acceptance, helped by W&A Gilbey's promotion, that small amounts of particular drinks were good for one and, on the other hand, strong opposition to this view because it was held that drink was the cause of much evil. In the times of Gladstone the former had been the dominant view, but supporters of the latter were growing

30. Advertisement featuring the two distilleries and the chateau.

and within the government too. In 1904 Balfour brought in a licensing act which reduced the number of houses that could sell liquor; but it was Lloyd George who had the most serious impact on the trade. He waged a vendetta against the drink trade, which he dubbed the 'drink traffic'.

Lloyd George's first serious move was made in a famous budget of 1909 which led to the Peers v. People election of 1910. He proposed to raise the duty on spirits from 11s to 14s 9d on the proof gallon and apply very heavy duties on all liquor licences to help finance the National Insurance Plan. This caused consternation at W&A Gilbey and Sir Walter, no longer a member of the Board, must have watched anxiously. According to Alec Gold's account the Board met almost daily and severe economies were contemplated, including the sale of the Pantheon (though no reasonable offers were received). Letters of protest were sent to the Prime Minister and the Chancellor of the Exchequer. Fanny Gold's diary of 1909 mentions (on May 6th) that her husband, Charles Gold, went with some others of the firm to interview Lloyd George about the Budget and they were received amicably. As a former Liberal MP, Charles must already have been acquainted with Lloyd George. The meeting was to no avail, however.

The general election was held and the people gave their support to the Budget. This led to much more than high taxes for the drink trade as the House of Lords, in rejecting that famous budget and not earning the support of the public in the subsequent election, lost their last real power. W&A Gilbey survived this first onslaught from Lloyd George, but there was another after Sir Walter had died. In 1915 Lloyd George tried to quadruple the tax on wines and double that on spirits, but the opposition was strong. These taxes were not introduced and Lloyd George's consolation prize, that a Scotch had to be a minimum age before it could be sold, did not affect W&A Gilbey, as they only put mature spirits on the market.

Whisky sales did fall after the Lloyd George budget, but W&A Gilbey were not put off as they diverted their efforts into the export market. They even expanded the business in other areas, becoming the largest distributors of port in the UK. In 1909 – 1910 they found another means to cut out the middleman, as they purchased the prestigious Port House, Croft and Co., in Oporto, Portugal.

Constitution of Whisky Questioned

Increased duties were just one of the problems faced by the W&A Gilbey whisky production. W&A Gilbey had three malt pot still distilleries, the traditional form of whisky production, but creeping onto the market through the last decade of the century were blends of the malt whisky and patent still spirit, usually called grain whisky, but sometimes referred to more picturesquely as silent spirits.

For the first time the firm of W&A Gilbey showed some reactionary tendencies, taking time to adjust to this particular new trend. Walter Gilbey in his book 'Notes on Alcohol' summarised their views:

The effect of Plain Spirit on the consumer is altogether different from that of matured Pot Still Spirit – i.e. genuine Whisky. The former merely stimulates the action of the heart; the latter, in addition, braces the nerves and other vital centres. Thus, Plain Spirit might fail to restore a patient in the state of collapse, where a matured Grape or Malt Spirit would succeed. This difference is due to the matured secondary products of Whisky.

W&A Gilbey held out for traditional production, failing to adapt to a new approach in the way they had in the past. Eventually, in 1905, W&A Gilbey bowed to, rather than led, public demand and started to use grain whisky in their blends. It was terrible timing, as the authorities suddenly questioned the validity of this whisky. Islington Borough Council accused off-licences of selling whisky which was not of the quality demanded and claimed that customers were being duped. The defendants in two test cases were found guilty, there were appeals, much furore and considerable publicity. Finally in 1908 a Royal Commission was set up with the aim of defining Whisky. The famous 'What Is Whisky?' enquiry began.

W&A Gilbey were described by that Commission as: 'the largest distributing business in the United Kingdom'[2] and were called on to give evidence. It was Alfred Gilbey's son and namesake who spoke for the company.

He explained that grain spirit made from maize was cheaper because the process was continuous, but that it lacked bouquet and flavour and was a neutral spirit, nearly pure alcohol. Pot still whisky had a fuller flavour, improved with age, and would take more dilution with water.

After calling upon the best technical, legal, practical and scientific evidence, the Commission allowed patent still as well as pot still to be called whisky. W&A Gilbey were clear to continue blending their whiskies and, thanks to the interest that had been aroused by the Commission, they were able to sell more of it.

An Acrimonious Ending

Walter Gilbey was the one who had led the company into this position of market leader, as he held the office of chairman for just short of fifty years. Sadly, he relinquished his position not in a blaze of glory, but after acrimonious disagreements.

He became concerned about the management of the company and in a memorandum in November 1899 wrote :

1. Numerous requests have been made to me from time to time by different Partners that I would reconsider the attitude which I thought it proper to adopt last year with regard to the motions by Mr Charles Gold and others for the rearrangement of our Capital. In view of the fact that some additional capital is urgently needed to carry on the business on a satisfactory basis, I have been considering the question afresh with the assistance of Mr Henry Grinling and Sir Ernest Clarke, whom I have previously consulted in these matters, and I now suggest for adoption by the Board the following proposals:

2. OBJECTS OF THE SCHEME – the chief objects which I have had in view in framing the subjoined Scheme for the reconstruction of the Company has been to affect existing interests as little as possible, and to endeavour to free the Share Capital – both Ordinary and Preference – from as many restrictions as possible consistent with safety. The Scheme will, I think, be found to provide for:

i. The obtaining of the new capital immediately necessary.

ii. The creation of further capital which can be issued in the future, as the business may require, without dislocating existing capital.

iii. The placing of the Company on such a footing that at any time it can be made into a completely public Company without the necessity for reconstruction.

iv. The provision of a proper Reserve Fund.

v. The reorganisation of the management of the Company's affairs.

3. CAPITAL OF NEW COMPANY – I propose that a new Company shall be registered with a Share Capital of £3,000,000, and a Loan Capital of £1,000,000, to take over the business of the old Company as from the 1st January 1900, such capital to be allocated as follows:

i. £1,500,000 in Ordinary Shares of £10. Each Ordinary Share in the old Company to receive two Shares in the new Company (thus doubling the Ordinary Capital). This will absorb £1,440,000 of the new Ordinary Capital: the remaining £60,000 to be held in reserve for future issue to those whom it may be desirable to interest in the business.

ii. £1,500,000 in five percent Preference Shares of £10. £720,000 of these to be allotted share for share to the Preference Shareholders in the present Company: the balance to be held in reserve for issue later on, as money may be required for the purposes of extending the business.

iii. £1,000,000 in four percent Debenture Stock. This stock to be irredeemable by the Company before 1 January 1920, but to be repayable at the Company's option after that date at the average price of the Stock of the three previous years: not being in any case less than the price of issue of the Stock, which I suggest should be £103.

a. £560,000 of this Stock would replace the existing 4% Debenture Stock, now repayable at any time at £103. The present Debenture Stockholders would have the option of taking £100 of the new Stock for each £100 of the old, instead of receiving £103 cash.

b. £80,000 to be issued in replacement of the existing Second Debentures.

c. £150,000 to repay Bank Loan, etc.

d. £210,000 to be new money required for the immediate purposes of the business.

4. DEBENTURE STOCK – A public issue of the four percent Debenture Stock to be made at 103 percent at as early a date as possible on a prospectus and a Stock Exchange quotation to be obtained for such Stock. The premiums received from the new subscribers for Debenture Stock to be applied towards the expenses of the reconstruction of the Company. I consider it important to limit our issue to the public to one Stock and to begin with the Debenture Stock, which is the best security we have to offer, and which there is no reason to doubt will be readily subscribed for by a desirable class of holders.

5. PREFERENCE SHARES – At the present market prices of similar Stocks, our Preference Shares may be regarded as worth something more than their par value. Of course the increase in the amount of Debenture Stock which will in future rank before the Preference,

diminishes to some little extent the security capital which the Preference represent; and had we been recasting the capital altogether, I should have been inclined to put out Preference Capital upon a 4½ percent basis, as representing the difference between the security of the two Stocks. But it is important to interfere as little as possible with existing interests and we had better leave, therefore, the Preference Shares exactly as they are with their 5 percent dividend. When the time comes for an issue of further Preference Shares beyond the £720,000 already in existence, The Board can decide the premium at which these Shares are to be placed on the market; but at present, as stated above, I regard them as worth a sum which would yield 4½ percent interest.

6. DISPOSAL OF PREFERENCE SHARES – I am ready to assent to the Preference Shares being freed from any restrictions as to transfer, which will enable the Partners to make such dispositions as they desire of their property amongst their families. I think it would be unwise to complicate any public issue of the Company's Capital by offering two Stocks at the same time: and, moreover, I am myself not desirous of parting with any of my own holding in the business, which I should be obliged to do to a considerable amount under the Stock Exchange Rule, which requires two-thirds of any issue of Shares to be offered un-reservedly to the public. But if, as I have every reason to expect will be the case, the public subscribed freely for the proposed issue of £1,000,000 Debenture Stock, I should be prepared to waive my own right under the prospectus to take up new Debenture Stock to the extent of my present holding (say £100,000) of the old Stock, if I could reinvest it (at a price to yield approximately 4½ percent) in Preference Shares of our Company now held by others, but which any of the holders might desire to realise in cash. If, therefore, any of the Partners think well to tender to me before the new Debenture Stock is advertised, any or all of their Preference Shares at the price of eleven pounds (£11) per £10 Share, I will take them up at that price to the extent that I may be relieved of my present Debenture holding by the applications of the public.

7. ORDINARY SHARES – I am ready also to assent to the Ordinary Shares being capable of devolution by will to any Member of any Partner's family, subject to the approval by the Board of the Transferee, and on the following understanding as to a Reserve Fund:

a. The old Ordinary Shares of £720,000 have yielded on the average a dividend of 22 percent. The doubled capital would therefore yield a dividend of 11 percent, if our profits should remain at their present level.

b. It is indispensable, however, in a business like ours, that we should have a Reserve Fund for the equalisation of the Dividends and general purposes.

c. I suggest, therefore, that the normal dividend on the new Shares should be regarded as 8 percent (equivalent of 16 percent on the old capital).

d. So long as the dividend has not fallen below 8 percent per annum, half the extra profits should go to a Reserve Fund. Thus, if 11 percent could be declared on any occasion, the Ordinary Shares would get 8 percent and half the extra 3 percent = 1½ percent. Total = 9½ percent and the other 1½ percent would go to the Reserve Fund.

8. RESERVE FUND – Of course, the allocation of a portion of the profits of a Reserve Fund will diminish the amount of the income actually realisable at the moment on the Ordinary Shares. Such a Reserve Fund ought to be regarded in the light of an Insurance and will be to the ultimate benefit of the younger Shareholders, rather than their seniors. But as its operation will diminish the immediate income of some of the junior Directors, I think their case might be met by an arrangement between the sons and their fathers for an additional allotment of Shares to the former to meet such a deficiency, as I am proposing to do in the case of my own sons, by the fathers making the sons an increased personal allowance.

9. MANAGEMENT – Whilst not desirous of limiting the amount of assistance given to the business by the older Directors, or interfering with the work which they have been accustomed to undertake, it seems to me indispensable for the proper conduct of our affairs that we should have a small body of the younger Partners acting as Managing Directors, directly responsible to the Board for the proper administration of the several Departments as set out below.

1. MANAGING DIRECTORS – I propose that the existing Board of Directors should meet only once a quarter, unless special necessity arises for more frequent meetings. The details of the business to be managed by five Managing Directors, to be appointed annually, such Managing Directors to devote all the time as may appear to them necessary to secure the efficient control of our affairs and each to take charge of a particular Department. Each Managing Director to receive £500 a year remuneration. The five Managing Directors (whose names are to be agreed upon before the new Company is formed) to be responsible for the following Departments:

    i. Finance and Agency
    ii. Advertising and Agency
    iii. Purchasing
    iv. Export and Stores Management
    v. Stores Office

11. HEADS OF DEPARTMENTS – The five Managing Directors to be assisted by the following Heads of Departments:

a. Secretary	Mr Burke
b. Cashier	Mr Brown
c. Accountant	Mr Carver
d. Book-keeper	Mr Macfarlane
e. Export	Mr Sleep
f. Purchasing	Mr Larking
g. Stores Management	Mr Webb
h. Stores Office	Mr Plowright

Each Head of a Department to receive, as such, £200 per annum in addition to his present salary, together with a percentage (to be fixed by agreement between the Directors) on the future profits beyond the average profits of the last five years.

I think it right to say that the above Scheme would be considered by the Board as a whole. I am quite willing to consider modifications of it in points of detail, but I should have to reconsider my position in making these proposals for what I believe to be the general good, if in any essential principle the Scheme now suggested were departed from .

Walter Gilbey

Two years later, in a letter written to Sir Walter, his friend and solicitor to the company, W.E. Gillett, mentioned,: 'the all important question of management upon which you feel so strongly.'[3]

Sir Walter thought that the Board took too little notice of his opinions, although there are plenty of refutations of this view. It is also important to take into account that he had a mass of other activities and, as Gillett said in another letter to him in 1905: 'your numerous very important pursuits and engagements of late years have quite precluded you giving that attention in detail to the very complex affairs of the business'.[4] Certainly, much had to be decided without him.

With very little material about this disagreement, and nothing being said about it at the time by those who wrote about the company, it is hard to assess whether it was just about an old man feeling dissatisfied with the way the younger generation were handling the company's affairs. It may have been that, in giving the Board a pretty free hand when it suited him to run other ventures, he did not like it when he found he had lost his power over them and could not push through issues he wanted. On the other hand, he might have been justified in his anxieties.

He was certainly not behaving like an old reactionary chairman when he tried to persuade them to make W&A Gilbey ready to be an open public company with a re-arranged Board of Directors. This showed positive thinking and that the old adventurous spirit was still ready to adjust to changing circumstances. It is difficult to know whether, if he had been successful, it would have led to more a lively and forward thinking Company through the 1920s and 1940s, making it a stronger force than it proved to be, or whether it would have led to the end of the family firm, as it did when the Company finally went public in 1946.

His disagreement with the directors came to a head in 1904. In October he resigned as chairman, but this did not lead to appeasement. In a letter on January 14th, 1905 he took matters to the extreme when he asked to give up his directorate and sever all interest in the Company. On the same day he wrote to Mr Gillett saying: 'quite recently the treatment of the directors towards me has been too cruel. In spite of all you have said and the advice you write me – I must get quite clear of all connections with the company.'

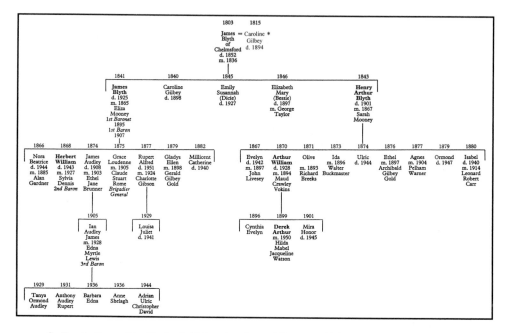

*C. Family Tree – The Blyths. * Eldest daughter of Henry and Elizabeth Gilbey (see page 20).*

This was a dramatic statement for such a conformist and its content and tone must have shocked the Board, who had been thought of as so family-minded. Henry Grinling, who had taken over as chairman, said in his letter of reply: 'your letter of the 14th instant announcing your retirement from the position of Director of the Company came upon us all as a great surprise.'

Following the bombshell of the resignation, A.J. Burke, secretary to the Company, wrote on January 16, 1905 to Walter Gilbey. He writes about the following points, which it is possible to surmise are the points that had disturbed Walter Gilbey. The first of these was a decline in sales by W&A Gilbey, but Burke finds a cause for this in the general depression and claims that, relative to others, they have acceptable records. The second was the question of restrictions on members of the family entering the business, as he discusses the case of Charles Gold, who wanted to bring in his grandson, Geoffrey, son of Arthur Gold. (Geoffrey eventually became a director.) The third was the question of Loudenne. It seems likely that the declining returns and the treatment of Sam Hucks, in particular, who Walter Gilbey held in high regard, and of Loudenne in general, were the major reasons behind his anger at the Board.

There is no doubt there were rifts within the family, especially between the two who became most famous outside the Company: James Blyth and Walter Gilbey. Nicholas Faith in Victorian Vineyard said: 'By 1904 they were, allegedly, barely on speaking terms – it is even said that they used different drives to the Chateau – even if that was a family legend, the visitors book shows 'Sir Walter's party' was quite distinct from 'Sir James and his friends'.'

Sir James was made a baronet for his services to agriculture, but there is a degree of mocking in Alfred Carver's recollections when he said that these services: 'consisted of keeping an expensive herd of Jersey cows and building a model dairy of Carrara marble in the grounds of Blythwood, which was superintended by Signor Fabbricottie, who owned the marble quarries in Italy.' It sounds a bit ostentatious for Walter Gilbey's tastes and then Sir James received even greater honours, a Peerage, for his services to the Liberal Party. It was an honour Sir Walter just missed, as we shall see later. Carver does add, and this is a strong statement for the discreet accountant: '[Sir James] attended more to social functions and less to business and spent heavily on dinner parties to political men and women – not much use to business'. The picture becomes clearer. The sober, upright and less honoured Walter Gilbey could easily be at odds with a nephew who was more of a bon viveur.

It seems, too, that it was James Blyth who was thought to have played a part in getting Sam Hucks ousted from Loudenne. On January 27 he wrote to Walter saying: 'You have been misinformed about my having had in contemplation for the last four or five years the removal of Sam Hucks from Loudenne'. Then he goes on to say that Hucks fired Bayle because: 'he was very impertinent and difficult to work with' and does not mention one of the reasons Burke gave in his letter about the Board meeting, that Bayle was extravagant in his methods of treatment of the vineyards. There is a definite colouring of the cases.

Blyth does go on to say, quite sensibly:

It seems however quite clear to me, that if we continue opposing each other, as we have done lately, that not only our incomes, but any reputation we had, must irretrievably suffer and, for the sake of our children, it surely is the duty of we senior members to try and prevent such a calamity, even if we should feel that others are more to blame than we are.

The Memorandum submitted to the Directors on Monday 20th February, 1905, by Sir Walter's solicitors, Baileys Shaw & Gillett stated:

Sir Walter Gilbey, after correspondence with Messrs Baileys Shaw and Gillett, has intimated his determination, having resigned the Chairmanship and Directorate, to divest himself of his Shares and Debentures in the Company.

His holding of £102,455 4% debenture stock will be offered for sale forthwith, or as Sir Walter shall determine in the open market.

As a large shareholder in the company, his decision caused some consternation, though at the age of 74 he is unlikely to have been making much of a contribution to the firm's administration. His resignation from the Board could not have been so disturbing. He had been in charge for 48 years.

Letters between Walter Gilbey and the Company's solicitors, Baileys, Shaw & Gillett,[5] pursue the matter of how he can rid himself of his Ordinary Shares (with a nominal value of £146,200), Preference Shares (with a nominal value of £190,000) and Debenture Stock (with a nominal value of £102,455), without exposing the rift publicly and causing a drop in their value. The

Directors tried conciliation, at one time offering an Honorary Chairmanship – but this was turned down.

They got very close to signing a deal, with his sons assigned the Ordinary Shares but the income going to him during his lifetime, the Debentures being retained by him and the Directors, other than the Chairman Henry Grinling, agreeing to guarantee him his income from the preference shares, so long as he did not sell them.

It should be noted that the Directors thought there was no need to guarantee the income from these Preference Shares as it was very safe, but Walter insisted, as he said the whole point of these disagreements were that he had no confidence in the future of the Company and its ability to pay the same interest.

After months of negotiation, in July 1905, an agreement seemed imminent, the Directors having even signed it, but then they received a letter from him, dated July 22, saying he could not sign as he had to be able to sell the preference stock. He appears to have lost all faith in the Company and was determined to safeguard his income and capital at any cost.

Walter then announced his intention of selling the Preference Shares and there was general incredulity and consternation in the letters trying to dissuade him. On October 18th he wrote to his own solicitor, Mr Wolfe,[6] saying: 'I intend to sell all my preference shares as speedily as possible. . . . In spite of what you say, but the time has passed to be prudent.' Then, on October 20, in response to pleas that this was going to have a disastrous effect on the family, he wrote again to Mr Wolfe: 'It is to the interest of my family that I am looking, and to them alone, which has decided me to dispose of my preference stock.'

Walter Gilbey's intentions were a mystery, for the predicted outcome of this action would be a depression in the value of the shares and a loss in the value of his and his family's capital. A person of his eminence trying to sell so many shares would have exposed the rift within the family and his lack of confidence in the Company.

Frederick Wolfe, his personal solicitor, was so concerned that he declined to send the Notice of intention to sell the Preference shares to the Company Secretary, Mr Burke, saying: 'I really cannot take any part in a step which in my judgement may be fraught with future mischief to yourself and to the Company and therefore to your family.'[7]

Walter Gilbey was not deterred, replying: 'I have no alternative but to sign and send the notice direct to Mr Burke, Secretary to the Company'.[8] It was duly received, with much regret on the part of Mr Burke.

W.E. Gillett, the Company solicitor with whom he had worked for thirty years, wrote a personal letter, referred to above, which included the statements: 'You are taking a course which is not up to your high standard of business morality, upon which you have acted all your life,' and 'Surely you don't want it to go down in posterity that you pulled down the splendid structure you built up.'

Heated exchanges and negotiations continued and appear to have ended with a reasonably satisfactory outcome.

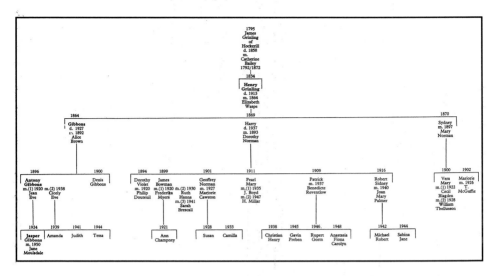

*D. Family Tree – The Grinlings. *Sister of Elizabeth Bailey (see page 20).*

There is very little information about this disruption. Carver, as a loyal employee, does not talk about it in his memoirs. It must have been a sad time though, as the letters of Walter Gilbey show emotion, which is never apparent in any of his earlier or later correspondence. He was very hurt and the concept of the family as a pillar of W&A Gilbey policy had taken a battering.

Henry Grinling, the cousin who went to the Crimea with Walter and Alfred, took over as Chairman and steered the company through those difficult times when Lloyd George was waging his wars on the drink trade. In March 1913 Henry was in the Boardroom when he had a stroke. He only lived for a few more weeks.

Alfred Carver said about Henry Grinling: 'Everyone liked Uncle Ben, as he was called, and his quiet calm manner was a distinct contrast to the eager, excitable character of the Gilbeys and Blyths.'

William Gilbey, the second son of Alfred senior, took over the chair for the last year of Walter Gilbey's life and was much respected for his shrewdness and sense of humour. He instituted such 'modern' developments as the Managing Committee, which met on Thursdays and to which the heads of departments reported on the past week's activities.

In the last decade of his life, with Henry Grinling and then William Gilbey taking over the leadership of W&A Gilbey, Walter could focus his energies on a mass of activities connected with the countryside. These activities had taken an ever-increasing proportion of his attention, since the Company had been established.

V
The Life of a Victorian Gentleman

Once W&A Gilbey had been established as a thriving concern, Walter Gilbey began transferring his successful tactics to country pursuits. This was provoked to some extent by weaknesses in his health, for which he had even gone to the length of bringing cows to his London home to provide him with fresh milk. In the main, however, the reason was that the business was no longer providing the absorbing challenge of the early years. He had found relatives who could do much of the work, so that business could become more of a means to the end of providing the funds to pursue his many other interests that centred around family, homes and country pastimes.

His passion was his horses. The *City Leader* newspaper of 1891 summed this up well: 'Just get Mr Walter Gilbey to talk about horses and it is as interesting as a finish of a neck and neck Derby.' He had a huge general knowledge, from shoeing to breeding, from Welsh ponies to thoroughbreds. He did not fall into the way of future generations of being an expert in one area only, which G.M. Young describes so aptly in his picture of Victorian times, *Portrait of An Age*, as: 'the Waste Land of the Experts, each knowing so much about so little that he can neither be contradicted nor is it worth contradicting.'

Walter Gilbey became an 'expert', but in a bedazzling range of activities, from lavender and jam to cattle and horses, from sporting artists to book collecting, from shooting and fishing to collecting rare birds – and he was expert enough to write books about various subjects, ranging from alcohol to cockfighting.

The pivot to his life, in line with Victorian principles, was the family. He was father to nine children, who were brought up in a disciplined household where routines were upheld and projects like holidays minutely planned months in advance.

In the country as a whole the last part of the Victorian era was a time of extraordinary change: with the switch towards democracy in politics, the shake up of religion by the theory of evolution, the transfer of emphasis on education from practical experience to specialisation and technical knowledge. The devastating agriculture depression had ended the long domination of the landed aristocracy and the poor were at last being given the opportunity to improve their position through education, collective bargaining and increased assistance from the State. With this whirlwind of transformation some secure base was needed. For the Victorians the family provided this, becoming a type of time capsule, with an outer wall to provide at least a temporary haven where there was stability, discipline, tradition and unchanged standards. For the Gilbeys their time capsule stretched around huge numbers, as Blyths,

Gilbeys, Grinlings and Golds built, bought or leased their residences around Bishop's Stortford.

Jersey Cattle

Walter Gilbey's first home in the country was Hargrave Park at Stansted, which he leased in 1864, and to which he could take those cows that had provided him with fresh milk in London. Even when he took his children to Brighton for a holiday, two of his own cows went with them! He wanted to build up a herd, but not an ordinary one, he wanted the best and this he achieved. John Thornton's *History of the Jersey Breed of Cattle* said: 'No herd has, however, been more distinguished or realised higher prices than that belonging to Mr Walter Gilbey.'

His methods were simple but strict. Culling was ruthless, with sub-standard cows sold or given away. Only high-quality cows were bought and Walter soon became known as a good customer for top animals. Records were kept of all offspring and their performance and the quality of the stock was tested in competitions. Essex County Show was the first at which Walter entered his stock and when he found that the low prize money attracted only a few animals, he sponsored higher prizes.

This financial boost had a startling effect on standards in the district. The demand for quality animals rose and drafts were sent in to Bishop's Stortford to be sold at the auction. Standards rose, prices were higher and this gave farmers the incentive to invest and breed better animals. Walter Gilbey, by setting an example and by providing financial incentives for other farmers to breed quality animals, had improved standards generally.

Hargrave was not the Gilbey home for long. In 1874, on the death of the owner, the lease was terminated, and Walter Gilbey, after a short stay at Norman House, Stansted, bought a house in Brighton. He stayed there for

31. The Essex Show years later with Sir Henry Walter Gilbey in the foreground, in a bowler hat.

three years (although history does not relate, we may assume that some cows went too). Sadly, the great herd of Jerseys had to be dispersed. Their sale made record prices and proved the success of the principles that he was to apply in many other fields: buy the best, cull judiciously and encourage competition through providing higher prize money, all of which raises standards and interest generally and in turn provides a good market for stock and a better return on investments.

Elsenham Hall

The estate on which Walter was to expand the use of these principles was the one where he stayed for the rest of his life – Elsenham Hall. It was on the Cambridge side of Bishop's Stortford, close to where he had been brought up and about 37 miles from London. He moved there in 1878.

It was an ancient site, as the Manor of Elsenham had been the home of the Barons of Folkestone in the eleventh century. The present hall was described by Nicholas Pevsner in *The Buildings of England* as a: 'largish symmetrical red brick mansion, late Georgian, castellated with three bay cemented porch between the two projecting wings.'[1]

It had, too, a history concerning the animals that were his great passion – horses. The previous occupier had been George Rush, a celebrated balloonist and a breeder of racehorses, including Plenipotentiary which won the 1834 Derby (this famous horse was buried in the Elsenham paddocks). More Derby winners were to be bred there, not in Walter Gilbey's time, but in that of Dorothy Paget, who owned it in the 1930s.

This land must have suited horses and in his 36 years at Elsenham Walter Gilbey was to produce top animals in practically every sphere, except racing. He nearly achieved that too, as his son, Henry Walter, only just failed to persuade him to buy St. Simon, which went on to win the 1884 Gold Cup at Ascot.

With his meticulous regard for quality, Walter made sure he ran an exemplary estate and extended it, building onto the house and eventually farming about 3,000 acres. As he was to say: 'There is now of course no need for me to make money but I like to see the estate turned to best advantage and I do not believe in working at anything for nothing.'

In addition the square, red brick house was made into a sizeable mansion. This was necessary because by the time he moved to Elsenham he had nine children, his wife Ellen having produced them in just thirteen years. The eldest five were all boys: Henry Walter; Arthur, the sensible business-like one, who went into the firm; Tresham, the country gentleman who hunted, farmed, ran a polo team and was a mainstay of local activities around Bishop's Stortford; Guy, who married the heiress to the Merryweather fire engine business; and Sebastian. Tragically this youngest son, when just 16 years of age, drank water out of the well at Elsenham on returning from a shoot. It was contaminated by a pipe to a septic tank and he, together with a member of staff, died from typhoid in 1896.

The girls were in the minority, the eldest being Maud, who shared her

32. Some views of the Elsenham Estate

33. First Sir Walter Gilbey and family, with husbands standing behind their wives. From left to right:
Top row: Tresham Gilbey, Dan Hine, Henry Walter, Emily Gilbey, Guy Gilbey, Arthur Gilbey, Len Routledge, Robert Barrow
Bottom row: Annie Gilbey (nee Barker), Maud Hine (nee Gilbey), Isabella Gilbey (nee Fowlie), Sir Walter Gilbey, Beatrice Gilbey (nee Gold), Mabel Kate Routledge (nee Gilbey), Rose Barrow (nee Gilbey)

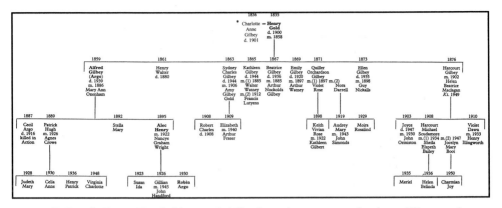

*E. Family Tree – The Golds, part 1. *Charlotte Anne, younger daughter of Henry and Elizabeth Gilbey (see page 20). Her husband Henry Gold was the elder brother of Charles Gold (see page 97).*

father's interests and became his main assistant; one year younger was Mabel; then four years to Rose; and the baby of the family was Emily.

Elsenham was enlarged to help accommodate them and to enable the entertainment of the mass of cousins who lived in the district and the ones who lived further afield, like the Alfred Gilbey family and the Henry Golds in the Thames valley. The additions were extensive. The ground floor could boast of rooms for every occasion, as there was a library, a dining, a drawing, a smoking, a morning and a tea room. On the first floor there were twelve bedrooms, together with a further library, on the half landing there was a billiard room, as well as three bedrooms, and on the upper floor there were four further bedrooms and eight servants' bedrooms.

Walter Gilbey built up a sheltered and comfortable existence for his family and staff at Elsenham. His attitude was: 'I like a comfortable house myself and I like to see other people comfortable,' but he then added the sting, 'if they deserve it. Some people do not deserve it'.[2]

The above attitude was illuminated by what became known in the press as 'The Great Egg Case of 1907'. His head gamekeeper and employee for 20 years, Herbert William Stride, was accused of stealing pheasants' eggs from Elsenham. At first Walter Gilbey did not believe that his trusted employee could do such a thing and it was the East Anglian Game Protection Society that had to bring the case for the prosecution. As the leading KC, Edward Marshall-Hall, conducted Stride's defense, it was thought that Sir Walter must have financed this. Stride was, however, found guilty, and convicted to 12 months' hard labour. Walter Gilbey realised he had been misled, and by even more than the Court unearthed, as Stride was convicted of stealing 6,750 pheasants eggs, but further evidence showed that the total was nearer to 30,000.

Stride then came into Walter Gilbey's category of not 'deserving comfort' and he withdrew all support, showing no sympathy for Stride's position when he came out of prison as a father of five children with no employment. He even took steps to get Stride's brother's tenancy revoked.

Walter Gilbey provided comfort for large numbers of those of whom he considered did deserve it and at Elsenham they usually sat down thirty or more for dinner each evening. The family were self sufficient within themselves for entertainment. Many cousins married each other. Walter's second son, Arthur, married one of Henry Gold's daughters, Beatrice, and two of Alfred Gilbey's daughters, Mary and Elizabeth, married Walter and Charles, sons of Charles Gold. Blyths and Golds also intermarried.

It is highly probable that the Gilbey, Blyth and Gold families in Essex were not considered socially acceptable by the local landed gentry in the whole period up to the first world war. In addition to their Liberal politics, which favoured free trade as against the Tory protectionist leanings of the agricultural landowners, reliant on their estates alone for their income, they also carried the dreaded stigma of trade. It is probable that Alfred Gilbey and Henry Gold, in making their homes in the Thames Valley in the 1860s, had done so in order to cut themselves adrift from their relatively humble associations in Essex. Certainly they appear to have been absorbed more quickly into the local society in which they found themselves than their Essex relations, whose origins were well known.

A grandson of Charles Gold, Jack Gold, now in his nineties, can well remember a fight at an Edwardian children's tea party in which his assailant, without venom or apparent understanding of what he was saying, called him 'a dirty little Radical'. This was clearly a description that the boy had heard his parents use about the Gold family.

Social life was therefore quite largely inwardly directed. A clear example of this is to be found in the annual races and sports held by the Stansted Polo Club. Throughout the 1890s virtually all the prizes were presented by the families' members and were won by other members of the same families. In the same decade, the younger members of the family formed a musical troupe – the GGG Minstrels – which raised money for local hospitals and charities in Bishop's Stortford, Maidenhead and Kensington. Both these activities saw the Thames Valley and Essex contingents of the families joining forces and close contact was maintained between them, with frequent visits between houses.

When Charles Gold's youngest son wished to marry a daughter of Sir John Brunner, one of the founders of the company which was later at the core of Imperial Chemical Industries, Lady Brunner insisted that the young couple should live at least twenty miles from Bishop's Stortford and Stansted. She doubtless regarded the families' self sufficiency as amounting to an unhealthy self-absorption and she got her way.

Walter Gilbey himself was not a witty conversationalist. Rather, he was an extraordinary mixture of eccentricity and the mundane. He kept to a pattern in his life from which it was difficult to make him deviate. Breakfast was always between 7 and 8am until very late in his life, when he let it slip to 8.30am. He was careful about food and, indeed, about his whole lifestyle: 'As to myself, its because I have been able to take care of myself that I've been able to take care of other things and other people.'[3] His food first thing in the morning was spartan, always consisting of coffee or milk with bread. Even at lunch and dinner he hardly ever ate meat, but consumed large quantities of fish and stewed onions and always finished his meal with plain Madeira cake. In contrast to this meagre fare, his drink was champagne and the occasional brandy.

Lunch was always at 1.30pm and dinner at 8.30pm in the summer and half an hour earlier in winter. He was punctilious in the extreme and nobody was allowed to delay these times. Any latecomer would find that the meal had been started without him.

Walter Gilbey always went for quality and the cutlery was magnificent gold plate at dinner, which had to be returned to the safe after use. The safe was a walk-in strong room that also contained his trophies and he would take visitors in to show off the accomplishments of his stock. Then one day a member of the younger generation thought it would be funny to shut the door when Walter and a lady were inside. Sir Walter did not think it at all funny and got in such a rage that he kicked at the door and damaged his shoes. It took some time to release him and his lady visitor, as the only other person with a key was the butler and he was in his home, on the other side of the park. The prankster was sent home the next day.

There were plenty of staff at Elsenham and all with clearly defined duties. Their master was said to be quite frightening, but only if they did not perform their duties well. He might have lost his temper occasionally, but he did not have the arrogant attitude that some Victorian heads of household possessed. He had, after all, been brought up in poverty and he never turned into a snob. Indeed, he enjoyed a reputation as a generous landlord and employer.

He was proud of his staff and wanted them, like himself, to be immaculately turned out. The tailors Tissimans made the uniforms which they all had to wear, which was of such a special mustard yellow cloth that there was allegedly a patent on it. There was so much of this colour around he was said to suffer from yellow fever; even his books were bound in mustard yellow cloth. The footmen wore livery with tail coats and there were three standards of dress. For special occasions, like Christmas, they even wore powdered wigs and knee breeches.

Walter Gilbey himself wore the flashy clothes of a Parisian dandy, quite out of keeping with his genial British attitude and straight talking in conversation. To add to the contradictions, these clothes did not vary in style or colour. All his coats were made of vicuna, a very soft wool. Buff yellow dominated and was the colour of his waistcoat, with a rust gold handkerchief tucked in the pocket. Underneath was a stiff collared shirt with a white tie and on top a frock coat. In the evening the yellow was not so obvious, as he put on a dark coat.

The clothes might have been all the same, but there were still cupboards full of them. He always wore the same type of boots on his tiny feet, a closely fitting style that were covered by his trousers and he had thirty or forty identical pairs of them.

Walter always looked immaculate and in his later years his few strands of hair were carefully brushed forward to hide his baldness. His face was clean shaven, except for a neatly trimmed moustache. But he never had a bath, instead his frail body (he weighed only about 7 stone) was rubbed down with a mixture of oil and turps. This used to be done in a big cabinet, using different brushes for different areas of his body. In his later years it was the role of his nurse, Miss Martin, to carry out these duties.

He had one unusual habit, although it was more acceptable in those days than now, as he was a big smoker of pungent-smelling cigarettes bought in Brighton especially for him. They were Turkish and wrapped in rice paper and he smoked them from a large amber holder which had to be cleaned everyday.

Walter Gilbey's eye-catching appearance and some of his unconformist habits were attention-seeking, but those expecting a radical, dashing personality must have been surprised. His actions were practical and his manners exemplary. He was reluctant to change his style of living and practised moderation in everything (except, perhaps, cigarette smoking). His way of life was highly traditional. He went to bed early and, though he gave parties, none were riotous or even frivolous. He promoted a great family life and a wide range of hobbies that were the epitome of an English gentleman.

His wife, Ellen, was a homely, motherly type. She had no pretensions to be part of a smart society and was happiest in the country, amongst her family and helping the poor; yet she had a graciousness which, when she had to play her part as hostess at major events organised by her husband, earned her the respect of royalty and aristocracy. She was a quiet and gentle person, who was relied on by her children and husband alike for support and advice. Not a seeker of the limelight, she was a background figure in the Gilbey entourage, a pillar to their activities and was direly missed when she died in 1896 at 63.

A typical obituary read:

Whether at Cambridge House, Regents Park, Elsenham Hall or at the Wine Estate in Bordeaux, Lady Gilbey was distinguished by that refinement of manner and that quiet tact which are so rare nowadays. She was an enthusiastic supporter of all her husband's schemes, whether they benefited the poor, agriculture, horses or his own business.[4]

Her homely manner was well exemplified in a short anecdote in the same obituary: 'On one occasion, when entertaining the Duke and Duchess of York at Cambridge House, Lady Gilbey inadvertently addressed the Duchess as 'my dear' and at once apologised. Her Royal Highness smiled and the Duke said quickly, 'I believe, Lady Gilbey, that she likes it.'

The villagers at Elsenham held many fond memories of all the work she had done to help them and they welcomed the pump Sir Walter built in the middle of the village in her memory. Its dome was finished in gold leaf, so bright that it had to be covered during the World War II Blitz in case it was used as a landmark for the bombers. One hundred years after its erection it is still maintained by Sir Walter's grandson, Walter Anthony.

Of all Walter Gilbey's children it was Maud who was closest to him and who shared his interests most fully. She made a good marriage in business terms, choosing Daniel Hine of the brandy firm, but the strict outlook of the Gilbey family must not have suited his bon-viveur attitudes. A more wayward character, he became the black sheep of the family, gambling, running into debt and not giving his wife the support expected of him. It was therefore natural that she fell back on her family, taking over the role of running Elsenham Hall and the stud. She was the one who loved riding, went hunting and could reel off the pedigrees of all the horses on the stud. Her father could depend on her strong character, for her nephew, Vincent Routledge, said: 'She ruled the house with a rod of iron.' Her sisters were a little jealous of her influence, but her own daughters were devoted to her.

With such numbers of children, grandchildren and cousins coming under the protection and hospitality of Elsenham, there had to be some people at the top who were strong enough to keep control. Walter Gilbey and his daughter Maud might have scared the young ones, but they would have had to be firm to maintain respect and discipline within that huge household.

At the same time the Gilbeys and their many cousins were kindly, good people who loved to laugh. Practical jokes were a feature of the numerous social events held amongst them. Typical was the time the Henry Golds held a lunch party. Mrs Gold was deaf, but much beloved, and she announced that she had two very fine chicken for lunch. Some of the guests caught an old rooster, put it under the silver cover and asked the butler, named Bird, to put one in front of the hostess. All of the guests except her could hear the scratching. Imagine her shock as she lifted the cover and the bird flew away, to the cheers of the assembled company and much laughter!

As the years rolled by, the offspring of the various partners must have found it more and more difficult to appreciate just what a big gamble Walter Gilbey had taken in those early years, with his brothers, cousins and brothers-in-law, and just how hard he had worked. The feeling began to creep in, as it always does with the new generations that had not created the wealth, that they had a right to more of the fortune, that there was no need for them to work hard and earn more. The worm that would lead to the eclipse of W&A Gilbey was at work by the end of the century. The archives are full of letters from various members of the family asking 'the guvnr', as he was commonly known, for more money.

The Collections

There appeared to be so much wealth. Apart from that massive income of around £100,000 per year, roughly equivalent to in excess of £5 million a year one hundred years later, Walter had been a judicious purchaser. He loved collecting, some of his greatest finds being his sporting paintings. It is only in retrospect that his foresight can be fully appreciated. During the last decades of the nineteenth century he picked up dozens of pictures by Stubbs, Morland, Sartorius, J.F.Herring Snr, Alkens and the like. He kept the Stubbs and Morlands at Elsenham, even building a drawing room on to the north-east, lit by a dome so that the Morlands could be shown off to their best advantage in the natural light. Morland was not in fashion in Victorian times, when he was dismissed as a painter of pigs and ponies. His real ability was not recognised until later, so Walter Gilbey was able to buy his paintings for

34. Eclipse by G. Stubbs. One of the paintings in Sir Walter Gilbey's collection

a few guineas and his mezzotints for shillings.

He had to pay more for the pictures of Morland's contemporary, Stubbs, giving the relatively large sum of 660 guineas for his famous painting of Eclipse – but still only a trifle of its worth today. It is not recorded how much he paid for others like that of Gimcrack, the winner of 27 races in 1764, or for 'The Farmer's Wife and the Raven' which illustrates Gays Fable and was hung in the dining room at Elsenham. As early as 1888, the magazine *Vanity Fair*, in publishing an accompanying text to its Spy cartoon of Sir Walter, stated: 'He has the finest collection of horse pictures in the kingdom.' By the beginning of the twentieth century, even after a Christie's sale in 1890, mostly of duplicates of others still in his possession, his sporting art collection was recognised as the finest and possibly the largest collection in private hands. The leading authority on Stubbs, Basil Taylor, wrote in his book, *Stubbs*, that Sir Walter was the most assiduous and resourceful of all the Stubbs collectors.

Pictures were not the only objects Walter collected and showed off in his rooms at Elsenham. He was a connoisseur by nature and in the library and the smoking rooms there were some great bronzes and many sculptures of horses and other animals, as well as snuff boxes and old watches. Then there was the furniture, for he started buying Chippendale and Sheraton long before they became fashionable. He had a flair for forecasting future fashions, a commercial sixth sense which helped him make his business a success and turn his rather plain house at Elsenham into a distinguished residence.

One of the most interesting rooms was the library. The bookshelves were full of works dating back to the seventeenth and eighteenth century, providing a library of sporting and agricultural subjects that could not be rivalled. In addition there were old sporting magazines, such as *Baileys*, dating back a hundred years or more, all of which were fruitful sources of material for the many books he wrote. A frequent phrase he used was 'Get to know your facts' and this is what he did as an author, providing remarkable detail by using these collections of magazines and books and by finding experts on each subject.

The Author

He was able, amongst all his other activities, to be an author on an extraordinary range of subjects. With an emphasis on facts he did not spend too much time on trying to be literary. His style is not very lively, but there is an extraordinary amount of information. A reviewer summed it up well with: 'Sir Walter Gilbey's contributions to the literature of agriculture are apparently as inexhaustible as they are uniformly interesting and instructive.'[5]

His early writings were associated with the business. It seems likely that *Treatise on Wines*, published in 1869 under the name of the company, was his first. There followed more books on alcohol such as *Notes on Alcohol*, but he soon ventured onto his favourite subject of horses. A reviewer from the *Norfolk News* in 1901 said: 'It may safely be said that what Sir Walter Gilbey does not know about horses is not worth knowing. On every variety of the equine species useful to man he has written with knowledge and insight; on riding and driving horses, on the great horse or destrier (the war charger of our forefathers), on young race horses, on ponies.'[6]

One of the first such books, and one very close to his heart, was *The Great Horse or Shire Horse*, which was published in 1888. This work caused a great deal of interest, as he claimed that the Shire was the purest survivor of the type described by Medieval writers as the Great Horse, tracing its development to his day. The book went into its second edition in 1900 and was one of three of his books republished by Spur Publications in the 1970s. The other two were: *Farm Stock of Old*; and one that created a stir at the time of its publication, *Sport in Olden Time* (cockfighting). Banned in 1849, cockfighting, Sir Walter pointed out, had left us with many phrases, such as 'cock', 'to pit against' and 'to show a clean pair of heels'. He also wrote about hounds, pigs, poultry and some fascinating and decorative books on the painters he collected; *Animal Painters of England*, in two volumes, *The Life of George Stubbs R.A.* and so many more.

Sometimes his books provoked new thoughts on subjects. One such was *Small Horses in Warfare*, published in 1900. This received reviews in most of the national papers as it called into question the fashion for big horses for the army, extolling the virtue of the smaller horse, for which there was so much foundation stock in Britain. A review in the *Livestock Journal* of July 1900 assessed: 'Probably no work on horses in modern times has attracted so much attention in so short a time as has Sir Walter Gilbey's book on the value of small horses for cavalry remounts.'

His book production increased dramatically at the beginning of the twentieth century when age was limiting his other activities. With the assistance of a diligent secretary he collected some extraordinary material and put it together into many publications and articles. In his lifetime he produced close to thirty books and booklets. The *Herts Observer* of 1900 said:

> The list of works from the pen of the popular baronet of Elsenham Hall is getting to be quite a lengthy one. Many of them, as well as the frequent contributions to agricultural journals from the same pen, have a most

practical bearing upon a subject of which the author has made himself an authority of the first rank; and are very valuable contributions to the practical side of a most important branch of agricultural development.

He was also a proprietor, as in 1894 he bought *Bailey's Magazine*. As usual with his enterprises, he improved the quality. He persuaded more eminent writers to make contributions. He made Tresham the manager, as he was the son who was the most ardent follower of country pursuits. Indeed Tresham not only went foxhunting, he also wrote about it, publishing a history of the Essex Foxhounds. Tresham's other passion was polo: he even had his own polo team, The Silver Leys, and was a leading breeder of polo ponies.

The Birds

The land surrounding Elsenham was rolling parklands noted for their fine cedar trees and, not surprisingly, some special Gilbey touches. Lining the drive were hundreds of pink roses that had been brought all the way from Bordeaux. There was an Italian garden, a summer house and an ornamental lake covering 3.5 acres, on which swam several unusual types of ducks.

Birds were another of Walter Gilbey's great loves. Thousands of pheasants were reared on his farms to give some great days of shooting for his son, Henry Walter, and his friends, with daily bags well into four figures. The park surrounding the house, however, was out of bounds to the shooting parties, as it was treated as a sanctuary for the birds there. At breakfast time Walter Gilbey would open the window, throw out some scraps and 200 to 300 pheasants would come running. He made sure his birds were well fed. Some visitors were startled to see a dead foal or pony hanging in a tree as,

35. Part of the aviaries at Elsenham Hall

when one small enough to handle died at the stud, it was the practice to allow it to rot and be used as food for the birds.

Walter was not an athletic sportsman, but he loved the country pursuits of fishing and hunting, which he did once a week with the Puckeridge or Essex Hunt. Unlike Henry Walter, however, he did not take to shooting driven birds. He did breed and train pointers and this led on to enjoying some shooting, but not with organised drives. He tended, within the limitations of Victorian thinking, to be conservationist. Most of his birds were bred to be looked at and not shot. He built huge aviaries and employed the well qualified Mr Gilbert, who had once worked in a zoo, to supervise this enterprise. There were many unusual species, some of which could not even be found in British zoos.

The Australian piping crow, Walter Gilbey claimed, would hold a flute in his bill and pipe 'Merrily danced the Quaker's wife' or some other simple tune. The Philippine Blood Breasted Pigeon was not so confident and could not be tamed like other doves. Similarly, the Indian Jet Black cuckoo sang sweetly but was very nervous. The Laughing Jackass, despite domestication, still went through the steps of killing the already dead mice that were fed to him, then gulped them down head first and a few hours later ejected a pellet of bones. The Indian Grey Breasted Drongo spent the summer days catching flies on the wing. But, to Walter Gilbey, the most beautiful and graceful bird was the Indian Hunting Crow, with its pale green livery, black cheeks, chocolate wing coverts and sealing wax red bills and legs. There were many more unusual birds which this extraordinary gentleman found, housed and made sure were given expert attention in his aviaries.

Another great interest for Sir Walter was lavender. He was by 1910 the largest grower of lavender in the country. This was not quite as important a status as it might appear, for at that time the popularity of lavender in England was rather low and little was grown or bought. As a scent it was out of fashion and its other more unusual uses, as a nerve tonic and an insect deterrent, were not promoted. It is very good for keeping gnats at bay and

36. The lavender fields

against the bites and stings of insects and was used for such much more frequently on the Continent than here. Sir Walter probably got the idea of growing it from one of his continental trips.

The Jam

The name of Elsenham, as opposed to Gilbey, was and still is today synonymous with quality jam. For years the two acres of orchards, planted mainly with plums and apples, kept Walter's large household supplied with fruit and increasingly with preserves. They were enjoyed so much by the household and persons to whom they were given, that Walter Gilbey's business instincts came into play and he decided to start commercial operations.

In 1890 he formed a company and increased the acreage of the orchards and the variety of fruits grown to include damsons, pears and then raspberries and blackcurrants. He even imported a special strain of strawberry from France, as his aims for this produce were quality, not quantity, and to provide a useful means of employment for local people. Women and girls were used seasonally for the picking, the men worked all year round and even the 'urchins' had a job in the autumn, gathering blackberries.

He built a factory in 1893 where the emphasis was on making the best possible jam, even if it meant higher costs. For this product, in contrast to W&A Gilbey's alcohol, the profit margins were not so important. A foundation of apple or plum pulp was used and only pure fruit was added, together with the best crystallised sugar. The mixture was then simmered gently in open copper preserving pans and the end result was a jam that the most famous shops, such as Fortnum & Mason, wanted to buy and which was exported to many of the British colonies.

ELSENHAM JAMS

THE ELSENHAM BRAND

GUARANTEE.—The Purity and Quality of all Jams are guaranteed under the Acts of Parliament, :: :: 38 & 139, 50 & 51 Victoria :: ::

made at the Jam Factory in the Orchards, the property of Sir Walter Gilbey, Bart.

To be obtained from Agents, or a sample dozen 1-lb. Jars assorted Jams will be sent, carriage paid, for **7/-** direct from

MR. H. COTTERELL, The Orchards, Elsenham, Essex

37. Elsenham Jam poster

The demand grew so much that the orchards expanded to cover nearly 40 acres, and by 1900 more than nine tons of fruit were boiled each year. After Sir Walter's death the production continued, but, without his business sense and marketing flair, turnover dropped.

In 1959 Elsenham Jams was taken over by Tony Blunt, who decided to promote the original high-quality recipes. He put the prices up, advertising it as the most expensive jam in the world. Renamed Elsenham Quality Foods, the company marketed a greater variety of products and the ingredients were bought from all over the world.

These have been the only major changes, as the factory still looks more like a kitchen and the recipes still date back to the original nineteenth century versions. Sir Walter Gilbey would be well pleased with the twentieth century developments to this, one of his many original ideas.

The Host

Walter Gilbey was a generous person who believed in the virtues of hospitality. Some of the occasions on which this was best shown were during visits from the Prince of Wales.

Walter Gilbey was undoubtedly a supporter of the royal family and, despite their rather different moral attitudes, a good friendship grew between him and Edward, Prince of Wales, and later on with his son, George V. The harmonising factor in this friendship was the horse, as both Walter Gilbey and the Prince of Wales devoted much attention to the breeding of these animals. The Prince of Wales, as leader of the 'champagne set', lover of parties and colourful extravagant occasions, may have found Walter Gilbey's rigid Victorian morals a little inhibiting. He showed many times, however, that he held this frail- looking businessman in high regard, and he personally pressed for Walter's baronetcy. He wrote a letter to ' My dear Wish' in October 1892, saying in the last paragraph: 'Hoping that she will not forget Mr W. Gilbey for a Bart.'[7] The Prince of Wales was said to have only agreed to become president of the Royal Agricultural Society if Walter Gilbey would act as his adviser.

The Prince was particularly full of admiration for Walter's contribution towards horse breeding in the UK and on one of his visits to Elsenham said that in his opinion the Stud was the finest in England.

Typical of a number of visits to Elsenham made by the Prince was the one in December 1889, when he watched an hour long parade of the stud's horses from the pavilion, followed by lunch in the house and then a walk around the paintings.

He learnt, too, to respect Walter Gilbey's assessments. When, as Prince of Wales, Walter Gilbey, as President, conducted him around the Royal Agricultural Show at Leicester, on 25 July 1890, they wagered a bet as to the attendance. The Prince lost and some months later a parcel arrived for Walter Gilbey containing an ashtray with a crown piece mounted in the centre and inscribed with the exact attendance of Leicester show: 80,602. This ashtray is still in the house of Walter's grandson, Walter Anthony Gilbey, to this day.

It is also of interest that the Royal Warrant, when it was bestowed on W&A Gilbey in 1900, was presented in person by the Prince, together with a signed photograph. No member of the royal family had made the bestowal so personal before.

The Prince also visited Walter Gilbey at his distinguished house in London on the edge of Regents Park, which had large enough grounds to boast of one of the few private tennis courts in the town. Known as Cambridge House, it later belonged to the Royal College of Medicine. There were huge rooms with tall ceilings, which were ideal to hang paintings by such artists as Herring, Sartorius and Bonheur. It was an excellent place for entertainment and the Prince of Wales was a regular visitor on many of the occasions when Walter Gilbey hosted events, such as the annual dinner given for the Shire Horse Society.

Walter Gilbey might have been eager to entertain royalty, but he was equally happy to provide hospitality for everyone from the various societies that he helped, including cab drivers. He organised a Gala Day at Elsenham for about forty officials of the Royal Agricultural Society. This was done in style, the officials being driven in carriages to the paddocks and then provided with a champagne lunch in the house. The afternoon entertainments were less grand as they were taken to the village's annual sports day where a novel class had been introduced at the suggestion of Walter Gilbey – a baby show.

The cab drivers were provided with a different type of entertainment when they visited Elsenham. They came each year, with the help of the Cab Drivers Benevolent Association. In 1895, 140 came down on the train from London and were met at the station by their hosts. Those who could not walk to the house were driven in carriages. All had lunch in a marquee and a speech made by the Earl of Warwick congratulated them on the care they took of their horses. They then saw the horses of the famous stud paraded in front of the marquee. The day continued with the opportunity to wander around the paddocks, garden, orchards and jam factory, before tea and the return to London. Such a variety of guests, from royalty to cab drivers, must have kept the Gilbeys and their staff well in touch with all walks of life.

The Philanthropist

A great day out, like this one for the cab drivers, was the sort of philanthropy that Walter Gilbey practised. He disliked making straight gifts of money. Even a plea from his friend the Countess of Warwick,[8] who was for a time one of Edward VII's mistresses, to help her through a time when she was short of cash, was met with a rebuff – indeed, he had plenty of practice at refusing requests for help. There are many letters from his sons and his son-in-law Daniel Hine asking for help to pay off debts, often to bookmakers. Walter Gilbey could be extremely generous, but his form of giving was aimed at maintaining the recipient's self-respect. He did not like simply to give money, but would provide help when appropriate and try to organise some

38. Visit of Cabby annuitants to Elsenham Hall, August 1895

form of financial contribution from the applicant, even if it was a few coppers.

One of his generous ventures included spending £20,000 on the Bishop's Stortford golf course and club house and then handing it over to a committee to administer. *The Observer* of 1910 stated: 'It is an admirable course, and in a season or more will take its place among the first rank of inland links.' The Earl of Warwick proposed the thanks to Walter Gilbey at the opening.

Another form of assistance he gave at this time was some land for the Thaxted Railway, ironically assisting the extension of the form of transportation that had ruined his father. He had worked towards getting this line built for twenty years, as it meant that the old and remote town of Thaxted would be connected to modern-day life and the farmers would have a cheaper form of transportation.

More directly at Elsenham he gave land for a cemetery and presented the

92

Village Hall to the village. At Bishop's Stortford he built the Kings Cottages Alms Houses in South Street, charging a rent of just six pence a week to the old people who occupied them. In the early 1960s, his Grandson Walter Anthony, who was Chairman, with Stanley Lee, the then Financial Controller of W&A Gilbey, started to bring about their complete modernisation. Walter Gilbey also gave land for the building of Rye Street Hospital and presented to the town the old Town Mill in Bridge Street. He then purchased the Stort Navigation in order to keep the navigation open to Bishop's Stortford. (This was not a successful venture as Brick Lock at Royden fell in and he sold the navigation on.) Walter Gilbey behaved like a lord of the manor and did, in fact, become the very first one of Elsenham, by purchasing the title from the Ecclesiastical Commissioners.

Early on in his involvement with agriculture, in 1869, he became a subscriber to the Royal Agricultural Benevolent Institute, which provided pensions to destitute farmers, their wives, widows or unmarried daughters when over 65 years of age. He was able to increase their coffers from 1887 onwards, when he gave the first of what became his annual appeals through the press to the clergy to give some of the offertories from the Harvest Thanksgiving services to this charity. His request worked, with the sums raised averaging £5,500 per year, compared with £1,250 before he spoke out.

In 1896 Walter Gilbey founded a Lectureship in the History and Economics of Agriculture at Cambridge University, the first holder of the office being Sir Ernest Clarke, secretary to the Royal Agricultural Society of England. Then, in 1898, he gave a stipend of £2,000 a year for a Reader in Agriculture at Cambridge and was thus a pioneer in improving opportunities for higher education in this field.

The Property Developer

Although work on the Gilbey family archive at Bishop's Stortford is still at an early stage, the extent of Sir Walter's financial interests is becoming evident. From his properties book it is apparent that he put about £½m into properties between 1888 and 1908. Many acquisitions were local cottages (35) and farms (22), but in 1898, on a larger scale, he bought 40 acres of land on the northern edge of Grimsby and developed it as a housing estate called Littlecoates, using street names of Stortford, Stansted, Elsenham, Harlow and Gilbey.

The Liberal

His version of philanthropy must have been a contributory factor towards Walter Gilbey's baronetcy, which was bestowed in 1893 for services rendered to the horse breeding industry. Another contributory factor was his staunch support of the Liberal party and the high regard in which he was held by W. E. Gladstone.

He was such a good supporter of the Liberals that, even after Lloyd George's attempts to restrict the 'drink traffic' and his People's Budget, Walter

39. Presentation of Portrait by Sir W. Q. Orchardson R.A. to Mr and Mrs Walter Gilbey by the Prince of Wales in March 1891.

Gilbey – unlike most nobility – did not switch parties. He even went so far as to openly support the principle of taxing the rich. In a speech at a Liberal meeting at Great Canfield he said he approved of what Lloyd George had done, adding: 'as to taxation, if it was not put on the rich, on whom should it be put?'

The reasons Sir Walter gave for this stance were:

I well remember the sad condition of the small tradesman and the poor fifty years ago. I may also mention the condition of the farmers. They were in a sad state. The livestock on their farms were few, excepting pigs. There were not as many store cattle and sheep on any tenant farms as can be seen now. At the same period local subscriptions were raised to assist farmers to emigrate, there being hundreds for whom there was no employment and funds were also contributed in London to aid the same cause. The altered conditions which have taken place during the last fifty years in the life of the rural labourer in the shape of better wages, food, clothing and housing should satisfy the minds of all the well disposed and it should be remembered that it is not the Conservative, but a Liberal government which has brought about all this, headed by that grand old man, the late Mr Gladstone and his worthy successors in office.

Walter Gilbey was not an active politician, unlike some of his relations. While he remained in the centre of the Liberals in Essex, he kept his speeches and campaigns focused more on agricultural and equestrian matters than on party politics.

The Campaigns

Walter Gilbey turned into a great campaigner and showed some considerable foresight in the subjects he selected. One that was unfortunately not effective was to adopt a 'Pari Mutuel or Tote Monopoly in British racing. He had been impressed by the effects of such a system at the Paris Horse Show, where he took his horses to win many rosettes and plenty of prize money, thanks to support from the profits of the Pari Mutuel.[9] In that country there were no bookmakers, so much more of the money earned out of betting on horses was used to help the horse industry. He tried to get the system adopted in this country. People such as Michael Clayton, during his time as editor of *Horse and Hound*, carried on the same campaign in the 1990s. If only Walter Gilbey had been successful when he tried in 1902, the British horse industry would be in a very different situation.

At the end of the first decade of the twentieth century there was a big scare about the dangers of milk drinking. We have already read of the importance Walter himself attached to drinking milk. With arguments raging, disturbing the market for milk, he produced, firstly, a pamphlet, 'Milk and Milch Animals' in 1908, claiming that the scare against milk as a source of consumption was groundless and he questioned sterilisation. He placed the emphasis on cleanliness and freshness.

He caused another great wave of interest four years later when he published a pamphlet claiming that pure milk is a vital necessity to the health of children and that the scares of infection through cows' milk are, in the main, founded upon the mischievous statements of the ill-informed. Arguments raged in the press at the time about whether or not milk was responsible for the spread of tuberculosis. 'The Scandal of Our Milk', 'Tuberculin Test Condemned' and 'The Importance of Milk' were typical headlines.[10]

He ran a campaign in 1890 to get horses shod in shoes that did not slip and, in the same year, created much interest on the subject of women riding astride.[11] He published views on swine fever in 1909 and even wrote about the educational value of museums. He was worried about the promotion of sugar beet in 1910, warning that the British climate, owing to its comparative lack of sun, is unsuited for the profitable cultivation of sugar beet for sugar purposes. This led to great debates. He might not have passed on too many views about how to run the country, but he was very articulate about his beloved animals and agriculture.

The Honours

Walter Gilbey's interest in so many subjects and his effectiveness in getting improvements made in neglected areas, like the treatment and breeding of horses, led to recognition. In 1889 a number of gentlemen formed a committee to devise a means of recognising Walter Gilbey's disinterested services in raising the reputation of England as a horse breeding country. There were 1,234 subscribers for portraits by W.Q. Orchardson of Mr and Mrs Walter Gilbey. The presentation was made at the Agricultural Hall.

The company were reminded that it had all started at a meeting of tenant farmers in 1871, when Walter Gilbey pointed out the loss to the country of buying horses abroad which could be bred at home. With sustained lobbying and plenty of personal action, Walter Gilbey had been the main factor in remedying this situation.

Walter himself said: 'If I have any share in restoring this once neglected industry and in making horse breeding more general, more interesting and more profitable I shall have amply reaped my rewards.'[12]

The Prince of Wales, presenting the picture, said: 'Mr Gilbey who has done so much for horse breeding throughout the country will give an impetus to what we so much desire, namely that we should have the best horses in the world bred in this country.' [13]

There were rumours that he was about to be made a baronet, but it was to be another two years before he received his letter from Mr Gladstone, in May 1893.

It was some measure of his popularity that the town of Bishop's Stortford and the village of Elsenham were so pleased with his baronetcy that they decorated their streets with flags and arches and there were many notices of congratulations to Sir Walter Gilbey. A banquet was held for him in the Great Hall at Bishop's Stortford, where there was singing, food and speeches. The toast to Sir Walter included this poem:

More than the laurel wreath,
More than the title won,
Is the approving consciousness
Of duty nobly done.
To this our hearts respond;
We know – we feel – how great his worth
And herein lies the bond
The honours they may fade,
Their glory pass away,
His deeds will live and bear their fruit
Through many a distant day.
His name will find a place
On the 'Victorian' page -
Will make a useful record there,
Worthy of this our age.
Stortford may well be proud
To honour such a son,
When our Most Gracious Queen herself
Proclaims his work well done.
Now raised to title rank,
Still wider grows his fame,
So well deserved – so justly won –
A stainless, honoured name.

His reply gives a little more insight into this modest, but determined gentleman:

I do not think I am blessed with genius beyond my brother townsmen,
but there is a time in the affairs of man that if he takes them at the tide
he brings them to success. Those things that I have undertaken I have

persevered with and made them a success.

Typical of Walter Gilbey, he ensured that as many people as possible shared in the pleasure of his baronetcy. He invited 800 employees of W&A Gilbey to come to tea at Cambridge House and, when they presented him with an illuminated address, he asked them all to tea at Elsenham. Consequently, on 12 August 1893, about 1,000 employees and their families turned up at his Essex home. It was a very special tea and true to Gilbey tradition it was done in style, with plenty of entertainments, from cricket and sports to swings and roundabouts for the children.

There was talk in the press of him being made a peer and there is correspondence from 12 Downing Street saying that he had been on the list, was on the one for the future, but had been passed over, for instance in May 1910, in favour of those who had been M.P.s. In 1911, he came very close again to becoming a peer, because his name was on the list, compiled by Asquith, of 249 men of Liberal convictions who would have been ennobled in order to pass the Parliament Bill in the House of Lords. In the event, this Bill, which severely limited the Lords' previous constitutional powers of being able to block legislation, was passed by 17 votes through the threat of a mass creation of peers, which was not, therefore, necessary. The list, found amongst Asquith's papers, also contained the names of the Honourable Herbert Blyth, heir to the existing Blyth peerage, and Sir Charles Gold. Very few peers, therefore, had been created in 1910, as the King had been conscious that the following year might require a large influx of new blood.

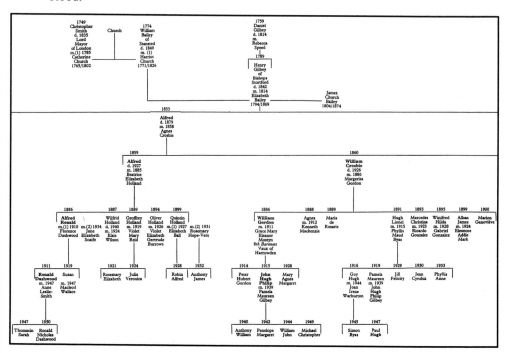

F. Family Tree – The Gilbeys, part 2

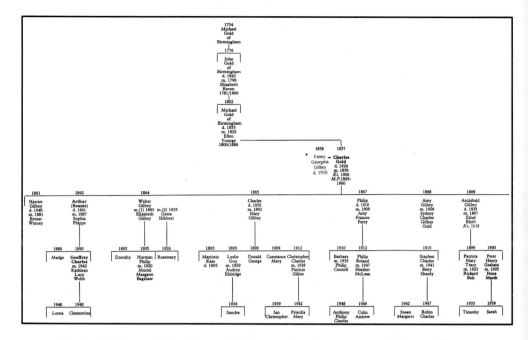

*G. Family Tree – The Golds, part 2. *Fanny Georgina, youngest daughter of Henry and Elizabeth Gilbey (see page 20). Charles Gold, younger brother of Henry (see page 79).*

Sir Walter showed a lack of opportunism in obtaining a peerage, as when asked to contribute to Liberal party funds in 1909, a time when the party were asking for substantial amounts to help them through the dramas of the Peoples Budget, he only sent £100. Sir Walter Gilbey was a philanthropist, a man of conscience, and he would only contribute towards a cause when he believed in its aims and not when it would bring him glory.

VI
A Breeder Extraordinary

Beyond the parklands of Elsenham Hall, down a drive lined with more roses, were the animals that brought Sir Walter Gilbey fame and a baronetcy – the horses. His grandson, Vincent Routledge, remarked: 'his sun went around those stables.'[1] The horses enjoyed facilities which it is doubtful any could rival at that period. His policy for the stud farm was to use his massive income to find out how to improve on current methods, then to apply the improvements to his enterprises and set an example that others could follow, all of which led to a general rise in standards of non-thoroughbred horse breeding in the UK.

The paddocks were small, usually around three acres, and divided by neatly-trimmed, four foot high hawthorn hedges with a fence on either side. An optimum number of horses for each of the paddocks had been determined as either two brood mares and their foals, or two or three colts, or four fillies. On the south side of each of these paddocks was a shelter with a raised floor so that there was dry standing. This was thought very important for sound, healthy feet.

The facilities played an important part in Sir Walter's principles of breeding, which he expounded in his book *Young Racehorses*. In this he said of the brood mare:

> from time of conception she ought to be allowed to roam in fresh untainted pastures; if pastures where horses have not been for the last three years, all the better. After foaling, the same policy is fulfilled for mare and foal. After weaning the foal should be treated as naturally as possible, turning out where herbage is succulent and is free to run

He put this theory into practice at Elsenham.

He carried out experiments to prove the dangers of horsesick pastures, where constant grazing by horses turns the grass sour and makes its growth patchy. His horses were turned out in model paddocks which were regularly rested and bullock and sheep grazed each year to keep the grass fresh. He found that the horses in these well-tended paddocks grew more bone, muscle and condition than those he put on horsesick pasture, which had been grazed by horses alone. 'I can attribute their superiority to nothing else than Nature's feeding.'

The Stables

A mass of stud buildings provided the horses with every type of modern facility, even including a rarity for those days, an indoor riding school, 140 feet by 40 feet, which was used for exercising and staging sales. Most unusual of all, however, was the Breaking and Driving School. Walter Gilbey had bought this extraordinary feature of the stud, an elaborate version of the modern day horse walker, from a dealer in London. It had been a major operation to transfer it to Essex.

The school was a circular building 100 feet in diameter with a smaller, enclosed inner circle. Horses were broken in the inner circle and then exercised and taught to go between the shafts of carriages in the outer circle, which was big enough for a coach to go round. The normal arrangement was to put the horses between shafts that were arranged along the spokes of a horizontal wheel, which went around and kept them walking. Six or seven horses could be exercised in this way and, when youngsters were being taught, an older horse was included as a calming influence. There were plenty of safety measures – a brake trip, walls built at angles and the ability to reverse the wheel when the horses were in the spokes.

The Breaking and Driving School was the most unusual feature of the stud, but the building where everyone congregated was the Pavilion, which lay just in front of the stables. Its walls were lined with the prizes won by the Elsenham horses and by the turn of the century these numbered more than 1,000. Outside was the exhibition lawn on which the horses were shown off to visitors. The setting was picturesque, with rose and lavender bushes scattered at carefully designed intervals. Peacocks strutted down the various walks and drives and, in contrast, the shy wild turkeys could be seen occasionally in trees and behind bushes.

There was a mass of stables, some so huge they were said to be ten times the size of the normal hunter's box, and these provided a more natural home for stallions and youngsters when they first came in from the fields. There were some smaller stalls, cordoned off with white cord, which required plenty of labour to keep clean. Everything that could be polished – and there was plenty of brass – shone brilliantly. By tradition there was an inspection by the house party every Sunday and then the straw was plaited at the edges and crests stencilled onto the floors.

The System

Walter Gilbey used these facilities to practice privately what governments in continental Europe were doing for European horses. He bought and stood at Elsenham the best stallions available and he employed a ruthless culling process to ensure that only the best mares were used and only the best young stock came forward to be sold at exclusive and highly publicised auctions.

The first stage of the culling was for the weaning foals. All those that were second rate were sent to Bishop's Stortford market and sold without reserve. The next culling was of the three and four year olds, when those short of top class went to Peterborough market, where they usually fetched prices which at least covered their rearing costs. Walter Gilbey estimated these at a mere £10 – £12 per annum (today they are more than £1,000 per annum). The best horses were either kept for his own use, or sold in one of his famous Elsenham auctions.

As with his first Jersey herd, Walter Gilbey's system included careful recording of pedigrees and performance. He kept his own stud books and, taking 1888 as a sample year, there were 15 Shire stallions, 51 Shire mares, 3 Thoroughbred stallions, including Pearl Diver who won seven races, 3 Hackney stallions, 4 Hackney mares, 1 Shetland stallion, 1 Arab stallion, 11 half bred mares (by Thoroughbreds and out of half bred draught or hackney mares), 1 Hunter mare (by a Hackney and out of a Hunter mare) and 5 draught mares with scanty pedigrees. It was quite a cross section of the equestrian world, from the massive Shire to the diminutive Shetland. Most had, prior to his interest, been relatively neglected and unfashionable breeds and they benefited a great deal from the support of such a high class promoter. He bred the pure breds, the Shires, Hackneys and the like, but he also wanted to breed the carriage and army horse which the British were importing in large numbers. It was for this that he used the Thoroughbred blood and not (with a few exceptions) to breed racehorses. His method to achieve this aim was judiciously to blend the blood of a Thoroughbred stallion with a draught mare to produce a half bred mare, who was then mated with a Thoroughbred or a Hackney.

The performances of his stock were noted in the stud book. To give some idea of his huge successes, between 1884 and 1887 his Elsenham stock won 96 firsts, 52 seconds, 21 thirds, three gold medals, and 14 championships. To illustrate how this success continued, and covered so many breeds and types, at the 1913 Royal show his stock won gold medals for the best Welsh stallion and the best polo and riding pony mare, a first for brood mares, 3rd and reserve with his two Hackney stallions and reserve with a Hunter brood mare.

The Shire

Walter Gilbey's first major venture into the breeding of horses was with partners in the 1870s. His farming at Hargrave had made him aware of the

40. *Prince of Wales inspecting Sir Walter Gilbey's stud at Elsenham Hall and watching the trotting out of a hackney stallion.*

41. *'Spark', Champion Shire Horse Stallion at London shows 1881-83*

high price of agricultural and draught animals for pulling heavy vans. In January 1877 he persuaded others interested in agriculture to launch the Bishop's Stortford Horse Co. Ltd., with a capital of £1200 being raised to buy two stallions. There were 12 promoters' shares of £50 each and 60 Preference shares of £10 each. All preference share holders were to send two mares to the company's stallions at a fee of 3 guineas, plus 5/- grooms fee (it was typical of Walter Gilbey's concern for those who worked for him that the groom's fee was twice the norm). The aim was that everyone would receive interest plus a bonus when the stallions were sold.

Despite a huge amount of energy expended by its chairman, Walter Gilbey, the company only lasted three seasons, but the shareholders did not lose out, as in August 1879 it was wound up with the share capital plus interest of 5% per year being returned to them. The experience of the venture made Walter Gilbey realise the importance of producing such stock, but he also realised that it would be easier to do so at his own stud.

The horses that were used by the Bishop's Stortford Horse Co. proved to be some of the foundation stock for the breed of Shire Horse and, as will be seen later, Walter Gilbey was instrumental in starting a breed society for Shire Horses.

His first well publicised private purchase was for the Shire stallion Spark. The record price, of 800 guineas, that he paid for this three year old colt helped turn Shire breeding into a commercial enterprise. His investment proved worthwhile, for Spark went on to be champion at the London Show and to produce good stock. *The Times* gave him very good support when describing the 1882 Cart Horse Show:

This horse is astonishing for breadth and depth of carcass, development

42. Shire Horse Show at the Agricultural Hall – The Prince of Wales looking over Sir Walter Gilbey's 'Staunton Hero'.

of muscle, perfection of shoulder, immense bone; and while his action in walking surpasses everything in the show for activity in stepping, he moves in trotting like a first rate cob. His colour is black with white haired feet and white stroke down the face – similar characteristics to those shown in the stud book authentic portrait of a Shire-horse in 1762.

An even more dramatic purchase by Walter Gilbey was that of Staunton Hero, who was due for export to the USA but whom he saved for Britain, bringing him to Elsenham in 1883. This horse, like Spark, became a champion at the London show, though he did not enjoy such success with his progeny. Keith Chivers in his excellent book, *The Shire Horse*, claims he was a martyr to Walter Gilbey's campaign to improve stock in Essex by making available top stallions. Staunton Hero was used on the local mares and they were not good enough to produce the show stock. He only stayed at the stud six years, then was the star lot at the second home sale, when he was sold to the Duke of Westminster for 500 guineas. This was a large figure in those days, but it does seem a little low when he had already won £543 in prize money.

Walter Gilbey started his own Shire horse stud book in 1880. Another great horse in it was Mars Victor, a stallion that he bought in 1891 for the huge sum of 1,500 guineas. It was his pedigree that helped to make him so valuable, as he was by Hitchin Conqueror, who is to the Shire horses as Hermit is to the Thoroughbreds.

Some measure of the success of Walter Gilbey's Shire stock is the awards they won at the London Show, where between 1881 and 1906 they accumulated 96 prizes. For the first decade of the Shire Horse Society they won more than any other stud except that of the Earl of Ellesmere.

SPARK (2497)—*STALLION. Foaled in* 1878 *Color Black*

Bred by Mr. WILLIAM RICKFORD ROWLAND, CRESLOW, BUCKS.

WON PRIZES

1878 As a foal FIRST—Royal and Central Bucks Show

1879 As a yearling {FIRST—Royal and Central Bucks Show
FIRST—North West Bucks Show

1880 As a two years-old {Was not Shown

1881 As a three years-old
- FIRST £20, AND CHAMPION CUP FIFTY GUINEAS }—English Cart Horse Society, London Show
- FIRST £10 AND SPECIAL £25 }—Essex Society, Southend Show
- FIRST—Royal Society, Derby Show

1882 As a four years-old {FIRST—English Cart Horse Society, London Show
SECOND—Royal Society, Reading Show

1883 As a five years-old {FIRST £30 PRESIDENT'S CUP £21 AND CHAMPION CUP £52 10s. }English Cart Horse Society, London Show

SPARK'S *Sire*—THE COLONEL (2101)

    g.-Sire—ᵃBROWN GEORGE (318)

      g.-g.-Sire—ᵇGLOUCESTER (942) foaled in the year 1853

        g.-g.-g.-Sire—WIRDNAM'S HORSE

ᵃ The Dam of BROWN GEORGE (318) by HONEST TOM (1106) by ROBIN (1862) by FARMER'S GLORY (831) by FARMERS GLORY (818) bred in the year 1825 by Mr. Ivens, Eydon, Northamptonshire

ᵇ The Dam of GLOUCESTER (942) by FARMER'S GLORY (838) by *GLORY (939) by K (1192) bred in the year 1827 by Mr. Grebby, Croft Marsh, Boston, Lincolnshire

* GLORY (939) bred in the year 1837 by Mr. R. Johnson Hilbrow, Haddenham, Cambridgeshire, won Prize in 1843 at Saffron Walden Show

SPARK'S *Dam*—ᶜDAISY (vol. 3) by KING CHARLES (1207) by EMPEROR (689) by MAJOR (1448) by MAJOR (1447) by HONEST TOM (1073) by HONEST TOM (1067) by ENGLAND'S GLORY (705) by HONEST TOM (1060) foaled in the year 1800 by BROWN HORSE (Milton & Colley's, of Bassingham, Nottinghamshire)

ᶜ DAISY (Vol. 3) bred in the year 1871 by Mr. Coleman, Sulgrave, Northamptonshire, won Seven FIRST and Five SECOND Prizes between 1876 and 1881, at Shows in Buckinghamshire and at Tring, Herts

43. Pedigree of 'Spark', Champion Shire Horse Stallion

The Hackney

The other breed in which Walter made some large investments was the Hackney, the high stepping breed that was driven to a light carriage. The Hackney was another British horse with ancient origins, tracing back to the trotters that were mentioned in a letter written by Dame Paston in 1465.

Walter Gilbey was recognised as the great breeder of Hackneys, for in *The Sketch* of 1897 it was said in relation to this breed: 'Sir Walter Gilbey is the most successful breeder and exhibitor of the day.' The *Essex Weekly News* on 28 December, 1912 said: 'The Hackney is the breed which he has done more to improve than any other man living.'

He aimed to breed a sound, tough animal and was willing to prove it. *The Sketch* article goes on to relate:

What the Hackney could do as a traveller was shown at the Crystal Palace Show when Sir Walter Gilbey's horse Old Times, sixteen years old and half trained, trotted three miles on a grass track in a fraction under 10 1/2 minutes carrying a 12 stone man on his back.

Walter Gilbey favoured the bigger, old-fashioned Hackneys, who trace back to the Norfolk Trotter, bred to pull the East Anglian farmers and their families at great speed. Many of the Elsenham Hackneys stood about 16 hands^2 high and one Spring Member was 16.3 hands high. These were similar to the types that were exported from Britain to improve so many of the breeds in Continental Europe, including the renowned Normandy horse and its offshoot, the French Trotter. In England the breed leapt into the headlines when Walter Gilbey paid the phenomenal price of £5,000 for Danegelt by Denmark, who traced back to one of the founders of the Thoroughbred breed, the Darley Arabian. More recently his pedigree included a dash of Walter Gilbey's Norfolk stock, but was dominated for five generations by Yorkshire ancestors. No one had paid such a price for anything other than a Thoroughbred and the

44. '*Danegelt*', *hackney stallion*

papers of December 1892 were full of this extraordinary action.

Danegelt was 14 years of age when he was moved to Elsenham. This, the most famous Hackney stallion of all time, was a substantial-looking animal and, although he himself did win in the show ring, it was his stock that brought him the most fame. He had been worked hard in Yorkshire, serving 200 mares a year at 10 guineas a nomination, but with great results, siring a remarkable 18 winners at the Hackney Horse Society's Show in 1894. Walter Gilbey was congratulated from many quarters for saving this great horse for British breeders. The Earl of Londesborough wrote to say: 'I must congratulate you on becoming the owner of what is certainly the best sire we have in Yorkshire.' The Prince of Wales' Hackney stud at Sandringham made an immediate booking for 10 nominations, regardless of whether the nomination was 15 or 20 guineas.

Danegelt might have brought attention to the breed, and to Walter Gilbey, but the latter owned many other winners. There was the smaller, 15 hands high Hedon Squire who represented the British breeds at the 1900 Paris Exhibition. He won everything there, taking the gold medal in the stallion class, the champion and gold medal for all breeds except that confined to the French, and Grand Champion and gold medal for all breeds including the French. A certain amount of showmanship was involved in this great victory, for while the Continentals were quietly leading their stallions around, Hedon Squire trotted spectacularly into the arena showing off his high stepping action and led by a whooping runner in cap, shirt sleeves and cloth gaiters. This noisy, active entry scattered the other horses and their owners might not have been too pleased when the championship went to the visitors. But to spectators and judges it was highly refreshing to see an animal move in such a dramatic fashion. The British papers were once again full of Walter Gilbey's efforts, which had shown that the British breeds could compete against the best from the Continent.

Gay Connaught, a half brother to Danegelt, also won many prizes, as did Bonnie Clara who won a first and gold medal at the Paris International. Then there was Antonius who was first and champion stallion at the Royal in 1910 as a three year old. He had a short but very great career siring many winners before his death as a seven year old. Such was his reputation that his death was recorded in *The Times* on 3rd March, 1914.

The Shetland, Welsh and Polo Pony

In contrast to the massive Shires, Walter Gilbey also promoted the smallest of the breeds, the Shetland. He used to tell a good story about one of his first Shetlands, which illustrates not only their diminutive size, but also the devastating nature of the streets of London: 'When I wished to bring a very small Shetland pony home to Essex, I was afraid to take him along Cheapside lest he should break his leg in the numerous holes among the stones. The difficulty was overcome by taking him through the City in a cab.'[3]

His best known Shetland came into his stables much later. Called Good

45. *'Shooting Star', Champion Welsh Pony Stallion*

Friday, he was a piebald stallion who won a first prize at the Royal Botanical Gardens show and was a popular exhibit everywhere. Just 9 hands high, he was claimed at that time to be the smallest stallion in the United Kingdom.

There was also the prettiest of all ponies, the Welsh, and again Walter owned the highest quality. His stallion Shooting Star was described at the 1912 Olympia show as: 'the finest pony in the world.'[4]

He had, too, some of the best stock for the breeding of polo ponies. The stallion Rosewater by Rosicrucian won more prizes than any other horse of his type and was the top polo pony sire at the turn of the century.

The Thoroughbred

The Thoroughbreds that Walter Gilbey stood at the stud were predominantly for cross breeding. His first successful one was Pedometer, but the next, Pearl Diver, had even better results. Pearl Diver was a powerful, rangy type who won Queens Premiums and sired many of the carriage horses for which the Elsenham stud was renowned. Walter Gilbey was a great promoter of the smaller Thoroughbred. In his book *The Thoroughbred and other Ponies* he expressed his concern about the importance attached to height. When the Thoroughbred was developed in the early eighteenth century, the horses stood around 14 hands high but by this time they were at least six or seven inches higher. He thought the stock had been bred to achieve greater height and greater speed, but stoutness, ability to carry weight and staying power had been sacrificed, and in his breeding he kept to the smaller horses. Many of these were used as carriage horses and at any one time there were always at least 20 matching greys in his stables for use in his carriages.

46. Ascot, the Royal Enclosure on Cup Day

47. Sir Walter Gilbey's postchaise

The Carriages

He certainly helped a huge range of British horses, from Arabs to those great Shires, and at one time was even an enthusiastic breeder of mules. Nor was it just horses that he produced, as he designed his own carriages. He was thought to be the only person outside the Royal family to drive around in a post-chaise. He was a well-known figure at Ascot and Epsom, not because he gambled or owned racehorses, but because he drove to them in his unique turnout. Four matching greys pulled his carriage and riding the horses were two postillions. The Prince of Wales' oft-quoted remark when he saw them was: 'Damn it, Sir Walter, not only do you match your horses, but your riders as well! How do you manage it?' Sir Walter replied, 'Breed 'em Sir!' (Two of the riders, the Patmore brothers, belonged to a family that had been in his employment long before the brothers were born.)

The respect with which he was held in the horse world is shown by this quotation from *Bailey's Magazine* of June 1919: 'There is no name more honoured in connection with the horse than that of Gilbey and probably no man ever lived who had a more comprehensive knowledge of every variety of the 'noble animal''.

The Sales

He also had sound commercial judgement and took steps to ensure that his huge investments in these noble animals did yield some returns. His methods created a better market for the stock, just as it had done for the Jersey cattle. He organised sales at which the quality was so good and the atmosphere surrounding the occasion so great that the prices set new records. This, in its turn, tended to create better prices throughout the country and for his next sale. It was a bold way of making his hobby help pay its way, at the same time as promoting the breeding and production of the creatures he held in such high esteem. Private sales caught on as a rather fashionable activity for the rich and noble during the 1880s and 1890s. Walter Gilbey's were the equal of anybody's in terms of extravagant displays, hospitality and quality of animals, although the Prince of Wales's at Sandringham must have been grander occasions.

Walter Gilbey first tried this remarkable form of marketing for his Shire horses in 1885. Catalogues were sent around the world and advertisements taken in the magazines of countries which had imported British Shires. The results were good, as buyers turned up at Elsenham from South Africa, America, South America and Australia. Most travelled down on the train, which was said to carry 600 people destined for this very special sale. Reports varied, but close to 2,000 people turned up on the day to view and to buy at the Elsenham sale. The marketing material boasted of Shires bred for their soundness, good feet, bone and substance and not, as so many were in Britain at that period, flashy lookers suitable for a quick sale. The stock for sale were a few brood mares plus the youngsters which had the previous season won 47 prizes between them.

It was reported in the press that:

Every facility and accommodation was offered to probable purchasers with hospitable arrangements for entertaining all comers. A commodious tent was erected adjacent to the spacious coach house and combined with it to provide a dining salon for 400. In the paddocks quarter of a mile away, overlooking the railway, was the sale ring with a large grandstand and a long line of farm wagons.[5]

Walter Gilbey invited a big house party, which included Lord Hothfield and Lord Egerton, and then gave a lunch for hundreds where the Moet champagne flowed with no restrictions. There were many toasts, but the auctioneer Mr Sexton hit the point when he said of Mr Gilbey that: 'he did not think another gentleman in the world would have had the pluck to offer his prize animals in this manner.'[6] Those who did not sit down to lunch still enjoyed excellent facilities, as there was a very large refreshment booth.

The crowd of 2,000 pressed around the sale ring to see the 40 Shires sold. Colonel Sir Robert Loyd-Lindsay, a major innovator in British agriculture and soon to be rewarded with the title of Lord Wantage, paid the top price of 475 guineas, a record, for a Shire mare. The average was £172. 2. 3¼d and this was the highest at any sale. The success of the Elsenham sale led to others staging similar events.

Walter Gilbey waited until 1889 until he tried again and he once more attracted buyers from all over the world, to whom the high class Shires and the munificent champagne lunch were very good attractions. In the lunchtime speeches Walter Gilbey, after many years of drawing attention to the problems in the British horse industry, was able to be more positive and note the improvements since the last sale. In 1888 he said that 10,000 more horses had been exported than in 1878, and of these, 1,500 were Shires, which was very good business for the breed.

The Prince of Wales was the guest of honour and also purchaser of several lots, including the mare Pride of Fleet for 300 guineas. Most of the buyers had titles and included the Duke of Marlborough, Lord Egerton, Lord Hothfield and Lord Wantage. The star lot was the great stallion Staunton Hero, who went for a record price of 500 guineas to the Duke of Westminster's representative.

These were good prices, but the average was not quite as high as at the first sale, possibly due to the inclement weather. It was February, there were six inches of snow on the ground and there was a very cold, westerly wind.

The Elsenham sales continued at about four yearly intervals, to give the stock time to be produced and grow. On each occasion Walter Gilbey showed off extraordinary hospitality, giving lunch to up to 700 people. This might have absorbed some of the profit, but it served his purpose of attracting the high and mighty to take an interest in the horses and bring attention to British horse breeding.

He began sales, too, for his other types of horses, holding one in September 1895 for his carriage horses and the Hackneys. In this sphere his status as the best breeder in Britain helped to attract even more buyers from overseas. All his best stock was kept for these sales and none had a reserve. He never sold a horse privately, claiming: 'I should never have a friend left in the world if I sold them horses!'[7]

The Prince of Wales bred Hackneys, Riding and Harness Horses at Sandringham and he too joined in the fashion for holding extraordinarily hospitable auctions. He held one in 1892, where Walter Gilbey was one of the main buyers, and he expanded the concept in 1894. A special train came from Cambridge carrying the house party, including many of Britain's aristocracy, the Prince of Wales himself, Lord Londonderry, and Walter Gilbey. The star guest, the Czarevich from Russia, arrived independently.

Fifty lots were auctioned, fetching £6,330, and it was the house party that boosted the funds, buying nearly two-thirds of the stock. The Czarevich paid the highest price of 450 guineas and Walter Gilbey bought three of the lots. The generous house party enjoyed plenty of perks as they arrived on Wednesday afternoon, attended the sale on the Thursday (which included a lunch in a marquee that could hold 1,000) and did not leave until the Friday.

Lord Belper was another to join the trend, holding a sale in February 1895 with a lunch for 600. Once again Walter Gilbey made a contribution, buying one of the lots. His free spending must have helped to make him an even more popular figure. He certainly was a major factor in the success of this means of selling horses, with his generous approach both to providing hospitality at his own sales and being a major buyer when others ran them.

Even when he got older and did not run sales for himself, he still used the auctions, sending shipments of horses to Peterborough and helping to promote a market for the breeds that he produced.

The Societies

As a breeder and a farmer with a business background, Walter Gilbey was in heavy demand to assist the various agricultural organisations, most of which had come into being to promote a more scientific approach to agriculture. The first one he joined was the Royal Agricultural Society (RASE), which had been started in 1837 to encourage and develop British Agriculture, largely at the instigation of Earl Spencer. He made his first major contribution when he joined its Mansion House Committee, aiming to raise funds for the Kilburn exhibition of the Royal Show. Held in the heart of the City of London, this show created great interest in agricultural matters amongst the urban population.

In 1881 he was elected onto the council and in 1889 he became a vice president, at the same time taking on chairmanship of the Show Committee. He was a key figure amongst the organisers of the Jubilee Show at Windsor and raised large sums from the City to turn this into the largest and most important show held by the RASE. Five years later he was instrumental, with the Duke of Westminster, in obtaining the freehold to premises at 13 Hanover Square for permanent offices and two years later he was made the President. This was when the Royal Show was held at Leicester and made a substantial profit of £3,600.

He kept up his interests in cattle, being a member of the British Dairy Farmer's Association from 1881-1886. He was also a member of the Smithfield Club, joining the Council in 1881, then becoming Vice President in 1889 and President in 1896. He became a Governor of The Royal Veterinary Surgeons College in 1886 and a member of the General Purposes Committee in 1887. He was also on the committee of The Farmers Club from 1885-1888.

During the 1880s and 1890s he must have led an extraordinarily demanding life, attending numerous committee meetings and later becoming the figurehead, as either president or chairman, for practically every society with agricultural connections.

One society that was only indirectly concerned with breeding, but still played a crucial role as the venue for their shows, was the Royal Agricultural Hall Company. Walter Gilbey became a director in 1883, Vice Chairman in 1884 and Chairman in 1890. It provided a unique site for agricultural activities as it was situated in Islington, the centre of London's shopping in the 1870s. Built in 1861-2 at a cost of £53,000, the original aim was to house the Smithfield Club's cattle show. Its smart surroundings and modern facilities soon made it into a popular venue for an extraordinary range of activities, from trade shows and exhibitions to Crufts Dog Show, the Military Tournament and the Shire, Hunter, Pony and Hackney Shows. In all, it covered nearly five acres with a main hall of 384 by 217 feet. One of the halls added later to meet the growing demand for its facilities was financed by Walter Gilbey and named The Gilbey Hall. Built in 1894, it was added to in 1907.

Although most of his work and honours were connected with the cattle and horses he reared at Elsenham, Sir Walter also did good work for chickens. It was through his efforts in 1894 that the Table Poultry Show was held in conjunction with Smithfield Christmas Fat Cattle Show under the patronage of The Prince of Wales. Whether coincidental, or due to this initiating, in the same year the Worshipful Company of Poulters gave him the freedom of their Livery Company, in recognition of his efforts for the encouragement of rural pursuits in general and the development of poultry culture especially.

It is a long list of involvements and honours for any one man, especially as he was still chairman of the largest drink distributors in the UK. To do all this work he depended on another of his assets: his ability to find talented, able people and delegate work to them.

Walter Gilbey may not have had the public manner and academic background of many more well-known personalities, but he had the judgement to focus on what was needed, the energy and determination to ensure it was achieved and a simple, honest manner, which earned people's respect.

VII
The Memorials

Walter Gilbey arguably did as much for the horse breeding industry (outside racehorses) as any other single person has ever done in Britain. Today his fortune may have been largely divided between the Inland Revenue and subsequent generations, his company absorbed in a world-wide wine and spirits group, his property and collections dispersed, but his outstanding achievements with horses have survived. It was he who played the major role in the multiplication of the breed societies in the decade starting in 1877 and most of these organisations are still thriving more than one hundred years later.

It was an extraordinary phenomenon for the horse world, this sudden spurt of rationalisation during just one decade of the late Victorian era. The societies formed then have been the backbone of Britain's horse breeding policy throughout the twentieth century. Sadly, the Victorians were so justly proud of the improvements achieved in the last part of the nineteenth century that they slipped back into a reactionary mode and saw no need for further changes. Walter Gilbey was the first to realise that the improvements made during that remarkable decade were not sufficient.

He was an extraordinarily forward thinking man and if the plans and ideas he suggested in the 1890s and at the start of the twentieth century had been enacted, the British horse industry would be much stronger today. Five or ten years after helping in the formation of all those societies, he started to campaign for more improvements, making speeches and writing letters to express unease, highlight problems and point to solutions. Amazingly, most of what he campaigned for is still wanted at the end of the twentieth century and Walter Anthony Gilbey, his grandson, is one of the campaigners pressing for their enactment.

Despite his pleas, the British breeding world made no further radical improvements, until their societies' centenary celebrations and movements towards harmonisation within the European Community provoked some more stimulating thinking. Most of the ideas enacted in the 1980s and 1990s in Britain are not original, but were in the main propounded by Walter Gilbey more than 100 years ago.

The Supply of Horses

Walter Gilbey was instrumental in organising that first great leap forward. He recognised the importance of the societies in an interview in 1890, when he emphasised: 'The revival of horse breeding in England has been almost entirely brought about by the horse societies.' The movement led to a dramatic increase in exports (in 1877-9, 10,398 horses were exported and in 1887-

89, 36,610). The policy he promoted was in two stages: firstly, to establish a stud book, so that the breeding could be done on systematic and intelligent lines; and secondly, to run shows which would be performance indicators, fulfilling a similar function to the racecourse test for Thoroughbreds. A newspaper report about Walter Gilbey said: 'he was the first to grasp the fact that the breeding of horses on intellectual lines opened a channel of relief to the tenant farmer,'[1] while another paper stated:

> The now influential breed societies which have during the last twenty years been formed to forward the interests of the old English breeds of horses, practically owe their existence to his foresight and energy. It is thought likely that if they had not been established the foreigners would have (as they had been doing) taken the best, to result in a rapid deterioration.'[2]

These various societies that he helped start and run produced a great change in the quality and quantity of English horses. Registered stock were more attractive to foreigners, who liked papers and pedigrees. Six years after the formation of the Shire stud book, colts were being sold at prices from 1,000 to 1,500 guineas and as much as 3,000 guineas was known. This was a huge increase in value.

Imports fell dramatically (in 1877, 30,525 horses were imported; in 1888, 11,505) and Britain was transformed into a major exporter of horses. Walter Gilbey, in the *City Leader* of 4 April, 1891, said: 'the country is now saving nearly a million a year on horses as compared with fifteen years ago.'[3]

At the same time as these societies were being set up, campaigns were being run to increase public awareness of the situation and to solicit help from the government. The government first considered the problem in 1873, when the Earl of Rosebery presided over a select committee in the House of Lords, including among its members the Prince of Wales. The committee reported that, although there was no scarcity of Thoroughbreds, there was of other horses, due to the export of mares to foreign countries, the increased profits on sheep and cattle which had caused farmers to switch out of horse breeding and the increased demand for general-purpose horses. Having highlighted the problems the committee then practised some proto-Thatcherism, concluding that private enterprise could correct the problems and there was no need for government interference. It did, however, recommend that the tax on horses should be abolished.

Walter Gilbey started his campaigns locally amongst the Essex farmers, pointing out the loss of purchasing power because we were not producing our horses at home, but instead had to import them. He built up local support, but it was when he spoke in March 1885, at the London Farmers Club on 'Riding and Driving Horses; their breeding and rearing', that his views became national. This talk was so important and had such an impact that this summary of it bears reproducing:

1. The decline of horse breeding is evidenced by the number of foreign horses imported of late years into this country.

2. The percentage of sizeable riding and, more particularly, driving horses is getting smaller every year and the prices paid for them greater.

3. The lack of success in breeding is in most cases attributable to: a) want of care in the selection of young mares of sufficient size, b) sacrificing too much to speed so that, in the craze for pace, size and substance have been disregarded.

4. To remedy this state of things and in order to breed horses that will repay their owners, there must be a change of system in the breeding and what is wanted is:

a. The judicious blending of the quality of the Thoroughbred stallion with the van mares or the lighter description of draught mares possessing frame, constitution, flat legs and plenty of courage.

b. From these half bred mares so obtained, cross-breeding can be resorted to by the selection again of the Thoroughbred and, for riding horses, an improved size, strength and constitution thus being secured.

c. For an improved supply of sizeable carriage and driving horses the Hackney sire can be used upon selected cross bred mares.'

Reactions were positive. That same year the policy that still exists today was started, in the awarding of premiums to Thoroughbred stallions to encourage their use on half bred mares and fulfil the demand for offspring of such matings.

Walter Gilbey helped to enact enormous improvements in British breeding, the establishment of stud books, the running of shows and in getting government and private funds diverted into helping half-bred breeding. This was, however, only a start, and he wanted to do much more.

He was quoted in the newspapers of 1892 as expressing anxiety that too little intellect and scientific evaluation was used: 'It is a regrettable fact that the English have not devoted much study to the breeding of horses other than racers and massive beasts of draught. The intermediate animals have been bred by accident or caprices and are of mixed lineage.' Further: 'Every farmer who possesses a mare, whether well or ill-shaped sound or lame, thinks her good enough to breed from.'

Just one year later he created a stir when he said that those premiums that promote the use of the good Thoroughbred on part bred mares were only the start of the answer. What was really needed to meet the increasing demand for the general purpose horse for riding and driving was a new stud book for the horses of mixed lineage. It was what the Continentals did – and it was what still needed doing in Britain 100 years after he first made the point.

Walter Gilbey realised the importance of cross breeding for foundation stock, but this was only the first stage. As soon as possible, breeders should be in a position to breed like to like, instead of relying on the cross breeding. As he so rightly said, which again still applies today: 'When we come to crossing one breed with another we are landed in a sea of uncertainty. . . . The breeding of half bred stock may be regarded as a lottery.'[4]

His statements provoked plenty of controversy. The letters page of *The Times* was full of it. In one reply to some of the correspondence, Walter

Gilbey finished by saying:

> At no period in history has the idea of perfection been more diligently sought and the particular aim during the past half century has been to attain perfection and to combine beauty and utility, and nearly all will admit the improvement in all animals, with the single exception of the saddle and harness horses.[5]

As it was in the 1890s, so it is in the 1990s, the Continentals are way ahead. Walter Gilbey in his book, *Horse Breeding in England* (published 1901), said that on the Continent: '

> They breed for business not pleasure; their aim is to produce the highest stamp of useful horse [and] They breed without prejudice. They do not pin their faith to one single breed and depend upon that to improve all other breeds. . . . The ground plan of the system is to raise the standard of merit in each breed, (1) by providing the best procurable stallions of that breed for public service at low fees and (2) by affording the owners of mares a certain range of choice in stallions, that defects may be eliminated or improvement obtained by judicious crossing.'

Europeans enjoyed another benefit from their more rational breeding policies: 'Foreigners' misfits are unlike ours. The foreigner may – he necessarily often does – fail to produce a youngster that will sell in the most remunerative market, i.e. as a carriage horse; but the misfit is not a weed, it is useful for general purposes.'

He also pointed out, somewhat ruefully: 'They have been buying British mares with good conformation for 60 years and since 1830 have been England's best customers for Hackney mares.'

In *Horse Breeding in England*, again, he says: 'Without wishing to see the continental system of horse breeding by government adopted in England, we in this Country may perhaps profitably study the foreign methods to the advantage of our private studs.'

He points out in this same book:

> For 50 years endeavours have been made to establish a better system of horse breeding in England; but nevertheless we are farther than ever from being independent of foreign countries; and horses for military purposes are those which we most lack.

That good start to the rate of reduction in imports in the 1880s had not continued and it was calculated that £16,240,700 was spent on importing horses in the last decade of the nineteenth century.

> A few years later, in 1913, he illuminated another weakness in the system: The endeavours that have been made of recent years to encourage English horse breeding have scarcely been well directed. What has been done is to increase facilities for production by placing good stallions in somewhat larger numbers at the disposal of intending breeders. This was helpful as far as it goes, but the scheme stops short just at the wrong point. What is wanted is a market, the farmer will not breed the horses if he cannot sell them. Create demand and supply will take care of itself.[6]

If only Walter Gilbey had been able to continue that renaissance of the horse breeding industry, Britain would not be in the sorry state it is at the end of the twentieth century, with such disappointing statistics as an annual Balance of

Payments deficit in equine trade of £31,600,000[7] and 90% of our top show jumping horses being foreign.

The Cart Horse Parade

Despite a frustrating disregard of his suggestions in the last 25 years of his life, the work Walter Gilbey did in his 40s and 50s lives on. Most of the organisations that he had played such a major role in instigating are flourishing today. The most unique – The Cart Horse Parade – had little effect on breeding, but led to extraordinary improvements in the treatment of horses.

> For a long time Walter Gilbey had been concerned about the care of horses: In my younger days horses on the street were, many of them, poor things, ill fed and badly treated; and while some people worked for the Society for the Prevention of Cruelty to Animals (SPCA) I set to work in another direction, to foster interest in the Englishman's innate love of a good horse and to encourage both the drivers and owners to take a pride in the appearance and well being of their charges.[8]

His approach was in keeping with his philosophy not to give money directly, but to set up systems and events where people could earn or win money and prestige if they worked for it. He achieved this through the London Cart Horse Parade, an event which made a major contribution towards improving the condition of the horses on the streets of London, as the drivers could see a material advantage to being kind to dumb animals.

It was not an original concept. Since 1863, Liverpool had celebrated May Day with Liverpool May Day Parade, in which decorated Cart Horses featured, and by the 1880s they were awarded rosettes if they passed veterinary tests. Manchester and Bristol copied this worthwhile humanitarian event, but to organise one in the more fragmented and larger city of London was not such an easy task.

It was direly needed; the figures prior to the parade spoke for themselves. In the 1860s it was estimated that 70,000 horses in London died prematurely or unnecessarily each year. Common causes were accidents, epidemics fuelled by poor ventilation and sanitation in the stables, poisoning from bad food and impure water, starvation from an inability to masticate and digest the coarse food and exhaustion from work that was too long and too hard .

The attitude towards the huge numbers of horses in the cities had to be changed. To most of their owners and caretakers they were not a source of pride, but a servant whose health and well being was of little importance. The extraordinarily effective way of achieving the necessary improvement was not to introduce legal rules and regulations, but simply to stage a grand annual parade. The improvements were made because the drivers wanted them, not because they were forced to.

In 1886 Walter Gilbey was made the chairman of the first London Cart Horse Parade Society. Its stated aim was to improve the general condition and treatment of the London Cart horses by encouraging the drivers to take a humane interest in the animals under their charge. Baroness Burdett-Coutts,

48. Sir Walter Gilbey at the Cart-Horse Parade in a brougham.

the great philanthropist who inherited £1.8 million in 1887 and used her considerable wealth to help charitable interests, was a major supporter. Known as the Queen of the Poor, she suggested her husband should be president. The parade secretary was W.H. Mole of the Royal Society for the Prevention of Cruelty to Animals (RSPCA).

The first parade was held on Whit Monday, 1886, in the grounds of Albert Palace in Battersea Park, with 113 vehicles taking part. Every driver who passed the inspection was given a cash prize and the total expenses of £53 were covered by Mr Burdett-Coutts & Walter Gilbey. The following year the parade was opened up to all cart horses stabled within seven miles of Charing Cross. This event attracted 383 horses and its popularity grew so fast over the following few years that entries had to be restricted to 25 per firm and a total of 1,000.

The day started with a veterinary inspection and then the three parade judges made their assessments. Good looks and conformation were not rewarded, but the judges looked for whether the horses were being well cared for, that they had shining coats, blemish free mouths, clean well fitting harness and were able to carry their load with ease at about 4 to 5 mph.

Walter Gilbey described the rewards:

Prizes and a rosette are awarded to drivers whose horses testify to exceptional good treatment and whose harness shows superior cleanliness, at a rate of 10/- for a single, 15/- for a pair and £1 for a team. To these awards the RSPCA adds a diploma or an ornamental brass tablet given to all drivers specially commended by the judges and they also receive a red rosette. In addition to these honours, the Shire Horse Society offers premiums of £2 each for the 3 best teams of horses, premiums of £1 each for the 10 best pairs and premiums of £1 each for the 10 best singles.[9]

These prizes were equal to several days' pay at the time.

In early 1888 Albert Palace was closed and, with the permission of Her Majesty's First Commissioner of Works, the parade was moved to the Inner Circle of Regents Park. This made possible what became a feature of the event, a grand lunch for the Committee, Judges and Officials in Walter Gilbey's London home of Cambridge House, in between the judging and the file-past when prizes were distributed. The event became popularly known as The Carter's Cavalcade, catching the imagination of the London public who turned up in large numbers to watch this colourful occasion each Whit Monday. One press report described proceedings thus:

> 'It is curious to watch the file of the competing vehicles as they pass before the judges, all of them loaded with a motley throng of men, women and children decked out in their 'Sunday best' and deeply interested in what is going on around them. It is a very solemn moment for them when they pass in front of the judges, there is an expression of rueful despair on the driver's face when he is inspected and has to move on without having a blue or red rosette handed to him.'[10]

Apart from the fun of participating, the glory of the rosettes and prizes, there was another attraction, as there was no entry fee and each driver received a gratuity to cover expenses: this despite expensive proceedings which must have depended on Walter Gilbey's generosity. Each year the crowd grew larger and the entries more numerous and of higher and higher standard, so more and more qualified for those coveted rosettes. It became such an occasion that it was deemed worthy of a special piece of verse in *Punch* in 1891:

> First rate English horses in holiday guise
> A sight, that, to please a true Britisher's eyes.
> And then the Society – surely that will be
> Supported by Britons – ask Good Walter Gilbey.

Some of the press notices of 1893 give an indication of the colourful and glamorous nature of the day:

> All the world and his wife, and likewise his pet dogs and his children, seemed to have assembled in Regents Park for the annual Whit Monday Cart Horse Parade. It seems to increase in popularity with Londoners of all classes each succeeding year.[11]

The Prince of Wales was a patron and came for a morning visit that year. His visit caused quite a stir, as it was the first time for many months that he had appeared together with the Princess and their two daughters. Like today's Prince of Wales, his marriage was not a happy one and although the press must have been less obtrusive then, it was still quick to criticise:

> The Prince of Wales appeared after a long absence abroad with the Princess by his side, though it must be admitted they did not seem in conversational mood, they did appear together in public. . . . The constant rumours about her health, her reluctance to return to England, the marked omission of the Prince to meet his wife at the station need abatement.[12]

In the afternoon the Duke of York (the future King George V), his fiancée, the Princess May (the future Queen Mary), and her mother, the Duchess of Teck, watched for two hours as the vehicles filed past. The Duchess of Teck presented half the medals, badges and certificates, but fatigue from stretching up to the huge drays made her hand over this honour to Princess May.

The Cart Horse Parade had shown how commercially-minded men could be encouraged to care for their horses and, as it did not cover the lighter

49. *The Whit Monday Cart-Horse Parade 1893 in Regent's Park, Princess May presenting the badges.*

horses that pulled the cabs, dairy, bakers and costers vehicles, it was decided to start a similar event for these. The Van Horse Parade, first held on Easter Monday in 1904, was started by James Buchanan (from the whisky firm) Lord Woolavington a great friend of Walter Gilbey's eldest son, Henry Walter, and Alfred Dyke Acland. The effect was similar to that for Cart Horses. Thoroughbreds and Hackneys pulling loads far too heavy for them became a rare sight. The popularity grew, too, after a start when there were just 132 entries.

Interest was stimulated when the King became President of the London Van Horse Parade in 1910 and at the 1914 event there were 1,259 horses taking part. Nowadays, as the twentieth century draws to an end, Battersea Park on Easter Monday is again filled with the horses and carriages. The two parades have been amalgamated and moved back to Battersea Park largely through the work of the founder's grandson Walter Anthony Gilbey, who has twice been chairman. The merging in 1966 produced the London Harness Horse parade, with 172 horses and 137 vehicles taking part that year. It has flourished and numbers have multiplied, so that twenty years later the figures have nearly doubled. Today the parade's educational role is minimal, as there is such a keen general interest in the welfare of horses. Instead it is more of a celebration of Britain's horses, now drastically reduced in numbers – from about 3.5 million horses in Britain at the turn of the century, to today an unsubstantiated figure that ranges between quarter and half a million. With the horse being used mostly for public relations, ceremonies, leisure and sport, this event is an important link with the past, reminding new generations of our treasured inheritance.

The Shire Horse Society

The Shire Horse Society, in the foundations of which Walter Gilbey played such a major part, is still flourishing. It is curious that the British, having reaped such great rewards for starting the first ever stud book – for the Thoroughbred – and having turned their racehorses into the most valuable in the world, should have taken so long to apply the same formula for improving a breed to others. It was nearly a hundred years after the first Thoroughbred was registered, that they tried out the method on heavy horses and the first in which Walter Gilbey played a part was that of the Shire Horse.

He described the history of the Shire in a speech in 1879 in this way:
I have taken some trouble to forage up history with regard to the breed of Shire Horses. I find traces of them as far back as 200 years. They were chiefly used for cavalry purposes, for carrying soldiers, who wore very heavy armour and consequently wanted very heavy horses to carry them. All writers of the period in authorised works then written called them 'The Shire Horse', from the fact they were bred in the Shires. The breed, however, fell into neglect in the nineteenth century when farming began to hit bad times, good stallions were sold abroad, good mares taken away from breeding and sent to work in the towns. Shires were

bred without concern about soundness. There was so little difference in price between a good animal and a bad one, that there was little incentive to take trouble about the breeding.[14]

A transformation of the quality of the Shire was achieved through the establishment of a society to record pedigrees and enable a more scientific approach to breeding, combined with an annual horse show where the prizes were high for the good animals and the unsound and second rate were shown up.

In the mid-nineteenth century the Shire was often referred to as the Cart Horse, which was all too appropriate with the deterioration in quality. Nevertheless this, the largest horse in the world, attracted a wide cross section of admirers and promoters, from the farmers and their employees, to the aristocracy and even the Prince of Wales. As Keith Chivers has said: 'This breed has done more than most men to break down the class barriers.'[15] The first champion in the mid-nineteenth century was the Earl of Ellesmere, who started buying them for his Worsley Hall estate near Manchester in 1869. He set out to breed them scientifically, selecting them on pedigree and conformation, and starting his own stud book. He also ran a sale in 1878, before Walter Gilbey started his own sales. The Earl of Ellesmere, however, used the sale as a culling process, putting in many of his weakest stock and prices were not nearly as high as those reached at Elsenham.

It was at a dinner before this first sale that the Earl proposed that a national stud book association should be started. There was such support for the concept that more meetings were held, a society incorporated and the rules for entry into the stud book established. Volume I stated: 'Conditions of Entry – That no Horse be admitted into the Stud Book having a cross of any other breed than that of an English Cart Horse for at least two generations.'

The Shire Horse Society attracted considerable interest, not least because

50. Shire Horse disturbed by the applause at a Shire Horse Show

of a great dispute about the name. Started as the English Cart Horse Society, it held its first AGM in May 1879 and a motion was moved by Walter Gilbey, who was on the Council, that the name be changed to the Shire Horse Society. He had the vision to realise the long term advantages of a more distinguished name than Cart Horse. The arguments raged, with Lord Ellesmere claiming not enough people knew what Shire meant and others expressing the shame at being burdened with a title like Cart Horse. When the vote was taken, a majority supported Walter Gilbey's motion, but a simple majority was invalid and it took many more discussions and meetings before the title was finally changed in 1883, the year that Walter Gilbey held the presidency for the first time.[16]

Walter Gilbey remained chairman of the finance committee from 1878 until his death in 1914 and he recruited some important members, including the Prince of Wales, who was not a mere figurehead, but an enthusiastic and active contributor.

The Society immediately promoted the use of showing classes to help improve the breed and, for their breed classes at the Royal Agricultural Society's 40th annual show at Kilburn, they trebled the prize money for the heavy horse classes. In 1880 the new society took the bold step of deciding to run their own show. They were the first breed society ever to do so and it was at a time when their 400 members were not working harmoniously together, as most had spent many hours in heated debates about the society's name. It was a precipitate move, as there was not even a defined conformation for the then Cart Horse (soon to be Shire), with no published stud books, and the decision was taken just three months before the agreed dates of 2nd, 3rd & 4th March. The venue selected was nowhere near where the Shires were bred and worked, but in the centre of London at the Royal Agricultural Hall at Islington. A main instigator of this daring move was once again Walter Gilbey, who took on the chairmanship of the Horse Show Committee.

Somehow they managed to make it work. The visitors included the Prince and Princess of Wales and the Lord Mayor, who came to see the 114 horses who had been transported by rail from all over England. Radical steps were taken to stamp out the notorious unsoundness of cart horses by stating that all animals had to be free from hereditary diseases, including ringbone and sidebone, which were rampant amongst the breed at the time. The first stud book was published on the second day of the show, proving to any doubting members of the public that the Cart Horse was not a common beast, but had an ancestry tracing back for many generations. After this first venture it was apparent that Cart Horse breeding could be turned into a fashionable activity and not merely a utilitarian necessity.

The second annual show in 1881 consolidated this trend with many more entries, probably attracted by the high prize money obtained largely as a result of Walter Gilbey's industry. As an additional feature, an auction was run on the last day of the show. When Walter Gilbey bought the show champion, the three year old Spark, for the massive sum of 800 guineas, there was much written about the show in the newspapers.

The show's success meant that the next year it could be extended to four days with judging on the first day, an auction on the last and two days for discussions, dealing and organising the hiring of stallions for the season. It was a very social occasion, with activities ranging from sophisticated lunches given by Walter Gilbey for the Council, to grooms and farmers finding it a great excuse to drink. This friendly atmosphere promoted dealing and in 1882 more than half the animals at the show were said to have changed hands.

Records were not kept of auction prices until 1895, when 121 animals were sold for £7,275. 11s – an average of £60. 3s. The show had been turned into a thriving market, providing yet another incentive to breed good Shires.

The Shire Horse Society made a notable contribution to British breeding. The smart London venue for their show attracted publicity and prestige. Prize money for the owners rose and in 1885 amounted to £646. 5s. Breeders too were recognised, gold medals being awarded to the breeders of champions. The society used the big stick as well as the carrot, as they introduced veterinary examinations in 1886 and then in 1887 accepted entries only for horses in the stud book.

In just a decade, the enlightened leadership of Walter Gilbey in the finance committee had produced mouth-watering prizes, attracting the best animals and making it worth buying and breeding better animals to win. Through his leadership of the horse show committee, the event was made prestigious and glamorous enough to attract the top animals and the fashionable spectators. The common and unsound breed of the 1860s and 1870s were now rare and the Shire was now the feature of a celebrated annual occasion. Walter Gilbey was recognised as the major contributor to the extraordinary transformation in the status of the Shire Horse and the consequent growth in its popularity. In 1884 there were 903 members of the society, by 1898, there were 2,237. Over this same period entries in the stud book rose from 1,423 to 3,581 and the prize money from £524 to £1,200.

When a promoter of the Percheron had the temerity to claim that this French breed was stronger and sounder than the Shire, Walter Gilbey issued an open challenge in the *Live Stock Journal*, offering £100 to the winner of a contest, or £200 if it was donated to the Agricultural Benevolent Institute. The tests were to be for weight pulled over a stated distance: but no one took up the challenge.

As early as 1883 the part played by Walter Gilbey had been recognised and when the Duke of Cambridge presented him with the Challenge Cup, won by his stock, he said about him: 'by the services he had rendered to an enterprise which had fallen away he has performed a national service.'[17]

The Shire Horse Society's tribute after his death in 1914 again illustrates his contribution:

> The value of Sir Walter's services to the Shire Horse Society can scarcely be over-estimated. From its earliest days he gave it the most generous support and the Society owes its remarkable success mainly to the great interest and enthusiasm which he displayed in its progress. One of its founders, he had from 1878 up to the time of his death, without a break, been a member of the Council, twice as President and later as Honorary

Treasurer. It was due to his interest and energies that the foundations of its present success were laid.

The Hackney

Heavy horses formed only one section of Britain's massive equine work force: another important division was filled by the lighter horses that pulled the carriages. In 1903, just before the motor car took over, there were 445,994 private horse drawn carriages and 127,410 for hire. The lighter versions of

51. The Empresses, Queen Victoria and Empress Frederick at the 1891 show.

these were pulled by Hackneys or Trotters, smart, fast horses that were fun to breed. These Trotters had a long history, so it is not surprising that their supporters followed the example of the Heavy Horse breeder to organise stud books and societies.

Again Walter Gilbey was a principal promoter of their formation, as he was a member of the first council and then President from 1889 to 1904. The momentum started at a meeting in 1878 at Downham Market in East Anglia, when it was proposed to establish a register for English Trotting Horses. For the next five years Henry Euren collected data for a stud book from newspapers, old hand bills and old stud cards. The records traced back hundreds of years and, although he concentrated on those horses of East Anglian origin, known as the Norfolk Trotter, there was a close relation in Yorkshire, known as the Hackney. Bred mainly in the East Riding of Yorkshire, the Hackney was derived mostly from stock acquired from East Anglia at the beginning of the nineteenth century. There was a difference in type, the Norfolk being more cob-like and the Yorkshire finer, but each traced back to the East Anglia stallion, the Original Shales, sired in about 1755 and which was by the Thoroughbred Blaze, who was a grandson of Darley Arabian, one of the three founders of the Thoroughbred.

During the eighteenth century these Trotters were big enough to be used for riding as well as pulling light carriages. The great expansion of this breed came during the coaching era, when the Macadam roads made it easier to pull carriages and meant these lighter harness horses had an important role to play. They were bred to be strong enough to pull the smaller carriages along this smoother surface, and when speed became of essence the Hackneys ancestors were ideal. As we have heard, Walter Gilbey's father had earned his living driving carriages pulled by some of these fleet footed animals, so it is no surprise that his son held them in such high esteem and did so much for their promotion. As in the time of Walter's father, these animals suffered losses in demand because of modernisation. In the nineteenth century it was due to trains replacing coaches, in the twentieth century from cars taking over from horses and trains. In both cases, demand for Hackneys fell and their numbers reduced.

When Henry Euren started collecting pedigrees and information they were still being used by the families of Yorkshire and East Anglia to pull the lighter, smaller carriages, the Landaus, Victorias and Broughams, and for cross breeding to produce hunters and army horses.

Euren's work stimulated much interest and grew to be beyond the capacity of one individual, so in 1883 a public meeting was held where the resolution was passed to establish a society for Hackneys, Roadsters, Cobs and Ponies and to publish a stud book. Members' subscriptions were to be 1 guinea a year. The following year the Yorkshire breeders joined them, after a meeting at the Agricultural Show at York. The name was changed to the Hackney Horse Society, with rather less turmoil than for the similar change within the Shire Horse Society. The Prince of Wales was the first patron and Anthony

Hamond the first President.

The organisers followed the same successful formula as the Shire Horse Society, publishing an annual stud book to establish the identity and pedigrees crucial to selective breeding. Then in 1885, one week after the Shire Horse Show, they started their own breed show at the same Royal Agricultural Hall, Islington, using the stalls and fittings already in place for the heavier horses. 95 stallions and 38 mares came forward for this first event. Once again, the man behind this important step forward was Walter Gilbey, who had been made Chairman of this show committee.

These stylish animals, with their spectacular, high stepping trot, had many fans. The Prince of Wales was himself one and for his stud, the Wolferton, which he had started at Sandringham in 1887, he bought the best strains. He produced some good winners and organised bi-annual sales where those keen to impress their future king could do so by showing an interest in the breed and buying some of his stock. This helped to add to the returns both of his own stud and of the Hackney breed throughout England.

The London Show became an increasingly prestigious event and in March 1891 a huge royal party appeared and watched for an hour. The group included two Empresses, Queen Victoria and Empress Frederick of Germany, and, of course, the Prince and Princess of Wales, who helped to answer queries from those of the royal party who knew little about the animals. Whether it was an indication of the limited popularity of the monarch at that time, or the huge attraction of the Hackneys, but a report stated: 'The cheers which were raised on the entrance of the Queen were less vigorous than those which greeted the Hackney stallions and mares.'[18]

This type of support turned the Hackney into an increasingly marketable animal, with many being sold abroad. The most popular of the two versions was the bigger stallion of 15.2 hands high or more, which in the show classes were usually trotted out in hand rather than shown pulling carriages. Walter Gilbey's Royal Danegelt and Antonius stood over 15.2 hands high and had plenty of substance. The foreigners bought this type for cross breeding and to introduce a higher stepping action and refinement into the heavier coach horses on the Continent. Even in 1911, when demand for horses was falling, pedigree Hackney stallions and mares were exported to Germany, Italy, Norway, Belgium, Holland, Russia, Spain, Argentina, Chile, Canada, Australia, New Zealand, Japan, South Africa and the USA. This Trotter/ Hackney blood can be found in the pedigrees of today's Selle Francais, Hanoverian, Oldenburg and Holstein breeds. The individual gold medal winner in the show jumping at the 1936 Berlin Olympics was Tora, a Holstein, who was by a Hackney stallion out of a Holstein mare.

The other distinct type of Hackney was lighter, smaller and a more showy animal. Its use was more restricted, being able only to pull very light carriages and tending to be more highly strung. It was, however, the more spectacular stepper, the one the laymen loved to watch, and in the twentieth century it became more and more popular as a show animal. Sadly, the heavier version faded out, largely through exportation and then being used so much for crossbreeding that they merged into other breeds. The lighter harness version flourished, however, supported by a big demand from the USA. At the 1911 New York show Hackney bred horses won 34 out of the 41 first prizes in the open harness classes and in 18 of the classes they won every single award.

The Light Horse

Another important sector in the horse world was that of the utility horses, the light horses used for the army, for general riding and for hunting. Once again it was Walter Gilbey who helped to arrest a deteriorating situation in that sphere, by initiating formal organisations, stud books and shows to promote these horses and to locate and reward the best of them.

They were only a few years behind the Shire and the Hackney and it was the latter's organisation that helped them to start operations in 1884. The crux of the scheme was premiums which were awarded to the Thoroughbred stallions suitable to produce hunters and half breds. The problem had been that, without support, it did not pay the farmers to breed these types of horses, so not enough were being produced and Britain was having to buy from abroad.

The first committee meeting was held at Tattersalls in November 1884. Foremost amongst the pioneers of the Stallion Premium scheme, which still flourishes today, were the Earl of Coventry, the Earl of Yarborough, Lord Hastings, Lord Middleton and, of course, Walter Gilbey.

They agreed to hold classes for Thoroughbred stallions as part of the London Show for Hackneys in March 1885. The primary objectives were to provide good, sound stallions for the farmers, at prices they could afford, and to achieve this all entries had to pass a veterinary examination to show they were free from hereditary or other diseases detrimental to the breeding of sound and healthy horses. Any premium winners then had to guarantee to offer 20 nominations to their stallion to tenant farmers' mares at a fee of no more than £2.10s.

Early spring was the best time to show off the stallions, as it was before breeders had made their selection of breeding stock. With a large number of stallions in one place it was easier to make comparisons and facilitate selection. The good financial rewards for prizes were aimed at inducing owners of higher class Thoroughbred horses to enter and a special class for stallions which had not been at stud was intended to encourage owners to send their racehorses directly from the track into the scheme.

The first show produced 35 entries, but there was controversy and embarrassment over an objection to the winner of the open class. The winner, Mulatto, was registered in the General Stud Book as out of a Thoroughbred mare, but by either Highclere, a Thoroughbred, or a cart horse. The mare had apparently spent some time with a cart horse stallion and, with no blood typing available in those days, nobody was sure whether it was he or Highclere that was the sire. Certainly Mulatto was a substantial type of Thoroughbred,

'Hedon Squire', Hackney stallion

just what was needed to breed hunters and army horses, but the Stewards of the Jockey Club were pedantic and ruled that he was not Thoroughbred and therefore not eligible for the Premium scheme.

The stallion standing second to him happened to be Walter Gilbey's Thoroughbred, Pedometer, and he was therefore upgraded to become the first ever winner of the premium scheme and as such appeared on subsequent medals.

Walter Gilbey chaired a general meeting held at the Royal Agricultural Hall at Islington after the show to assess the value of this first venture. Following a discussion a proposal was made to form a society for the improvement of the breed of Hunters, known from then until the present day as the H.I.S. (Hunters' Improvement Society).

Plans were drawn up that summer for the second show, but the next important meeting was in December when, in line with Hackney and Shire experiences, there was a motion to change the name, this time from Hunter Improvement Society to the Horse Improvement Society. A Colonel Ravenshill opposed the motion and was successful. It took more than a hundred years before its name was changed to the National Light Horse Breeding Society, though it is still known under the initials H.I.S.

Once again, there was influential support, as the H.R.H. Prince of Wales became the patron, along with H.R.H. Duke of Connaught and the first President was the Earl of Coventry. Walter Gilbey, however, was the driving force and at a General Meeting in March 1886 Colonel Ravenshill proposed a vote of thanks: 'to Mr W. Gilbey for his great assistance without which the society would not be in existence.' Walter Gilbey became one of the first presidents, in 1889.

In those early years it seems the general standard of stallions was not good, with many failing the veterinary examination and not enough attention being paid to their preparation. It is interesting that the type of Thoroughbred was often one we could benefit from today. Huguenot, who was a premium winner, stood 16 hands high and in such good proportions that they said he would have been well able to carry 15 stone to hounds. He had run on the flat over hurdles and across country before retiring to stud.

The H.I.S was not the only society operating premiums, as the Royal Agricultural Society, under the aegis of the Duke of Richmond, had awarded them to stallions at their Newcastle show in 1885, but in 1889 amalgamated their scheme with the H.I.S. This led to a considerable expansion and at the following show, at the Royal Agricultural Hall at Islington, there were 388 horses.

The largest part of the funds eventually came from the government, as in 1887 Walter Gilbey compiled statistics to show to parliament, highlighting the plight of the half bred, as opposed to the Thoroughbred, and showing that the country could save money by halting the trend of an increase in imported horses and promoting the trend of an increase in exports. To do this, a larger production of home bred utility horses was needed.

A Royal Commission was established under Lord Ribblesdale and the stated aim was:

> to make the breeding of half bred horses possible and reasonable for the farm community, whereas before the commission, the breeding of these horses by the farming community was hardly possible or reasonable.
>
> Let us stimulate and provide for foreign demand of English produce and let us recognise clearly that the stallions and mares it has paid the foreigners so well to come and buy may pay us still better to keep and breed from them.

The end result was the diversion of government funds from racing into breeding premiums, amounting to £5,000 from the Treasury and £3,500 from the Queen's Plates at race meetings. To these were added funds from private sources, such as the Royal Agricultural Society. From 1889 premiums stood at £200 each, a considerable sum in those days, and with the added perk of having the title of Queen's (and after Victoria's death, King's) Premium. The Royal Commission took over the financing of the premium scheme until 1929, when the Hunter Improvement Society took control again.

The London Show where the premiums were awarded flourished, with more and more entries and classes for mares as well as stallions. In 1893 there were more than 100 stallions with a total of 609 entries. These horses and their inevitably large entourages of country people, plus the spectators, were too many people for the Hall. There were complaints about the difficulties of moving around, so it was decided to separate the Hunters from the Hackneys and start a third week of equestrian activities in the centre of London.

This gave an impetus for further expansion and classes were introduced for youngstock, riding horses, horses likely to make Officer's chargers and, in 1902, a novel concept in Britain, two jumping classes. Royalty were frequent visitors to these shows, which buzzed with activity. The Hunter's

Improvement Society had built up a showpiece which produced untold benefits for their members. Surprisingly, they never tried to establish their produce as a breed, continuing to rely on the Thoroughbreds from the racetrack and cross breeding them with the half bred mares. The concept of trying to breed like to like, half bred to half bred, which was so successful on the Continent was never proposed – except by Walter Gilbey.

Walter Gilbey continued to be concerned about the supply of horses in Britain. The Hunter's Improvement Society and the Premiums had made a contribution, but it was not enough. The supply of horses was the first subject which drew public attention to his interest in breeding horses and it was the last subject about which he talked publicly. He was asked just before his death about the supply of horses, at a time when the subject demanded even more serious attention because of the large losses of horses through the war. His comments appeared posthumously in *Country Life* and *Horse and Hound*:

> It is obvious, owing to the enormous shrinkage in horse flesh through the war, that we shall practically be denuded of horses in this country and I earnestly hope that the Government will take this matter in hand at once, if in the future we are to have horses, either for our cavalry or for hunting purposes. To make breeding pay it is manifest that more money will have to be provided by the Government for this purpose, as the principal breeders of the country being farmers it goes without saying that they will not continue to breed if it is not profitable to them. They have ceased to breed to any large extent for the past few years, because the prices they should be getting for their horses have not been paid. We have not been able to compete with foreign nations in the purchase of horses as other Governments have given much higher prices for their horses than our own.

Today we need to substitute 'Sport' for 'Cavalry' and, of course, with modern techniques, cavalry war no longer denudes us of our horses, but much of what he said still applies. There is a huge deficit in our balance of trade for horses, due in large part to the horses about which he was so concerned – the light horses. Walter Gilbey played the major role in establishing the British breed societies, but he knew this was not enough. We are still fighting the battles he campaigned for a century ago.

He might not have achieved all he wanted, but nothing can take away from the enormous impact he had on British horse breeding. He was the key person in creating the structure under which today's horse world still operates. The memorials to his work are still flourishing, and continue to show his great contribution to the horse world.[19]

THE FIELD

THE COUNTRY NEWSPAPER

WITH WHICH IS INCORPORATED "LAND AND WATER"

VOL. CLVI   No. 4066.   SATURDAY, NOVEMBER 29, 1930.   REGISTERED.   PRICE 1s. POSTAGE {INLAND, 1½D.; CANADA AND NEW-FOUNDLAND, 1½D.;   FOREIGN, 3D.}

SIR WALTER GILBEY, BART.

A staunch believer in the future of the Totalisator. His chocolate and yellow striped jacket has been prominently displayed on the Turf for many years. He has rendered immense services to the breeder of the heavy horse, the hunter and the racehorse

A portrait from life specially drawn for the "Field" by Frank Slater

53. Sir Henry Walter Gilbey, from The Field *newspaper*

VIII
Maintaining the Status Quo

The press was full of news about Sir Walter Gilbey in the months that led up to his death, at the age of 83, on November 12th, 1914. The reports had appeared throughout the first months of the war whenever he had a relapse and again whenever he recovered enough to take one of his nap-inducing rides in his car. They covered stories about his stock that continued to win at the shows and about his campaigns to save Thaxted church. They discussed his articles on horse painters and those about his pet subject, the dire state of the horse supply. He had become a highly newsworthy personality and, although his body became weaker, his mind was alert to the end of his long and active life.

A mass of obituaries in the national and local press included such headlines as 'From Clerk to Millionaire', 'The Great Merchant's Life', 'A Fine Old English Gentleman', 'A Great Agriculturist', 'Great Business That Began in A London Cellar' and 'Grand Old Man of Agriculture'.

The *Pall Mall Gazette* put it most concisely: 'A very vital and valuable type of Englishman was exemplified to perfection in Sir Walter Gilbey, whose death is recorded to-day. A daring and consummate man of business, a kindly squire, a stout-hearted sportsman, and a powerful friend of agriculture and the horse, he was an influence in innumerable directions and one that made for good temper, national health and general progress.'

It was into these illustrious shoes that Henry Walter, now Sir Walter, the second Baronet, stepped at the age of 55. Until that time he had not generally made a strong impression. In his own words, in a letter to his father asking for money in 1900, he said: 'I daresay I have done nothing for either you or myself to be particularly proud of in my life and work, at the same time I don't think I have ever done anything to disgrace the name and I pray to God I never shall.'

Henry Walter said of himself in his unpublished autobiography: 'I was no youthful prodigy of learning and I must have broken the hearts of a succession of tutors.' Any signs of an adventurous spirit were dampened, both during his upbringing, which was very different from his father's, and by the attitude of his father's generation towards his generation when they joined the family firm.

The old saying, 'Clogs to clogs in three generations', stems from what seems like a self- destruct mechanism. It starts with the determination of the first generation to protect their offspring from the trials they themselves had faced in childhood, though in fact it was just these trials that had helped to turn them into entrepreneurs willing to take risks. Then, as the children grow older, there follows parental disillusionment – the disappointment that the

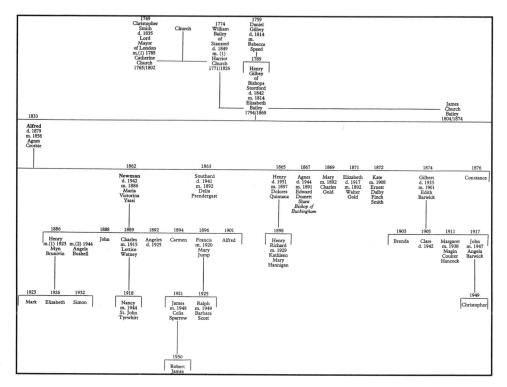

H. Family Tree – The Gilbeys, part 3

offspring do not live up to expectations, followed all too soon by efforts to prevent them from ruining the business and wasting the hard-earned capital. The end result is a person like Henry Walter.

His secure, disciplined upbringing had stifled the intuition and adventurous spirit needed to make money. He was, however, a personality and he turned into one of those British eccentrics whom the papers love to write about, especially when, at the age of 55, he emerged from his father's shadow, was free to run an estate, make use of the title and become an important figure in the great W&A Gilbey business.

It was a difficult start for Henry Walter, not least because it was in the early stages of World War I. Further, although he inherited the property, a house and three thousand acres, under his father's will,[1] the contents had to be divided between the rest of the family and that meant selling at a time when few British people were in the mood to buy valuable luxuries. The wonderful paintings and furniture did not realise their true value. Then, to add to the problems, the house was commandeered for the war effort, the farming could not be made to pay and the wine and spirits business faced war time difficulties.

Sir Walter had given up Cambridge House some years earlier and its contents were sold in 1910. The Elsenham sale involved 129 pictures, including no less than 28 by Stubbs and 24 by Morland. The highest price for a Stubbs was £753 for 'Eclipse', although four Morlands made higher prices than this. If it had been possible to keep the collection intact it would have represented a memorial to the first Sir Walter which would by now have probably outstripped even his achievements with horses in the public mind. Stubbs is currently regarded by leading art critics as the finest of all eighteenth century English painters, superior to Gainsborough and Reynolds. As it is, many pictures in the collection are now in the United States, some of them forming an important part of the Mellon Foundation collection.

Henry Walter did not relish the challenges in the same way his father had done, nor did he have the same verve and insight . He kept the name in the public eye, but the fortune began to decline during his remaining life, 30 years which encompassed immense social changes, including the Great Depression of the 1920s and 1930s and the Second World War.

As suggested previously his upbringing did not encourage the necessary drive for self improvement, but instead bred an attractively honest satisfaction in himself: 'I am very fond of myself. I know I should not say it, but it is true. And so I looked after myself.' He also enjoyed the opportunities he was offered: 'I was born with an immense capacity for enjoying the good things that came my way.' At the same time, he was extremely conscientious about his role in business.

In contrast to his father's, Henry Walter's own education was the most fashionable available, yet it failed to develop so effectively acuteness, intuition and business instinct. Its benefits, however, were useful contacts and familiarity with the standards and ethics that would make him at home amongst the grandest in the land. His education started with tutors at home and continued at Harrow Public School where, he said:

> I worked just hard enough to keep out of trouble and on the whole got on extremely well with my school-fellows, though I must confess that I achieved a little more popularity than I was entitled to, owing to the fact that occasional letters from my Dawson friends [the Racehorse trainer's family] contained the hint of matters appertaining to the Turf that did not always prove unprofitable to my House chums.

Henry Walter, however, became best known at Harrow because he fought the last public fight. His description in the autobiography he wrote at the age of 78 bears repeating, revealing a little more about that curious character.

> I had been bathing in the 'Ducker' and on coming out of the water into a keen wind, discovered my towel was missing. When I found a certain youth by the name of Peter McKie had thrown it into the pool, I retaliated by giving him a hefty kick in that part of his anatomy which nature had designed for that purpose. The following day I received a properly worded challenge to fight it out with him in the Milling Ground, which was traditionally reserved for that purpose. Between the challenge and the day fixed for the fight at the end of the term I may say I was not made any happier by the tales of the prowess of my opponent, who, I was informed, had been taking regular boxing lessons and I had not.

Not only did the whole school turn out for this Roman holiday, but the news had spread throughout the Town and when the eventful day

54. Argo Gold, Henry Walter Gilbey, Florence Crawfield and an unknown woman. (Dublin, 1880.)

arrived it appeared that every errand boy and 'townie' for miles around had assembled to watch the contest. This was conducted with all the formality of the prize ring, except that we used bare fists. It was indeed a great scrap. We were fairly evenly matched and the ding-dong fight went on for what appeared, to me, ages. At first I was slightly overawed by my opponent's alleged skill, but we soon warmed up and whatever science he may have possessed was soon forgotten and the affair developed into a proper slogging match, much to the delight of the crowd. In the end I emerged a definite, though battered, victor.

There was so much publicity about this event that Harrow banned fights at the Milling Ground, but it did prove that Henry Walter was tougher and more athletic than at first appeared; and it was an event that made his father proud of him. Henry Walter remembered, with considerable warmth and satisfaction, that it helped to mitigate the poor academic results.

The biggest influence on Henry Walter was undoubtedly his father: 'I had a clever father who encouraged me to learn life by mixing with people and in business he was a firm believer in personal contact,' he wrote in his biography. 'Another thing that I learnt from my Father was the importance of proper attention being paid to dress. He himself was probably one of the best attired men of his day and he always insisted on those of whom he had control being suitably attired for the occasion.'

Henry Walter left Harrow at 17 to round off his education with some travelling. The United States was chosen as the country from which to learn, with his cousin, Ernest Watney, an older travelling companion. It was a great adventure, the journey across the Atlantic on one of the early Cunard liners taking 10 days. Although New York and the East coast were relatively sophisticated, the West, as he said, was 'wild and woolly'. The news-papers had frequent stories of blood-thirsty encounters with Indians who were frequently on the warpath. Denver and St. Louis were still frontier towns. The two headed West on stage-coaches and there was plenty of excitement. The drivers often vied with each other to set the fastest times across bumpy tracks, which sometimes had yawning precipices on either side. The two went on buffalo hunts outside Denver, to the races, saw Spelterini walk a tight-rope across Niagara Falls in the wind and enjoyed the tremendous hospitality for which the Americans are famous.

Henry Walter, who was now 18 years old, came back bubbling with enthusiasm about the opportunities the Americans had to make fortunes. His mind had been opened and he recognised, unlike so many Victorians, that although England might still be the centre of the world, competitors were developing.

His mind was broadened still further when he was sent off to Tours in France to learn the language. He found there some other young Englishmen, which made it difficult to practice French, but easy to have a good time. Henry Walter learnt a lot about the ways of the world whilst in France. His second wife said that this included getting to know an actress who took a great fancy to him. In her skilled hands his early experience of sex was so good that it made him assert that his first wife was a severe disappointment.

Henry Walter appeared to have made good use of these travels, as he started his career in business bursting with bold ideas about promoting exports. However, he received little support from the first generation, who must have by then forgotten about the business gambles they made when they were in their twenties. Henry Walter's positive, enthusiastic thinking was soon curbed, but although he lost some of his ebullience, true to family principles he persisted. To prove his belief in the importance of exports he offered to work for commission, but the Board turned down the proposal (sadly for him as this would have eventually given him a good income). His persistence was respected, eventually, and he was allowed to promote some exporting.

His initiative did lead eventually to big increases in trade. The expansion started with Australia; success there led to the appointment of agents in many countries. The part Henry Walter played in these developments was rewarded by his father, who increased his allowance, gave him some shares and – most touchingly – one of his best horses.

However, despite this success, the older generation dampened the bold thinking of the second generation who began to settle for a secure, conservative approach. Henry Walter's education might not have stimulated boldness, but it was much more this stifling reaction from his seniors, whom he respected so much, that finally made him a person who avoided risks rather than taking on challenges.

With his father in the chair of the business Henry Walter was given a moderate allowance. He was also a partner in the firm from 1885, a director from 1893 and a shareholder, so he was able to lead a relatively comfortable life, without any incentive to rebel or go to another business to make more money.

Henry Walter's heart was not in the business, yet he worked at it conscientiously from the time he returned home from his travels until he died, which amounted to well over sixty years. His conscience lay with the business, but his heart was with sports and the good things in life.

The Sports

He placed great emphasis on sports and attributed his health in old age to keeping fit through exercise. Speaking at a W&A Gilbey Social Club Sports Meeting in May 1925 he said:

> Sport makes the man, not the man the sport, and if the heads of commercial undertakings would join their employees in a day's sport now and then, we should hear very little of labour unrest. In the field of sport you can usually discover the best in a man, a business chief can find out more about the grit and value of his work people on any field of sport in a few minutes than by months of association in the office or warehouse.

Like his father, he was not an athlete. He played golf, but it was his determination to improve his game that produced the results rather than his swing which was, like his personality, somewhat unusual. For five years he had a pack of Beagles, hunted them himself and paid for their upkeep. He often rode, at first hunting until a severe accident in the field, after which his riding was largely confined to hacking in Rotten Row. He drove carriages, but he was not a great horseman; he lacked those vital good hands, and, despite his enormous affection for horses, did not have an empathy with animals.

He did, however, have an exceptional eye and was one of the leading shots in England. His father, Sir Walter, had leased the shooting rights over 8,000 acres from other landowners for the benefit of his sons. Henry Walter had grown up on an estate that had some of the best shooting in England and at fifteen was allowed to join the shooting parties. It was a marvellous opportunity, as there was an extraordinary number of targets. Today a good bag of pheasants is around the 500 mark, but in those days there were occasions like December 13th, 1906, at Elsenham, when it was as high as 2,311, with eight guns.

The other advantage of having such good home shooting was that the

55. Sir Henry Walter Gilbey at W & A Gilbey's sports at Hendon

guests returned the invitations. Henry Walter became his father's deputy when it came to shooting, both supervising the days at Elsenham and accepting the invitations from some of the best shoots in the country.

Nor did he confine his shooting to game, as during the eighties and nineties live pigeon shooting was still acceptable, legal and even fashionable. He was a regular competitor in the matches at Hurlingham and in 1890 won the International Hurlingham Cup against the best pigeon shots in the world.

His love of sports, of doing well in them and his rather bombastic approach towards trying to achieve this aim led to his nickname of 'Champs'. He always gave the impression that he could do things better than anybody else and would back himself to win. 'I bet you' was one of his most frequent phrases, usually emitted excitedly and in rising tones, but out of conviction, not anger. He would bet on sports and he would always bet to defend the name of W&A Gilbey. When someone made the mistake of saying that W&A Gilbey port was rubbish, Henry Walter immediately challenged him to tell the difference between it and some of the best ports. Henry Walter won his bet, but then he knew the drink business, and it is very difficult to tell the difference between ports if a large number of them are drunk in quick succession.

The Racing

He would bet on himself at the drop of a hat, but he was not a gambler and he pursued his favourite sport, racing, because of the horses and the people, not because of the bookies. So highly did he rate this activity that in his autobiography he devotes fifteen out of the twenty-two chapters to it. He enjoyed it because: 'There is no place like the racecourse to test a man's character' and 'The common interest of racing seemed to engender a camaraderie which I do not think exists to quite the same extent in any other sport or indeed in any other sphere of life.' He certainly spent much of his time on the racecourse and in the homes of trainers and owners. He never missed the Derby or a Royal Ascot, and was a regular visitor to Newmarket. There he used to stay with top trainers Richard Marsh and Peter Gilpin, while for Goodwood he joined his greatest friend, Lord Woolavington, who held famous house parties at nearby Lavington Stud.

There were quite a few people in the Gilbey offices keen on this pastime. There was always an exodus from the Pantheon over Ascot week and on Derby day. It was Henry Walter's cousin, Argo Gold, who first lured him into becoming a partner in some horseflesh. At that time it was really beyond Henry Walter's modest income, so he kept it quiet from his family. Those first racehorses were steeplechasers. He did buy some winners, which helped to get him 'hooked' on racing and ensured that they did not drain his finances, but he was soon to divert into flat racing. He chose as his trainers the Cannon family from Stockbridge, who were great jockeys as well as producers of racehorses. He kept horses in training with them for

56. 'Burnside' with Steve Donoghue up

57. Jack Sirret, Sir Henry Walter Gilbey's jockey

what must be a record 49 years.

His prominence in racing came from his loyalty to the sport, not his successes. He never owned a top horse, but this was not too surprising as he would not, or maybe could not without stinting other activities, spend more than £1,000 on any animal. Realising he could only aspire to modest ambitions, he sought out 'genuine' horses, usually geldings who could win handicaps, preferably over long distances. His favourite, as it was with the general public, was Burnside, who ran 88 times in total before he was retired, aged eleven, in 1934. This horse won twelve races, was placed in forty races and became 'the Newmarket specialist', particularly over the Rowley mile. The jockey with whom he was most associated was Jack Sirret who rode him 49 times and became so fond of Burnside that he named his house after him. Burnside was everybody's favourite, winning the admiration of the general public, especially the small punters, as they found that a few pence on him gave them a good run for their money. He was named the working man's horse and epitomised what Henry Walter looked for (and not just in horses): reliability and a stout heart.

Henry Walter did have one horse that made the Derby. With his father's death he found he had more cash during the war than most people and he bought a number of horses, including Paper Money by Greenback, who cost less than 500 guineas, but proved good enough to enter in the 1919 Derby – the first to be run at Epsom after the war – and started second favourite. It must have been one of the most exciting days of Henry Walter's life, as his horse was always contesting the lead and finished a close 3rd to Grand Parade. Paper Money won some important races and at the end of his career on the racetrack was sold for a handsome profit to be exported to New Zealand, where he became one of the leading sires.

Henry Walter himself was a very popular figure on the racecourse. The *Sporting Times* of April 1920 remarked: 'The Turf is all the better for men of the Gilbey stamp to patronise it.' It became an annual tradition for him to give a broadcast on the wireless, advising people on what to back for the Derby.

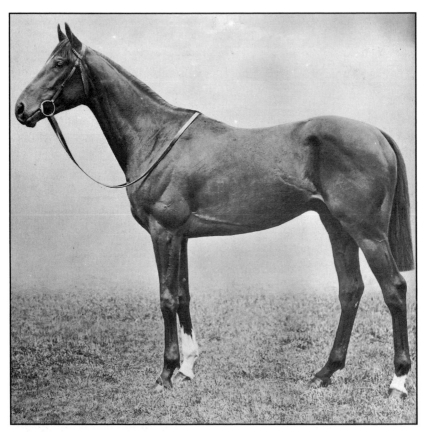

58. '*Paper Money*', *Sir Henry Walter Gilbey's racehorse which came third in the 1919 Derby*

The Marriage

Henry Walter admitted towards the end of his life that: 'the racecourse was where the most enjoyable days of my life have been spent.' It was this love of racing, and of sports generally, that set him apart from his wife, Isabella May Fowlie, often referred to as Ella. They had been married in his wife's home town of Surbiton on 26 January 1884, when he was 25 years of age. It was the groom's parents who entertained in the evening, with a supper for 50 at Elsenham and, unusually for most families (but not the Gilbeys), the staff sat down for that huge dinner as well as the guests. The next day the newlyweds headed off to the country where Henry Walter had had such fun in his bachelor days, France, to Paris first and then the Riviera.

They must have made a handsome couple. They were both tall and she was fair and very pretty. She was unlike other people who had attracted Walter in his past, not jolly and sporty, but erudite and artistic; and her special talent was as a needlewoman, a craft at which she became good enough to exhibit at a Paris exhibition. She was, like Henry Walter, highly principled, but in rather a different direction, holding some 'funny' ideas by Victorian and practical Gilbey standards. She was an ardent Christian Scientist, for instance, and refused to see doctors. The problem was that they were opposites. That might have helped them to fall in love, but did not encourage them to become companions. Not even their friends got along.

Henry Walter not only enjoyed contrasting interests to hers, hunting, shooting and racing, but his excitable bombastic nature must have been very difficult for a sensitive, artistic lady to handle. These were Victorian times, however, and a failed marriage was a disgrace and, for Henry Walter, with his sensitivity towards failure and his eagerness to impress his father, the thought of failure must have been a dreadful threat hanging over him. On the surface he weathered it through with his confidence in himself and his principles, but it would have been yet another factor in hampering his development of leadership and bold risk-taking nature. Divorce was impossible, so, after 18 years of marriage, from 1902, the two simply went their separate ways, living in separate rooms, with separate lives and Ella hardly ever went to Elsenham. They reached such a stage that when they were together they were said never to speak.

Then, in 1904, the inevitable happened for a man who enjoyed women and a social life. Henry Walter was attracted to a lady, a Mrs Ethel Mary Mavor. He became so fond of her that she accompanied him to many social gatherings, even to Ascot, Monte Carlo and the Opera. Curiously, however, her husband often came too and sometimes her child as well.

Lady Gilbey

Ella was not as accommodating as Mr Mavor. She tried to produce hard evidence of adultery, but failed. Nevertheless the very open friendship soon became a subject for idle chatter and it was all too much for her. In 1907, she wrote to him from the Bath Hotel in Felixstowe:

> Dear Harry
> You may be surprised at receiving a letter like this from me, but I feel the time has come when I must write and ask you if you intend to go about with Mrs Douglas Mavor in the way you have been doing this year. Last spring you went to Monte C with her – Newmarket – and at Easter here – where both your names are in the Visitors' Book. Ascot, Newmarket, abroad this autumn, and again at Newmarket. You take her to all the theatres and public restaurants chaperoned by Rose. I constantly meet you together and the situation has become quite impossible. Your servant is allowed to pack Mrs D. Mavor's photograph every time you leave home – and it is left on the top of your portmanteau for all the servants to see. This I have often seen myself, I have already allowed things to drift, hoping there might be a change – but now I have quite made up my mind and mean to stand it no longer and am prepared at any cost to stop it – you have both your boys' future to consider and, instead of their respecting you, you are showing them an unpardonable example in every way. Many people are talking about you. . . .
> Ella M. Gilbey.'

They decided to separate legally, but it took four years to agree terms, as Henry Walter aggravated his wife by refusing to stop seeing Mrs Mavor.

The separation became official in July 1912. After this, Mrs Mavor became more and more of an open companion, staying at Elsenham when it became Henry Walter's home; and by then her husband rarely came along.

Lady Gilbey adjusted to her new status of separated wife and her health improved. Then, in 1922, the divorce laws changed. For the first time a husband could be sued for divorce on grounds of adultery and Lady Gilbey began collecting the evidence she had found difficult to establish in those, for her, very unhappy years at the turn of the century.

It was easier to find this evidence in the years following the separation. Staff were willing to confirm that he called Mrs Mavor 'Ethel darling', that he went to her bedroom at the flat in Down Street and that a handkerchief bearing her monogram was found under his pillow. There was plenty of evidence, too, that he had lavished money on her, buying her smart clothes. These were not, however, clear grounds for divorce, as, after the change of law in 1922, adultery had to be proven. Mrs Mavor was no longer a likely adulteress, as she had had a number of operations and her health had deteriorated. Although they were still very fond of each other and frequent companions, they had become unlikely lovers.

Lady Gilbey decided to try and strengthen her case, as adultery was questionable, and sued in addition for cruelty. It was these allegations of cruelty that startled and deeply disturbed Henry Walter.

The case was called in March 1926. Henry Walter admitted adultery prior to 1922, but denied any after this date and denied even more strongly the cruelty. The plaintiff's claim was that he had inflicted mental cruelty through his neglect, lack of affection and refusal to break off the relationships with Mrs Mavor, all of which had serious effects on his wife's health. A prime piece of evidence was an emotional letter from her personal maid to Henry Walter in 1912,

> Mrs Gilbey is really very ill and no one knows it better than I do; you may remember some years ago she had a very bad attack brought on entirely by your cruel treatment; her present condition is also due to you and you are daily increasing your torture. . . . M Trippas.

Friends and relations of Henry Walter were called who said they had never observed anything cruel or unkind in his treatment of his wife and that he was a very generous and kind-hearted man. Mr Willis, Henry Walter's lawyer, claimed the case had been brought to humiliate him through cross examination as his wife had known the facts for 20 years. Henry Walter claimed that she had tried to thwart him and, long before Mrs Mavor came on the scene, she had been so rude to his friends and relatives that they had stopped visiting his house.

Finally, it was because his behaviour with Mrs Mavor had been so insulting to his wife that the case went against him. Indeed, in Victorian times, Henry Walter's public association with Mrs Mavor was a grave insult to his wife. The jury found that he had both committed adultery and been guilty of cruelty to the petitioner.

Henry Walter continued to hold great affection for Mrs Mavor. They did not marry, perhaps because she did not want her own marriage broken, or

59. Mrs H. W. Gilbey (nee Isabella Fowlie), by Maude Warsfold, 1909.

perhaps because she was too old for it to be worth going through the trauma of divorce. In any case, Henry Walter took care of her family and in his will left an annuity for life to her daughter Rosemary.

The scandalous divorce would have been hurtful to any normal man, but in addition there was the sacrifice of those racing privileges[2] that meant so much to him. The marriage had been bad enough, but this divorce must have been even worse and because he was the sort of person who did not confide or expose difficulties, it was hard to assess the effect of it on him. He was a product of the Victorian public school system which developed the 'stiff upper lip' approach to difficulties. Whether it was the divorce or age, he became bluffer, more outgoing and more active in his campaigning.

The marriage did not even produce happy children. They had two sons,

Walter Ewart and Eric. The youngest, Eric, was killed in 1915 by a sniper's bullet when going to rescue one of his riflemen at Aix La Chapelle, while Walter Ewart proved to be his mother's boy. Henry Walter at first indulged him, then, realising they had little in common, became less and less generous and eventually (though with some justification) financially unsupportive. Ewart achieved little; he enjoyed drinking and spending freely. His father was said to have bailed him out of debt, then disowned him and refused to speak to him again. Ewart married Alice Sim, who was popular with the Gilbey family, but this marriage ended in divorce even more quickly than that of his parents. Mother and son, having both suffered the traumas of failed marriages, then took up residence together at Ascot.

The great Gilbey concept of the family had been given a severe battering. Those huge family gatherings, which were such a feature of life at Elsenham with the first Sir Walter, were not maintained by the second baronet, although there were plenty of parties for his friends. His disastrous personal family life and poor relationship with his heir meant that he hardly ever met his grandson, Walter Derek, who was born in 1913. Walter Ewart died a year before his father's death and so never inherited the baronetcy. Derek, therefore, whose parents had divorced when he was nine, was the third holder of the baronetcy. He remembered just three meetings a year with his grandfather, always prior to returning to Eton. He would go to the Gilbey office just before the start of each term and receive 10/- from his Grandfather before setting off to Eton. On one occasion he called without an invitation at his grandfather's flat, who ' blew my head off.'

The dreadful result of Henry Walter's attempt at family life had generated much hate and there was a split throughout the family. The two brothers who were then most influential in the business, Henry Walter and Arthur, favoured different sides, Arthur being very friendly with Ewart and the first Lady Gilbey. This division helped to fuel a volatile relationship in the business. Vociferous disputes were common in the boardroom. People around the two protagonists would tremble from the vehemence of it all – but suddenly the two brothers would slap each other on the back and head off to have lunch together, usually at the Orleans Club. These two leaders of W&A Gilbey Ltd. were not, however, real friends and they did not socialise out of office hours, nor visit each other's houses. Derek Gilbey, whose father and grandfather had both been divorced, was the unfortunate victim of the splits and his impression of his family was that everybody hated each other. There had been a serious erosion of the family cohesion which had been such a major contributor towards W&A Gilbey's earlier success.

Closest to Henry Walter was his brother Tresham, who was three years his junior. They shared a love of country sports and, although Tresham put most of his energies into polo, his house at Bishop's Stortford was still a useful base for Henry Walter, as it was only 20 miles from Newmarket. Tresham enjoyed what had been so severely missing in Henry Walter's life, a happy marriage. He and his wife Annie, daughter of Sir John Barker, founder of the major London store bearing his name, were a devoted couple. Tresham, as a younger son, did not go into W&A Gilbey, but instead helped his father-in-law, becoming a director of Barkers.

The Farming

Henry Walter himself started life as a country squire in the first autumn of World War One when he inherited Elsenham. For the part of the estate which he did not directly own, Henry Walter had to share decisions with his brothers. His new life began badly as he was one of the first to pay the higher death duties imposed to help finance the war. He lacked the support of his own family and he had to cope with his sisters, particularly Maud, who for so many years had run Elsenham and had now inherited little in proportion to his own inheritance. He could not provide the secure, contented family life that had been the feature of Elsenham for more than 30 years. This undoubtedly produced some resentment from the mass of brothers, sisters and cousins who made up the extended family around Bishop's Stortford.

The new baronet had the Home Farm and 1,000 acres to run; the remainder was let to tenants. He set about the task of running the estate with enthusiasm, obtaining the best advice, employing skilled labour, keeping efficient accounts and spending much of his time supervising the activities. It was, however, primarily wheat-growing soil, and it only paid in exceptionally good years. After the First World War, losses built up. He was reluctant to follow his usual maxim, which was applied ruthlessly to his racehorses, to cut his losses as soon as there was a real risk of failure.

The land held a fascination for him and, as he said: 'It was hard to loose grip of it and all its pleasant associations.' He knew that he had inherited a model estate, but from his tenants' accounts he realised that he was not alone as they, too, faced similar financial problems. It was a terrible period for British agriculture; more and more landlords were selling their estates. Henry Walter's campaigning spirit was aroused and he started to draw public attention to this great tragedy for British farming.

In 1922, in the *Pall Mall Gazette*, he was quoted as saying: 'There is not a landowner in the country whose income is derived wholly from agricultural land, who is receiving an income from his estate and not a cultivator who is losing less than something like £4 an acre on cereals.' When talking at Smithfield Show that same year, he added: 'Agriculture cannot be in a more grave and precarious position.'

He himself eventually accepted defeat, giving up his role as country squire in 1927 and selling the land to the tenant farmers for practically any price they would offer. He said in his Memoirs: 'I am sorry to say that all of them lived eventually to regret their bargains. Knowing the capabilities of my former tenants I know it was not their fault.' Henry Walter struggled on with about 500 acres, but had to face losses of £1,000 a year. Eventually he decided to sell and move to a flat in London, saying, 'Legislation, particularly since the war, imposing, as it has, such excessive burdens on the land, point the way to complete ruin.' Elsenham, one of Britain's most famous model estates,

60. Sir Henry Walter Gilbey

was put up for auction and was bought for an amount representing the previous value of the land alone and taking no account of the value of the buildings.

Having had such a dismal experience as a landowner, Henry Walter felt compelled to expose the problems facing British farmers. He set about collecting facts and figures, obtaining direct answers from more than 60,000 people connected with farming. He was allowed sight of the accounts of some of the major estates, which 'certainly made appalling reading.'

He was determined to get those in power to listen. 'I persisted in my humble way at every available opportunity in placing the facts before the public and suggesting the remedy.' The only remedy he could suggest was simple assistance to the farmers, through tariffs or subsidies; but this was when free trade was still being fought for and the thought of such protection aroused enormous hostility. He became dubbed the 'Doleful Baronet' – though not amongst the farmers, with whom he became a very popular figure. It is clear today that his campaign was before its time. Tariffs and subsidies were introduced and Henry Walter had the satisfaction of seeing he was right within his lifetime, but only after one of his most valued inheritances had been lost.

It might dutifully be argued that Henry Walter was not a gifted agricultural administrator, but he did practice the theory passed on to him by his father to find and use experts in each subject. He simply had the misfortune to be given his opportunity to farm through some of the worst years in the history of British agriculture and the loss of this part of his inheritance was due mostly to circumstances beyond his control. Despite looking more like a London man, he wanted to be – and could in more fortunate times have been – a country gentleman.

The Clothes

Henry Walter's appearance was not quite so debonair as his father's – and he did not look like a Parisian dandy – but it was equally distinctive and he was, if anything, even more fastidious. He was so insistent on having highly polished shoes that he had them varnished. In dress he developed his own unique style and never varied it. His hats were specially made by Henry Heath in Oxford Street and he often wore a billy-cock bowler with a turned-up curly brim. The reason was, quite simply, he said: 'because I like it and because I believe it suits me.' Robert Lillico in Maddox St. made his numerous suits, which were unusual. He wore a striped waistcoat, with initialled buttons, finishing in a single point below his waist. All his shirts were hand-made, with rounded detachable collars. The suits were single-breasted with five cloth-covered buttons on the sleeves and his overcoats had velvet collars. This apparel, of course, aroused considerable interest, but it was the carnation that became most famous. He was never without one, in a buttonhole which had been made especially large, with a bar at the back so that the flower would fit neatly. Nor was it any carnation, but the dark-coloured Eastern Wonder sent to him every other day. By the time he was 80, he calculated that he had worn 30,000 carnations. It was a practice he had begun at 18, because his mother had chosen carnations as the flowers she always wanted around her.

Like his father, he wanted to stand out from other people. He aimed at an appearance that was immaculate, a little eccentric and that would make people take note. He was willing to go to extraordinary lengths to uphold this approach. He even had his car, a Daimler, specially made with a higher ceiling in order to accommodate him while wearing his hat.

An article in Man and His Clothes in 1926 selected Henry Walter as the man with the strongest individual taste in clothes in the sporting world. Sir

61. Sir Henry Walter Gilbey (left) at the Harness Horse Parade

Henry Walter explained: 'men's clothes are the visible signs of the artistic expression of the wearer. My idea is to blend my own individuality with the atmosphere of my surroundings.' He was unhappy about modern trends. 'All round the City there is a constant eye-sore of gaudy, flashy colours, savouring more of the apparel of a country boxing booth than a man engaged in serious pursuit of business, which demands an atmosphere of soberness and reliability.'

The Campaigner

Henry Walter got on well with the press and the general public. The way he dressed attracted attention, which helped with public relations. He was honest, outspoken and loved being unusual and this made great material for the journalists. He kept the name of Gilbey in the limelight, which helped to get his many campaigns across to the general public. As with his father, most of these campaigns were associated with agriculture and horses and he carried on much of his father's work. He was twice President of the Hunter Improvement Society, of which he was made a Life Honorary Member (one of only three). He was Chairman of the Royal Agricultural Hall, President of the London Cart Horse Parade for 25 years, member of the Council of the Royal Agricultural Society, Governor of Smithfield Club, on the Board of Governors of the Royal Veterinary College and was President of the Shire Horse Society in its Jubilee Year of 1928.

Like his father, too, he was instrumental in the foundation of some organisations, the most important of which was the National Horse

Association. He was concerned that the horse industry as a whole was not well represented and put forward the idea that the various societies and organisations should get together to form a national association, like that already existing for cattle. There was considerable support for the project, especially after a scare when it was thought docking of horses' tails would be made illegal. This made it apparent that such moves from the Government needed to be met by lobbying from the as yet ill-organised horse industry. At the 1922 Royal Show, 14 societies were represented to found the National Horse Association (NHA) and to elect Henry Walter as the first Chairman and Reg Brown, a clerk at the Hunter Improvement Society, the first secretary. More societies joined in and by the autumn it consisted of a dozen breed societies and 15 other organisations from the horse world.

The general aim was to stand up for the horse breeding industry, but specifically to further the welfare of horses and ponies and the interests of horse and pony breeding generally.

The NHA was made up of representatives of societies rather than individuals. These societies often pursued their own group interest, but, whenever there were real dangers they became more united. Two of the initial successes of the NHA were preventing an entertainment tax being levied at agricultural shows and, even more seriously, preventing the banning of horses from towns.

In June 1925 they opposed successfully the move in the House Of Lords to license the horses in London and to gradually cut down numbers by not giving a replacement licence when an animal died. Horses were said to cause traffic jams; but when investigations were made into the relative costs of mechanical and horse-drawn vehicles in Glasgow it was found that the horse cost 3s 7d a day and the motor 5s 1d. Thanks largely to campaigning by the NHA, led by Henry Walter, it was realised that horses still had a part to play in towns.

More threats to the horse industry followed. There was a proposal to ban horses from Oxford Street and Regent Street, but Henry Walter and the NHA lobbied and compiled figures to show the importance of the working horse population, which represented a capital value of at least £10,000,000. Their efforts were successful and the ban was not imposed.

The NHA represented the industry, but education in the training of horses and riders was needed and in 1925 the Institute of the Horse was formed. It was to act as a repository for the accumulated knowledge and traditions of horsemanship and as a centre of information on all matters concerning the horse, its training and management. In 1947, with the Olympic Games to be staged in Britain the following year, the strongest possible organisation was needed.

The NHA and the Institute agreed to amalgamate to establish, as a registered charity, the British Horse Society. Reg Brown moved on from the NHA to become the first secretary of the BHS and the first president, W.J. Cumber, came from the Shire Horse Society. Today the BHS must be the most important equestrian organisation in the country, with its charter covering the original aims of the NHA and the Institute: 'to promote the interests of horse and pony breeding, to further the art of riding and to encourage horsemastership and the welfare of horses and ponies.' However, it has been in the world of sport and welfare that the BHS has been strongest, not in the area that Henry Walter played a leading role – the breed and breeding societies.

Henry Walter, through the NHA and individually, was a leading campaigner for the right of horses to stay in the streets of towns. He followed the techniques of his agricultural campaign, collecting much data to support the case for horses and then using it in a large number of speeches and articles. He concentrated on five main reasons:

1. Horses are the most economic form of transportation in much of the work in cities.
2. Horses are best adapted to moving heavy weights in circumscribed areas.
3. Horses are essential to the small businessman and contractor.
4. Horses do not give the same wear and tear as heavy motors and are therefore less of a burden on the ratepayer
5. Outlawry would damage horse breeding.

These are the arguments that helped delay the departure of large numbers of horses from our streets and, in addition, he made speeches at events with which he was connected, like the Van Horse Parade.

In 1925 the 862 entries for the Van Horse Parade meant it was allegedly five miles long and, speaking at the luncheon that day, Henry Walter said in his usual outgoing manner: 'Horses are a necessity, and attacks that have been made on them absolutely nauseate me. I have been in consultation whether I should answer them officially but I think they are beneath contempt. You have shown by your parade what horses can do.' After this occasion cartoons appeared, showing horses pulling cars.

The Dress in Rotten Row

Henry Walter's colourful character was a pivot around which many others helped to make their legitimate campaigns successful. They were premeditated and carefully planned, but Sir Walter became even more famous for a campaign which arose from a spontaneous outburst at a press luncheon in 1932. He had been increasingly disturbed by the deterioration in the way in which people dressed when they went for their rides in Rotten Row. With his high standards, he felt it disgraceful that those who went riding in a Royal park should not pay attention to their turnout. On the way to this particular lunch he saw some particularly poor examples and realised it was a subject he could include in his speech. He did so, pointing out that some riders were wearing only pullovers or sleeveless blouses and many had no coats and hats. Elaborating on this, he said: 'This is a real eyesore to our lovely park. It will be bathing costumes next.' He called the badly dressed riders 'Hottentots' and foresaw London and other big cities becoming a 'wilderness of slouch hats.' He believed that riders and drivers were much more reckless when they were not wearing hats.

Nobody, including Henry Walter, was prepared for the reaction. The press found that they had some magnificently funny material. It caught everyone's imagination and, though Henry Walter at least thought there was a serious element, it was a rare opportunity to make people laugh. The next day all the papers covered the speech under headings like 'Charge of the Hatless Brigade' and 'Rotten Row Traditions Totter'.

By coincidence, that same day the famous actress Evelyn Laye and the actor Frank Lawton were photographed in The Row in what Henry Walter would consider improper attire and this gave even more lively material to the great Rotten Row dress bombshell.

More material was provided the following week when Henry Walter went to Rotten Row to point out to photographers the riders whom he considered suitably dressed and he added the much quoted: 'All sorts of people are after my blood and I do not want my new topper bashed in.' The stories even appeared in China and Japan. In South Africa he was dubbed 'The Censor of the Row', in the *New York Tribune* the headline was 'Hatless Riding debated in London' and in *The Calcutta Statesman*, 'Sir Walter Gilbey condemns Outrageous Dress'. In Budapest Peter Lloyd's article said: 'England's troubles cannot be very great if the whole of the press can devote itself to a discussion on correct dress in Rotten Row.'

Nor was it just the press. Music hall comedians, actors in plays and cartoonists found it hilarious. Even his family joined in, with Ronald Gilbey composing a song which became a regular feature at all functions connected with the drink trade.

Riding in the Row

Just listen to Sir Walter now if riding you must go.
Don't dress up like a Tallyman each morning in the Row,
Don't throw and wave your arms about as if you're doing Morse.
Don't come out in your night-shirt, it's an insult to your horse.

Each mother to her daughter, as she dresses her with care,
Says, Try and keep yourself done up, you'd better now beware.
Sir Walter will be in the Park, now just you think of that,
You'll know him by his buttonhole and curly bowler hat.

So don't go bumping up and down, or you'll get very sore,
Just try and look as though you have been on a horse before.
Remember when you do get home I'll give you such a smack,
If when you pass Sir Walter you should fall off on your back.

I've seen a great improvement since Sir Walter's been about,
For no-one hardly ever has his coat on inside out.
They'll soon all look like Melton, then a hunting we will go.
Sir Walter will be Master of the Pack in Rotten Row.

They're used to hunting in the Park, so you need have no fears,
For many years the wily fox has stalked the little 'deers',

62. Sir Henry Walter Gilbey judging turnout in Rotten Row in the early 1930s

They nearly always go to ground or on a seat that's free,
Sir Walter's sure to find a fox under a leafy tree.

For many years the Empire with its home in Leicester Square,
Some ladies used to wander in the promenade round there.
The London County Council said the ladies all must go;
But Sir Walter is the gentleman who purified the Row.

There was so much fun to be had that the subject would not die and stories
appeared with headlines like, 'World Storm Over Rotten Row Dress Critic'

and 'The battle of the Rotten Row.' *The Evening News* were rude enough to say Sir Walter's hat was an atrocity and ought to be in the British Museum.

Henry Walter revelled in it, although it did lead to a good deal of extra work. He received hundreds of letters, mostly supporting his cause, but some of them abusive. Henry Walter was up to countering these. One gentleman said that Sir Walter acted as if he owned Hyde Park and the Row. Henry Walter replied that if he did he would be sure that this critic would not be in either again.

He also became an accepted expert on dress, with many writing to ask advice on correct riding attire and even about how children should ride. Sir Walter so enjoyed all of this that he started to offer trophies for the best turned-out children and it was natural that he was often asked to judge these new types of events, which did achieve the result of raising standards of turnout.

The following year the Rotten Row Horse Show was started, with prizes for the best turned-out horse and rider, the best seat and control at park paces. Of course it was Sir Walter who was the judge. At the great Royal Richmond Show a class was introduced for the most suitably dressed boy and girl and again the judge was Sir Walter.

He also received a great many photographs of riders in Rotten Row. He collected more than six hundred of them, dividing them into 'Graces' and 'Disgraces'

After a year or two, people began to forget about the matter, but Henry Walter knew he had a good subject and at the Richmond Royal Dinner in 1935 he launched another outspoken attack:

> monstrosities seen daily in Rotten Row are pullovers, blouses without sleeves, ties flying like flags and trousers like sailors pants. Bah! only sights for heathens.

This was more good material and the press responded as he had no doubt hoped, with one wonderful example in America's *Philadelphia Inquirer*. A full page article with coloured pictures was headed 'Crabby Old Sir Walter Tongue-lashing the Riding Cuties' and went on to say: 'The Victorian Gin King shudders at bare legs, rubber boots and sweaters, but just wait until he meets Central Park's lady centaurs.'

From the original spontaneous outburst in 1932 his views consolidated and it was the touch of pomposity, the willingness to be made fun of, that gave so much fuel to the comedians:

> I considered it an indignity and an insult to our Royal family for some to turn out in the Royal Parks in the manner they did, particularly as so many foreigners make a point of visiting the Row for the purpose of witnessing the best type of horses and riders. Whatever must they have thought of the outrageous appearance of some of them who were perhaps suitable for the sands of the seaside but no-where else?

It shows the fickle nature of fame that, with all his good works, it was this rather ludicrous campaign for which he is most remembered. In a time of catastrophic economic upheavals, it must have been such a relief to find a subject which could make people laugh. It did have an effect, as it led to more thought being given to turnout, but it also illuminated the unusual character of Henry Walter – the importance he attached to correct attire, his forthright manner, his lack of concern when people made fun of him and his complete confidence in what he believed was right.

Henry Walter must have been feeling a trifle more frivolous at the time of the Rotten Row Saga as, despite being in his seventies, he was courting Marion Broadhead, a Yorkshire widow 35 years his junior. He had not lacked domestic care as a divorcee, as he was looked after by an extraordinary assembly of characters making up his loyal and long-serving staff. Nor was he short of female company. Despite the disastrous relationship with his first wife, he attached great importance to the ladies, putting them on a par with horses and wine. This quotation, from a 1935 speech, was repeated by him many times: 'Throughout my long life I have been closely connected with wine, women and horses. They are the three most delightful things in the world.' At another time he said: 'Women are expensive but they are worth every shilling you spend on them.'

The Second Marriage

He might well have happily remained an aged bachelor who enjoyed the good life, if it was not for the disappointing relationship with his only living son, Walter Ewart. He wanted another son and Gilbeys are not put off by difficulties; he made light of being a septuagenarian. Nor was it a sudden spontaneous decision, as he courted Marion Broadhead for five years before he made her his second wife.

It started at the Majestic Hotel in Harrogate, where she and her mother were playing bridge with Arthur Gilbey. Henry Walter returned to the hotel after a great victory in the Ebor horse race and said to her 'I put £5 on for you'. She realised he had taken a fancy to her, but her arthritic mother, who was more his age, thought his attention was to her.

The actual proposal came about four years later, in May 1934, when he took Marion to a family occasion: a sale of Tresham Gilbey's polo ponies. True to Gilbey tradition there was a big luncheon, followed by the sale, and while she waited inside with the ladies someone said, 'Champs was seen bidding for the best polo pony.' This aroused her interest, as it did not seem much use, to a man who lived in London and only owned racehorses, to have a polo pony. She was startled to discover the answer as he met her in the hall with the greeting, 'I have bought Mayflower II for you' Not being quite so besotted by horses as the Gilbeys, but a practical Yorkshire girl, she found a horse less of an attractive present than Henry Walter had anticipated, especially since she had noticed it was a nervous chestnut with a wall eye. She was so shocked she dropped her creamy coconut cake on the floor. With the Duke of Gloucester about to arrive and many important people milling around this was an embarrassing faux pas amongst the manners – conscious Gilbeys.

63. Sir Henry Walter Gilbey and his second wife Marion

She was not in a happy mood as they got into the car for the return journey and as soon as they were alone attacked Henry Walter about the purchase. He smiled and replied, 'What about getting married? You know though I am a very selfish man.' It was, in keeping with the man, a curious proposal and, because she hated the idea of moving from Yorkshire, one that she took time to accept.

Selfish 74 year-olds might not fall truly in love, but he was undoubtedly besotted with the lady. In the months leading up to the wedding he wrote

64. Sir Henry Walter Gilbey, Lady Gilbey and Walter Anthony Gilbey in 1935

almost daily letters to her whenever they were apart. He always addressed her as 'My Dearest' and, for a stoic Victorian, was warm with his words: 'It was a joy to hear your voice last night.' 'I am so fearfully distressed to hear about you still having that awful sickness.' 'All my very best love. God Bless you always and give you all you desire.'

They were married on August 10th, 1934 at the Huddersfield Registry Office. He acquired a stepdaughter of eight years old and she a stepson nine years older than herself. They honeymooned where they had met, at Harrogate, and when the press asked for comments Henry Walter, as usual, gave them some quotable ones: 'She has a wonderful temperament. I am a great believer in temperament – temperament in people and in horses;' 'I am quite sure we shall be happy. We are both fond of golf, gardening and of course horses;' and 'I am a temperamental sort of person and a man with a temperament needs someone to look after him.'

It was a big challenge for her to move into the household of such an inflexible old gentleman whose life was ruled by his principles. She had to deal with staff who, like him, had become set in their ways. They did not appreciate having a wife and her young child around. Routines were disturbed. Then there were tricky little matters, such as when she first paid the fishmonger and was given a handful of bank notes. The staff had been taking a commission, which had been a useful addition to their wages. They were not too pleased about being found out and very disturbed about the loss of income.

The new Lady Gilbey had to deal with a large number of unusual characters: a chauffeur, butler, footman, cook, kitchen maid and housemaid. The butler, Ronald, had been in the Navy and, true to that profession, suffered from periodic attacks on the bottle. His remedy for a hangover was Worcester sauce. The footman, Hart, had only one eye, having lost the other in the war: he had been Eric Gilbey's batman when Eric was killed at Aix la Chapelle. Trail, the chauffeur, was rather lame and it probably hurt him to change gear, so he avoided this manoeuvre by warming up the car for an hour before setting out. Having a large car, he then managed to further minimise stopping and starting by staying in the middle of road and frightening any smaller cars into swerving out of the way. Sir Walter thought this was highly accomplished driving, and took no notice when Lady Gilbey called him a 'road hog'.

There were plenty of such matters in which the new husband took little notice of the view of his new wife. He had always been fastidious and his life was ruled by inflexible principles. These included the admirable ones of honesty and of mixing with all classes, but also rather more outlandish ones, like never using a towel twice, always changing for dinner even if he was on his own, never drinking before noon, refusing to go to cocktail parties and, of course, his concern with the correctness of dress.

Lady Gilbey was to suffer on a number of occasions for the latter. Once, rushing to the fishmonger to get some fowl dressed, she did not have time to pay much attention to her attire. She met Henry Walter walking with Lord Lucan and, on catching sight of her, he pretended he had not seen her. In his view she looked far too common to be acknowledged as his wife. She remembered, too, a horrible day at Royal Ascot. Even though they could not go into the Royal Enclosure because of his divorce, he insisted that she wore a long dress on Tuesday and Thursday, regardless of the weather. Practicality was not part of his vocabulary and on one rather wet day she had to wear a long, white pleated dress which soon turned into a limp soaking mess. The only way she could get around was to hook it up under her coat – but only when he was not looking.

The Office

Henry Walter had a rigid routine to his day. The major adjustment he made on getting married was that in the evenings, following one or two hours' bridge at his club, he would come home after the game and not stay on for club dinner. His weekdays revolved around his work at the firm. Until he was 80, he was taken to the office by Trail and, although he did let the hour of departure from home slip to 9am when he reached his 70s, in his younger days he was there before the staff arrived.

He had his own office and although he was rarely seen he was often heard. He had a loud voice and a hot temper and most of the staff remember vividly those tirades which made people fearful of him and eager to obey. Some, like his younger brother Arthur, knew that he meant no harm, but, lacking great intellect, it was his means of getting his opinion across. Arthur was the businessman of the family, who had inherited some of his father's acumen. He was one of the few who used to stand up to Henry Walter's outbursts as they echoed around the Pantheon.

Arthur Gilbey was chairman for a short time after Henry Grinling. Henry Walter was put in the post for the following year, but then William Crosbie Gilbey, son of Alfred Gilbey, took over. Arthur Carver, chief accountant of W&A Gilbey, described him as: 'beloved by all . . . a genial personality and of buoyant spirits.' He died suddenly, aged 66, in 1926. By this time the members of the second generation eligible for the post were dwindling.

The last member of the first generation, Lord Blyth, died in 1925, having spent most of his later years concentrating on politics, which had brought

65. The opening of Blythwood Dairy. Back row: Henry Parry Gilbey, Sir James Blyth, Sir Walter Gilbey, Lady Gordon Lennox, Mrs Gardner (daughter of Sir James Blyth), Lady Dorothy Nevill. Front row: Earl of Warwick, Prince of Wales, Countess of Warwick, Lady Blyth.

66. The Blythwood Dairy

him his title. His sharp brain, coupled with his specialisation in wine buying had enabled him to make a great contribution to the success of the firm in its early years.

When Britain and the world were heading towards those devastatingly difficult economic times of the 1930s, Henry Walter took over the position his father had filled for so many years. There were few of his generation to compete with, or to support him.

Arthur Gilbey's memory had been severely damaged as a result of an accident when a car had knocked him down in Hyde Park. Alfred Gilbey, William Crosbie's elder brother, had died in 1927 and their brother Newman had become ineligible because his son Harry had left the business and set up in opposition. Argo Gold suffered from arthritis, which restricted his mobility severely; Arthur Gold had died in 1901; the second Lord Blyth, Herbert, was confined to a wheel chair following a polo accident; Gibbons Grinling died in 1927; and Arthur Blyth died in 1928.

Good health was an important qualification for Henry Walter Gilbey for the post of chairman and it kept him there until his death in 1945. He was highly conscientious in this important role, but, as he was the first to admit, he was not particularly intelligent and while his upbringing and the vagaries of life had produced an honest, eccentric campaigner, it had not bred a sharp businessman. He had not experienced, as had his father, the dreadful consequences of not adjusting to change and he had grown up into a man who stuck to his principles, defended tradition and based his decisions on achieving security, rather than on foresight, acumen and adventurousness.

He played safe and had plenty of noisy battles with the third and even fourth generations, who were now well represented in the firm. Typical of these disputes was one about the capital which he wanted tied up for security, but which the young wanted to use to invest and buy retail shops.

As chairman he got his way and the £1 million in question was invested in Government Securities. It helped W&A Gilbey weather the depression and to keep going through World War II, but this failure to invest in their future in better times became one of the causes of falling profits on the home market. Relationships in the business were not easy, as family bonds are not the same as business ones. Henry Walter knew the younger generations all too well, he was familiar with their idiosyncrasies and weaknesses and he found it difficult to give their ideas the respect needed to build up more businesslike relationships.

All was not completely stagnant, however, because members of the third generation, assisted by some able managers, were active under Henry Walter's

67. Walter Anthony Gilbey on a horse in the gardens at Portman Square London W1 with Orchard Court where his parents had their flat in the background.

and Arthur's leadership in setting up local gin distilleries in Australia, Canada and, after prohibition was lifted, the United States, in order to counter the threat to the export trade posed by new competitors' local production. Alec and Geoffrey Gold, in particular, spent long periods abroad supervising these important initiatives and the Hucks family provided the technical engineering support.

Henry Walter kept W&A Gilbey going, but his important contribution was in obtaining publicity for the company in completely different spheres.

Henry Walter kept the name of Gilbey in the public eye. He was for W&A Gilbey what Commander Whitehead has been for Schweppes. He was vain enough to enjoy publicity and clever enough at getting on with all types of people to work well with and understand the press. They found him a great subject, always ready to speak out. A typical occasion was when in 1922 he was asked to propose the toast at the Gimcrack dinner. Not being a member of the Jockey Club he was able to be more controversial than past speakers and, to quote the December Country Life: 'He achieved the distinction of introducing a very slight wave of constructive criticism. The effect was the same as the throwing of a stone into a very placid pond.'

His main pleas were the licensing and taxation of bookmakers and the use of this money to aid breeding: to set up a British form of France's pari mutuel (French for mutual stake), as his father had argued a quarter of a century earlier, to introduce stipendiary stewards to racing and to change the constitution of the Jockey Club so that its membership could be enlarged. He did a great deal for the horse industry and, although none of these points was adopted as an immediate result of his speech, it is only the pari mutuel that has not yet been enacted today.

It was as a promoter of good dress sense that Henry Walter became best known. Soon after their son, Walter Anthony, was born in 1935, Henry Walter

and Lady Gilbey, making their weekly visit to the Plaza Cinema, met the Prince of Wales who congratulated Henry Walter on being the father of a young son and said: 'When is he going to ride? Now see to it that he is properly dressed when riding in Rotten Row.' Henry Walter was well prepared to see to

*68. The original cartoon by Lowe which appeared in the
Evening Standard*

this as he had the album with more than 600 cuttings illustrating the 'Graces' and the 'Disgraces' that he had collected during the Rotten Row dress controversy. He intended that these would be a way of teaching his son good horsemanship and the correct dress to wear when riding.

Having a son at seventy-five years of age gave him great joy, but even on the day it happened it did not disturb his diary too much. He went straight from the birth to a meeting of the National Horse Association, of which he was chairman, and said 'I have a new member – my son. . . . ' Young Walter was the 1,000th member of the association.

It was quite an achievement to have a son at this age. In a speech in 1935 he explained that his recipe for a long life was adequate, but not too much, sleep, a temperate approach to life, avoiding heavy meals and harmful quantities of intoxicating liquor, not overtaxing the strength in outdoor games and not keeping late hours. He kept reasonably thin, going for walks wearing two or three sweaters. He led a busy active life and emphasised the importance of daily vigorous use of the brain. He also valued congenial friends and meals with cheerful companions. Finally, he talked about suitable recreations and recommended card games, because the competition encouraged the use of the brain.

Another of Henry Walter's great loves was the circus, especially the horses. He was a good friend of Bertram Mills and President of the Circus Fans Association of Great Britain, of which he made his young son a member within two weeks of him being born. The young Walter Anthony much enjoyed an annual trip to the circus and continued to do so after his father's death.

It was quite awe-inspiring having such a father, who was both old and very proud, but who lacked any warmth towards or understanding of the young. Walter Anthony was summoned daily in early evening to see his father in the drawing room, but he had a tendency to hiccup when nervous and became more and more nervous of these occasions because his father did not like hiccups. It was usually quite a brief meeting.

The Second World War came when Walter Anthony was just four years old and he was evacuated to the country near Melton Mowbray. His father remained in their spacious London flat at Orchard Court, Portland Square and carried on with his same routine of going to the office and the club in the evening. Eventually, however, he was persuaded to rent a hunting box on the outskirts of Melton Mowbray to which he, his family and staff moved. However, once the worst of the bombing was over, he soon returned to London – indeed too soon, as a nearby bomb blast shot Henry Walter along a corridor of his flat, which shattered his stomach and caused him to become thinner and thinner until his death in 1945.

There were some splendid obituaries for this colourful character: 'He was one of the most picturesque figures in public life. – The Victorian Beau Brummel dashing airily on the stage on which he saw a generation whose dress horrified him. He belonged to a past age.' 'His readiness to express downright opinions kept him in the limelight.'

At his request, his racing colours were buried with him. The gesture showed where his real love lay. His car was painted in his racing colours of yellow, brown and cherry and three quarters of his unpublished autobiography was devoted to his times on the racecourse. There amongst the trainers, the jockeys, the rich and the poor, the special Gilbey gift of mixing with everybody, from cockneys to kings, came into its own. There, too, his strict adherence to tradition and his eccentric attitudes did not isolate him, as the racecourse is full of extraordinary characters. It was also a sphere that his father had not ventured into and the respect people felt for him had been generated by his own personality. He used his facade of the bombastic, overpowering personality to compensate for the features he did not inherit from his famous father – judgement, acumen and intelligence. Yet, although not of the same calibre as his father, he was a unique and memorable character and he made important contributions towards the development of the agricultural and horse industries.

IX
The Demise and Eclipse of W. & A. Gilbey

In Alec Gold's book, *Four In Hand* (1957) celebrating the centenary of the firm in 1957 he wrote:

> What would please the first Sir Walter and his brothers most would be the sight round the table of the grandsons and the great-grandsons of the men with whom they had started their venture a century ago; Gilbey, Blyth, Gold and Grinling – the same four names, not one dropped out and not a single new one. The clan still holds together. The House of W&A Gilbey is a family business still, welded and maintained by long-tried trust and consanguinity. There lies its strength, its charm, its future.

In that centenary year its tangible assets amounted to £10 million, it had a vineyard in France, large stocks in Oporto and Jerez, distilleries in Pietermaritzburg, Cincinnati, Melbourne and Toronto, and it had received Royal Warrants from Queen Victoria, Edward VII, George V and George VI. W&A Gilbey represented so much of what was valued in post war Britain: emphasis on the family concept, safeguarding of traditional principles, economising rather than needless spending, suspicion of rationalisation and revolution, need for a well-rounded approach to life so that work hours should not be too long, profits that gave a steady income and secure employment for nearly 1,000 people in Britain and more overseas.

Eleven years later these attitudes had been destroyed. The family board members were outnumbered, with only three remaining, and within another four years there were none. W&A Gilbey had been caught up in the whirl of modernisation, the primacy of profits, the appreciation of the price of the shares on the stock market and good bottom lines to the accounts, at the cost of all those traditional values. The business of the intervening years had been a long series of hunts for partners, mergers, contested bids and agreed bids.

Many of the reasons for these extraordinary changes did not lie with W&A Gilbey, but with the new standards set in Britain of the 1960s. Improved communication and a future within the European Community ended this country's insular status and were the beginning of the end for the complacent attitude that 'British was best' and 'what was good enough for our grandfathers is good enough for us.' Britain had to face up to competition from rationalised, energetic economies like Germany and Japan and had to take a fresh look at the methods and approaches she had used which might have enabled the Victorians to make their fortunes, but under very different circumstances.

In many ways W&A Gilbey epitomised the reactionary approach. They did make changes, but these tended to be too little and too late. The new generations lacked the drive and adaptability of the founders, which had led to such huge success. They made half-hearted reactions rather than bold initiatives. In the early days, the company's reaction to the potential disaster of phylloxera had earned them a fortune. Yet in the 1920s, when there were obvious signs of a need for change, they moved only in a very limited way which left them with neither traditional strengths nor innovating energy. They aggravated all parties without finding a solution to their fundamental problem.

Their target became the wholesale market. They still sold to those within the trade, but no longer through the agency system which had reaped them such high rewards in the days before mass advertising. W&A Gilbey had switched more and more towards general advertising rather than relying on personal contacts by agents.

Realising that they were missing out on the growing opportunities for retail trade, they started by targeting for the first time the on licenced trade from pubs and hotels, rather than the off licences. This change was mainly instigated by Ronald Gilbey (son of Alfred junior). Ronald was very personable and a great after-dinner speaker, so he was able to win over friends and contacts to develop this side of the business.

In the off licence trade there were significant changes afoot, with multiple stores and chains of shops forcing the smaller retailers out of business. W&A Gilbey were losing their customers and the brewers were gaining them, as many of these 'strings of shops' were owned and developed by breweries. The W&A Gilbey Board did react, but only in a half-hearted way. They acquired some shops – the family business of T. Foster & Co – but this business only had 33 branches and these were confined to London and the south. Not only had W&A Gilbey been too timid and gone in at too small a scale to have a real effect and compete with the breweries, but they caused serious aggravation. They had placed themselves directly in conflict with other retailers, as they were on one hand in competition with them and on the other trying, as wholesalers, to supply them. This double role lost them many customers and in retrospect was one of their most serious mistakes. They alienated many of their retail customers, without providing large enough outlets for their produce or increasing their bargaining power with their competitors, the brewers.

The tendency towards bigger and bigger units accelerated after the war and spread to wholesale business as well as retail shops. It became more difficult to accumulate funds for investment, with individuals having to bear the huge increase of the tax burden and, if there was a death, relatives were unable to pay death duties while keeping small businesses afloat. Alongside these difficulties was the growing complexity of business, requiring specialists in taxation, legal matters and advertising, which a small company could not afford. The economies of scale under post- war conditions were undeniable.

W&A Gilbey followed the tide of bigger and bigger units. They tried to keep pace with the big breweries, who were buying more and more pubs and off-licences (which, once 'tied' to the brewers, ceased to stock W&A Gilbey products). W&A Gilbey even put their retail outlets into a joint company with the Canadian House of Seagrams to give them funds for the purchase of more shops and provide more outlets for whisky for their lines. As had been the case from the 1920s, it was too little too late. These limited attempts at retailing were also a constant drain on the profits and cut the cash resources of the company, so that none was available for other investment.

Another major change which was the seed for their downfall was the decision to go public. This act was forced upon them after the Second World War, as increasing death duties and taxes were draining the cash supplies of the various families who made up the clan. Taxes rose to 98p in the pound, for the very highest earners in the late 50s and early 60s and, together with death duties, forced many private companies to go public during these times and lay themselves open to take-overs. Until 1946 the Ordinary Shares of W&A Gilbey had been subject to severe restrictions and could only be transferred to male members of the family in certain lines of descent. It was decided in the summer of 1946 that the Ordinary Shares would be converted mainly into participating Preferred Shares, with a small block of Ordinary Managing Shares. At the same time W&A Gilbey applied for a quotation on the Stock Exchange for the Preferred Shares which, after the Board meeting of August 26th, 1946, became free of all restrictions of transfer. The Management shares were retained by the Directors with the intention of ensuring control by the family over the business – but that was not to be.

These were the seeds of the demise; yet there were plenty of healthy developments which overcame any feelings of impending doom. Wine duties were reduced in 1949 by Sir Stafford Cripps, giving scope for lower prices and attracting new drinkers. Restaurants sold carafe wines at much lower prices, pubs offered wine by the glass and W&A Gilbey, renowned for their cheap, reliable products, became one of the main suppliers, aided by their own source in Loudenne which could be shipped in cask and was therefore cheaper than bottle-shipped wines.

W&A Gilbey also capitalised on another of the policies for their original success by finding a new product and offering it at a good price. In the summer of 1953 they launched Smirnoff Vodka, at a party with balalaika music for a thousand guests. This brand had been originated by the Smirnoff family in pre-1917-Russia and taken to the United States of America after the Russian Revolution. Some vodka had come to Britain for drinking Russian-style – gulping it from a small glass – but now it was marketed for mixing and became extremely popular in such cocktails as 'Bloody Mary' (for which drink W&A Gilbey's, true to their upright reputation, used the name 'Red Snapper').

W&A Gilbey's greatest post-war success was, however, its overseas companies and exports. As soon as barley could be freed for whisky production, the government encouraged whisky exports, as this was a major dollar earner in a time of dire need for that currency during the late 1940s.

69. *The Directors of W & A Gilbey Limited in 1957, left to right: Top row – Anthony Grinling, Derek Blyth, Gordon Gilbey, Jasper Grinling, Robin Gold, Derek Gilbey, John Gilbey. Bottom row – Sebastian Gilbey, Ronnie Gilbey, Arthur Gilbey, Alec Gold*

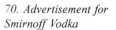

W&A Gilbey, too, had their own distillery plants in Australia, New Zealand and Canada and produced local whisky brands for these markets. The Canadian company, in particular, enjoyed a sustained and substantial growth, producing rye whiskeys called Golden Velvet, Black Velvet and Golden Special. There were clever innovations, like blending an Irish whiskey especially for the American palate and emphasising its Irishness by selling it in a bottle wrapped in Irish tweed and sealed with a green ribbon. The end result of these activities were good profits that helped to subsidise the losses on the home market, but these were in the main only paper profits, as the overseas units did not return them to the mother company, but kept them to invest in their own production.

The losses on the home front were not occasional, but went on year after year only alleviated by the annual Christmas boom. Cash was getting very short and with only non-voting shares on the open market, it was difficult to raise capital. In the 1950s W&A Gilbey took the first of their desperate measures, selling the American rights to their gin. They sold it with the right to a royalty, but this was at a fixed rate per case of gin sold so that their income failed to keep pace with inflation.

The shortage of cash was aggravated by the government tax policy, which did much more damage to W&A Gilbey than the loss of their traditional customers, the individual retailers. The directors were taxed at the top rate of 98p in the pound and one year there was also what was called a voluntary contribution or a special levy, which brought it to over 100%. Also the Company was subject to Excess Profits Tax which was levied on profits made in Canada but not remitted to the United Kingdom.

The problem was that through all this whirlwind of changes in attitudes and structure of business, W&A Gilbey hung on to their old formulas and the ways in which they had run the business for a hundred years or more. The Board and the management was structured to stifle any dynamism which would have helped to cope with change.

The Board was only open to a father and one son of each of the original families. It was affected by family jealousies. The aim of chairman Ronald Gilbey (grandson of Alfred) was not strategy and planning for the future but 'to keep the church in the middle of the village', that is to get the various members of the family to co-operate and work together. His nature helped this aim, as he had an abundance of charm, was affable to everybody, was immensely popular and frequently asked to speak at Licenced Victuallers Associations, which was very good for W&A Gilbey trade; but although this tendency was good for family accord, it was not the sort of character that was needed to cope with the increasingly cut-throat nature of business.

He was not so astute at taking sound decisions on the business front, or giving his Board the leadership they needed through these difficult times. In his private life he followed the Gilbey tradition of a great interest in horses, and in particular the racehorse, a love which he shared with his brother Quinney, a famous Racing Correspondent.

Helping Ronald Gilbey from his generation were: Alec Gold as finance director, Tony Grinling in charge of home sales, Gordon Gilbey, who looked after the wine buying, and Sebastian Gilbey, who dealt with production. From the next generation there were: Ronnie Gilbey (son of the chairman), who

City Banquet Notables

Mr. Edward G. Hemmerde. K.C.

GEORGE GREEN 37

Sir Samuel Brighouse.

Mr. R.D. Gilbey.

Mr. John Morgan.

Mr. Thomas Tushingham, Chairman.

Mr Ronald Gilbey. The President.

71. *Cartoon from the Liverpool Echo*

looked after home trade, John Gilbey (son of Gordon), who was on the buying side, Arthur Gilbey (son of Sebastian) who was in charge of exports and the vital overseas companies, and Derek Gilbey (grandson of Henry Walter), who assisted him in this field. Younger members of this generation were: Jasper Grinling (son of Tony) on the marketing side and Robin (Bobbie) Gold (son of Alec), who covered the home market.

In a Board of eleven there were five fathers and sons, admirable perhaps, but it no doubt made for vigorous discussions. The directors were born to their place on the Board, they had not earned it through talent, so some had assets that were little use in business. Gordon Gilbey was an expert on wine, built up useful contacts in Spain and France and married the Baroness Vaux of Harrowden, his son John later becoming Lord Vaux through the female line. Tony Grinling was popular, but not such a strong character. Sebastian Gilbey, son of Sir Walter's second son Arthur, had inherited the family passion for horses and a love of the good things in life. He used to drive his team of horses to the office in Camden, causing quite a sensation in the streets of London, which was useful to the firm as it advertised the business. However, it was hardly a major board level contribution to the management of a multi-national company.

Alec Gold was probably the

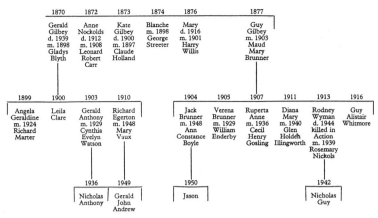

I. Family Tree – The Golds, part 3. This shows the younger children of Charles and Fanny Gold (see page 97).

most able. He was certainly a hard worker, but this only aroused suspicion amongst the others who were less so and when it came to selecting their next chairman he was passed over, to his bitter disappointment, in favour of the young Ronnie. It was said the other members were frightened he would make them work too hard, whereas Ronnie was himself a lover of an easier life. He led the Board through its last years with charm and relied on loyalty rather than dynamic leadership to keep his support. Sir Derek Gilbey, the third baronet, never took over the chairmanship that his grandfather and greatgrandfather had held for so many years, but he was a great support to Arthur on the export side.

Arthur Gilbey was a great entrepreneur, setting up some excellent deals, including the Smirnoff Vodka licence, but he did find the necessary follow-up more difficult. He relied on an assistant to tie up the loose ends. Arthur died very young, at just 44 years of age in 1964, largely due to the deprivations he suffered as a prisoner of war in the Second World War. His death was a serious blow to the company, as his wise counsel and large numbers of international contacts were invaluable and, for W&A Gilbey, irreplaceable.

The youngest generation did show glimmers of the dynamism that the firm so direly needed, but the family atmosphere and their fathers' presence made it hard to bring forward innovative measures. The most effective were Jasper Grinling, who was creative and hard working, and Bobbie Gold, who was particularly intelligent.

In the 1950s and early 1960s the Board of W&A Gilbey were kindly people for whom the firm provided a way of life for part of the week (rarely five days), where some work was done in the mornings prior to meeting together in the Directors' dining room, with its magnificent view over London. There was sherry before the meal, wine with it and port at the end, so, although making good use of their produce, it could not have been conducive to an afternoon of hard work. It is a far cry from the hectic schedules of modern day directors.

The directors were supported by managers and staff who were taught to say yes, to never speak first, to address directors as 'Mr', followed by the

72. The Gilbey Coach in Regents Park, London with Ronald Gilbey driving and Sebastian Gilbey sitting behind him. From an original oil painting by Lionel Edwards R.A.

Christian name, and generally to inhibit any signs of creativity, independence or dynamism until they had progressed to the top of a clearly-defined scale of promotion. By that time they were in their fifties or sixties and, perhaps, too old to exhibit any sign of innovation.

W&A Gilbey managers might have enjoyed a happy, secure working life, but it was frustrating for anyone with talent or initiative. They were meant to obey, not manage; they lost their drive and problems took a long time to resolve.

Arthur Gilbey was the first of the directors to try to change this long tried and tested system and to find some young managers with potential from public schools. These new managers included John Patrick, Dick Bowes, Eustace Crawley and Simon Bradley. W&A Gilbey was changing, but yet again it was 'too little, too late'. Those managers who joined in the early 1950s rose through the ranks, but were too young to save W&A Gilbey.

Amazingly, the standards were so old-fashioned that even in these post war years (1945-1964) steel pen nibs were de rigueur and biros were banned for use in the books. Some of the desks were the same tall ones with high stools used a hundred years before, although the 'new' W&A Gilbey house, built in 1937 at Oval Road, Regent's Park, was a modern building with contemporary, 1930s, furniture, much of which was moved on to the 1963 building at Harlow. Time was not as precious then as it is today and there were plenty of opportunities for practical jokes that would never be tolerated in a modern office. A popular one was to balance a book on top of a door, so that the unsuspecting person who entered next found it landing on his head.

W&A Gilbey might not have promoted energy and dynamism, but it was a wonderful place to work. There was complete security of employment. It was joked that the only way of getting dismissed was by stealing company property or assaulting a director. W&A Gilbey went to the length of taking back every one of its employees after the two world wars. Workers expected to spend their lives with the company and many gave over 50 years' service. Some families spanned generations, for example John Carver, the Chief Accountant, was the third member of his family to hold that position – the Carver family had worked at W&A Gilbey for a total of 100 years.

The Directors knew the names of all the employees and often their families too, so with this feeling of conviviality there was no question of strikes and only a few workers even belonged to a Trade Union. Certainly a Trade Union official might have found cause to strike for higher wages, but he would have overlooked all the other benefits of being W&A Gilbey workers. They were able to draw on a pension fund after 1952, and it was one that did not differentiate between manual and clerical staff. This was backed up by ex gratia pensions for those retired persons not drawing a reasonable income from the fund. There were good canteen facilities and when, in 1963, some of the staff were moved to new premises at Harlow, the W&A Gilbey Social Club was provided with new premises to help them integrate into their new surroundings.

There were many examples of important assistance, such as the employee who contracted TB and was sent to Switzerland, at the firm's expense, and employed again when she returned. Some with financial problems were bailed out by W&A Gilbey and one with a back injury was given private treatment. Once you were a W&A Gilbey employee there was security of work and a knowledge that the company cared. This caring policy created enormous loyalty and pride, features which inhibited militancy, but which were damaged in the whirlwind of mergers and take-overs of the 1960s.

W&A Gilbey stood for much that was worth preserving, but not all of the ways they had done things in the past were worth keeping. They had taken too long to realise this important point but were doing so as they went into the 1960s, the decade that was going to give the world new standards and destroy one fine product of the Victorian era: – W&A Gilbey.

Changes were beginning to happen within the company. The younger directors were aware of the changing needs of business and were beginning to have an influence: more of the long-standing traditions were about to be broken.

It had been a policy that only one son was allowed in the business, but Sir Walter's grandson, Walter Anthony Gilbey, born so late in Henry Walter's life that he represented the third generation amongst directors who were themselves fourth and fifth generation, was determined to end such a restriction on getting into W&A Gilbey. He was not allowed in, however, as his half nephew, his father's grandson, Sir Derek, represented his family's line.

This caused consternation in his family and his mother's subsequent letter to the chairman Ronald Gilbey catches the importance her son attached to getting into the family firm.

I was very disappointed and sad on Walter's behalf when I received your letter, as from being a very little boy his great ambition has been to one day work for 'Gilbeys'. I knew of course, that his Father had appointed Derek before he was born – but as both his Father and his brother Arthur Gilbey were in the firm I had hoped you might have been able to find a place for him, particularly in view of his excellent school record and the fact that he will be such a very large shareholder.[1]

This first interview was after Walter Anthony's school certificate and two years later he tried again, but was still rebuffed. This time Walter himself wrote and showed the strength of his feelings:

Dear Uncle Ronald,

Thank you for seeing me yesterday. I was very disappointed that the result of our talk was not more satisfactory. I do hope the Board will change their minds, in any case I shall not change mine.

Walter Anthony Gilbey had inherited the old fashioned view that it was his duty to carry on the family traditions. His interests lay, like those of his father, grandfather and great grandfather before him, in the wine and spirit trade and in the horse world.

Walter A. Gilbey was not put off by the refusal of the Board to let him join. Becoming one of the firm was his ambition. He wanted to bring W&A Gilbey up to date, without destroying its traditions, and to become its chairman. He set out to acquire qualifications that would make him useful to the firm, firstly joining another Gilbey who had been refused entry. This was Mark Gilbey, who had set up his own wine company, Mark Gilbey and Co.. After a short time there, Walter A. Gilbey went on to join the merchant bankers Kleinwort Benson. Then W&A Gilbey's policy forced the retirement of one of their most able members, Alec Gold the finance director, as directors had to retire at 65. Nobody in the family had the qualifications to take over his role, except Walter, and he held 10% of the shares. After his seven years with Kleinwort Benson, one of the managing directors of that firm, Sir Mark Turner, gave a favourable report of his ability and the directors waived the rule that only one descendent of each director could join the Board. In 1961, at 26 years of age, he achieved the first stage of his ambition and joined the W&A Gilbey Board. He was the first Director to have received outside financial training for that role.

It must have seemed like a good time to be joining the Company, as it was waking out of its complacent acceptance of traditional approaches. The dangers of a take-over were being realised and the directors were becoming jittery about the company's position. The younger directors were being given more freedom to reorganise the business and found themselves able to force the pace. To bring W&A Gilbey into the modern world Walter, with his training in the City, knew they needed more than a Chief Accountant (a post held by John Carver). In keeping with the W&A Gilbey approach John Carver had been born to the role, being the grandson of the firm's first accountant. Walter recognised the need not just to keep the accounts but to monitor cash flow, the raising of finance, investigating acquisitions, costings and general financial policy-making. There was new blood coming into the firm and plans were afloat to move its main operations from London to Harlow (which was nearer the Gilbey heartland of Bishop's Stortford), although the choice of

Harlow was a result of Socialist legislation controlling the re-location of industry and especially of new office building.

This new and more open attitude included the use of outside consultants drawn from the company's auditors, Turquand Youngs and Co.. One of their recommendations was the creation of the role of Financial Controller. This was the sort of new appointment that Walter A. Gilbey wanted, provided it could be appropriately filled, and he was very pleased to select Stanley Lee. Stanley was the son of a toolmaker and the grandson and great grandson of vat makers who had made vats for W&A Gilbey for decades. A Grammar school scholar, he joined the company in 1951 and qualified as a Chartered Secretary two years later. During his ten years with the company he had run the punched card accounting machines, which were the fore-runners of modern computers. He was generally recognised as being dynamic, with a critical turn of mind and brusqueness of manner coupled with frankness rather than diplomacy. He was, however, both qualified and capable and was just the man needed to produce and implement the sort of new financial policies that Walter A. Gilbey wanted. He did the work so well that he held the position for more than two decades. He retired from the post of Finance Director of International Distillers & Vintners Ltd. in 1984, following major heart surgery.

W&A Gilbey made another revolutionary break with tradition when they bought Osborne and Son Ltd., Jim Peppercorn's family business with a chain of retail shops. J.K. Peppercorn was invited to be the first outsider to join the Board. He had the right credentials: being from public school and the Chairman of the Wine and Spirit Association.

The reason for the take-over was to strengthen W&A Gilbey's hand against the growing power of the breweries. With more retail outlets, they believed

they would be in a better position to set up reciprocal deals, taking the breweries' goods in exchange for their taking W&A Gilbey's products. The concept of matching the breweries' was a good one, but its implementation, both as to purchase prices and to extra stocks and sales ledger debtors, added to the company's growing liquidity problem, resulting from inflation and enormously increased duties and taxes on wines and spirits. In April 1962 there were £4,500,000 of secured and unsecured loans and overdrafts.

The whirlwind of take-overs in the business community was gathering force and sending gusts in W&A Gilbey's direction. The pressure was on to get bigger and bigger in order to ward

73. John Carver, Chief Accountant of W & A Gilbey Ltd, the third member of his family to hold the position

off marauders. The breweries thought that small family units could not survive – although Youngs and other firms have proved them wrong. During the 30 years following the 1950's the number of independent breweries was reduced by three quarters and at the same time the ever-enlarging breweries started to intrude more and more on the wine and spirit trade, as they saw the profits to be made. Allied Breweries acquired Grants of St James and Bass Charrington took over Hedges and Butler. Adding to the difficulties caused by changes in the wine and spirit trade, was the end of retail price maintenance and the growth of competition from supermarkets taking out retail wine and spirit licences. These led to cuts in both wholesale and retail profit margins. Pressure on W&A Gilbey was increasing hourly, to which the fashionable answer was growth.

W&A Gilbey toyed with merging with a leading brewery, Ind Coope, with each party holding shares in a new joint company, in which Ind Coope would have dealt with all beer and pub matters, leaving W&A Gilbey as sole suppliers of wines and spirits in the Ind Coope-tied and managed public house and off licence estates. The merger would have had trading repercussions with other parts of the trade (who were not friendly) and meant the end of the 'family' control of the British W&A Gilbey business. In fact, Ind. Coope became Allied Breweries (now Allied Domecq) and ran its own wine and spirit business, much to W&A Gilbey's detriment. W&A Gilbey believed themselves to be secure against the threat of a take-over, as all voting shares were held by the Board, but their confidence was shattered when E.P. Taylor, the Canadian brewery magnate, made approaches regarding a take-over. The Board took fright, fearing that they would have a very bad press if they refused to recommend a bid to their shareholders and were to block it through the holding of the Management shares. Walter Anthony believed that with the large family non-management shareholdings (he held nearly 10%) and the many loyal shareholders, they would not be put in this position, but his youthful defence of the family firm was not heeded and the Board looked hastily for a desirable partner with which to merge for their mutual defence.

The Board's aim was a merger that would give them the strength to resist any hostile bids, but in hindsight their next move was their most serious mistake. Instead of joining forces with a brewery whose operation would complement their own activities, they chose to merge with a competitor in the same field. To add to the risk this move entailed, the family took the far-reaching step of relinquishing their control over the voting shares. In the words of Walter Anthony: 'they gave away their birthright for a mess of pottage by quite unnecessarily relinquishing their voting control'.

They chose a competitor because, as wine merchants, they preferred to remain wine merchants than join forces with the less grand breweries. When Robin Gold reported that United Wine Traders Ltd. (UWT) would like to merge, the announcement was welcomed, as their Directors seemed to be like-minded wine and spirit merchants. There were three original United Wine Traders Ltd. companies: first was Corney and Barrow Ltd., run by the Stevens brothers (who had another plus in the eyes of W&A Gilbey as the original

74. Stanley Lee, Financial Controller of W & A Gilbey and International Distillers and Vintners Ltd, subsequently Financial Director of the latter

brothers (who had another plus in the eyes of W&A Gilbey as the original Barrow was related to the Gilbeys by marriage), second was Twiss & Brownings & Hallowes Ltd., who were wine wholesalers, whose major attraction was the Hennessy Brandy agency, which was run by Geoffrey Hallowes (husband of Odette, the French Resistance heroine) and, most importantly of all, the third company was Justerini and Brooks Ltd., which owned the pale whisky brand, J & B Rare, which was enjoying a phenomenal growth in the USA, providing big profits for the company.

Cecil Berens, an executive with Hambros Bank, was brought in to be Chairman and to weld together this new group, UWT. He was supported in the role of vice chairman by Freddie Hennessy, an English member of the famous Cognac family. Freddie was bright and had the traditional upbringing that W&A Gilbey respected: Eton, the Guards Armoured Brigade and then the wine trade. He was wealthy and had excellent connections.

The advantages to UWT of the merger were that W&A Gilbey had the distilleries to supply the whisky for J & B, an established loyal staff, substantial assets, successful overseas companies and a great name. W&A Gilbey was acquiring a fast-growing international brand, J & B, and the Hennessy agency. It was a merging of similar companies with like-minded leaders.

Young Walter Anthony, whose life was focused on upholding the family name, and the newly appointed Financial Controller, Stanley Lee, were very unhappy about the merger. They objected strongly, with a host of arguments, pointing out that the J & B success produced 90% of UWT profits, putting that group in a very vulnerable position compared with W&A Gilbey; the latter were a virtual wine and spirit trade investment trust, with interests around the world, numerous brands and vertical integration, from the vineyards to the shop counters.

In a paper showing that the merger was more advantageous to UWT than the number of young and dynamic directors and executives; its proposed modern warehouse and bottling plant; the reorganisation of the sales policy and organisation; the streamlining and modernisation of the office organisation; new developments in the overseas markets; a new feeling of confidence and determination amongst the managers; and the growth of Smirnoff vodka sales.

The paper showed that W&A Gilbey's net tangible assets were worth approximately £8,800,000, while UWT's were only worth £1,100,000; that the capital value of royalties on Gilbeys Gin in 20 countries was considerable; that the consolidated revenue reserves amounted to well over £3 million, while UWT's were a mere £13,000; and that profits were rising in 1960, being some £27,000 better than in 1959, while estimated profits for 1962-63 were £1,140,000. Walter Anthony said, at the March Board meeting:

> The proposed merger with UWT lacks justification on the grounds that we can not continue alone or that we are in danger of being taken over.
> It should be on account of whether it is in the best interests of the company that the issue should be considered.

Walter Anthony, the youngest director, was the only one on the Board against the merger; but the paper that he produced in support of W&A Gilbey's position showed just how much the company was changing. There was every indication that it was on the point of emerging as a modernised company.

In April 1962, after two months of negotiation, W&A Gilbey and UWT merged to form the holding company, International Distillers & Vintners Ltd. (IDV).

The two chairmen produced the joint statement:

75. Walter Anthony Gilbey and Miss Jenifer Price on their engagement in 1963

We are both delighted to have reached terms for what will, in effect, be the largest merger to take place in the wine and spirit trade since the last war.

This is in no sense a take-over deal, but a blending of our interests in what is virtually a 50/50 transaction. The companies in the group will retain their separate identities together with their present managements and staffs, to whom the merger should offer greater scope and opportunity.

The chairmen both thought that they could carry on as they had done in the past – that they could remain 'bachelors after they were married'. However, it is not possible to carry on as before after a merger, not if the merger is to be effective.

Walter Anthony was to learn later that, although he himself did not advocate the need for a merger, if there was to be a merger there could have been another, more suitable, option to the UWT merger. Tom Fogden, the Managing Director of W&A Gilbey in Canada, the most profitable and powerful overseas unit, could have come to the rescue and got together the money to make a counter bid. He had the loyalty, as he had started as a clerk in the export department in the UK and he had the finance, as his dynamism had turned the Canadian plant and a major distillery into a significant money earner. It would have been a complicated manoeuvre, but the subsidiary could have taken over the parent company.

International Distillers and Vintners Ltd. became the new name for the holding company for the merged operations and Cecil Berens became Chairman. Freddie Hennessy and Ronnie Gilbey were the two vice Chairmen. Most of the older generation of the W&A Gilbey Board stepped down, with Alec Gold, Sebastian Gilbey, Tony Grinling and Gordon Gilbey all going into retirement. From the other camp all the UWT Board remained, but on the management side it was W&A Gilbey people who took over. They had built up a good team and this was recognised by UWT. John Carver became Chief Accountant, Stanley Lee was Financial Controller and Frances Edmund Lee was Company Secretary. Walter Anthony, despite his objections to the merger, became Financial Director.

It soon became obvious that, although UWT made a major contribution to the profits, thanks to sales of J & B whisky (largely in America), their management was weak and old-fashioned. By comparison, although only by comparison, W&A Gilbey were a paragon of efficiency; but as there was very little merging of activities, both carried on very much as before, in line with their initial intention. There were few changes to the structure and little improvement in efficiency. The merger did not stimulate direly-needed new innovative marketing policies and no strategy document was produced. Everything went on pretty much as before – even the losses for W&A Gilbey in the retail sector.

The key problem was that both parties wanted to remain separate, so that the benefits of a merger were only partially realised. The Board members thought the merger in itself would be enough to avoid take-over threats and did not take note of the dangers the merger had created, through loss of control over voting shares, nor the dangers of not consolidating their position and adopting a tougher and sharper policy to increase profits and improve ratios. Any company is vulnerable to take-over, so long as someone else is bigger than them. Although IDV did take over some companies, like Peter Dominic and J & H Brookes, to try and make themselves less vulnerable, it was not enough to avert the danger.

To be safe in that time of take-over mania, a company needed to be controlled by voting shares; by remaining private or through family control. W&A Gilbey had thrown those options away. The other two alternatives were to get so big that others could not swallow them, or to keep profits growing so well that nobody thought themselves capable of doing better, so that the shareholders were too happy to contemplate accepting a bid.

Walter Anthony, who had pointed out the dangers of a merger with UWT, did not realise how imminent they were. His finance department did come up with ideas – some were accepted, but the more revolutionary were turned down, including two important options for reducing their vulnerability. To get the home trade into profit, Walter Anthony suggested a scheme of joining up with three of the biggest breweries in joint ownership of retail shops, thus giving W&A Gilbey the direly-needed outlets for their produce. The other idea was to get three of the major breweries to buy into IDV, as with three masters there would be less chance of domination and the breweries could put their wine and spirit departments into IDV in exchange for shares.

Walter Anthony did not, however, concentrate entirely on the business, as he was intent on making his name in other spheres. In politics, he was elected onto the Berkshire County Council. His long-term objective was to become chairman of IDV and he believed that political qualifications would help him in this objective.

Merger approaches were made to IDV by a number of companies, but they were all turned down and, although IDV's limited growth in profits did give rise to the possibility of take-over by companies like Beechams, none had materialised. In the mid 1960s the future looked more promising, as IDV began to slowly merge into one whole, rather than two separate units. It was being run in a more technical manner – although at the cost of human management. Profits were increasing, if slowly, thanks to J & B and W&A Gilbey of Canada. Most directors were content that things were marching along well, when on 21st June, 1967 the company was suddenly taken aback by a share exchange offer valued at 17s 5d a share against 13s 6d on the market (before the bid) or 16s for cash. The bid was from Showerings, famous for their Babycham product, and it galvanised the IDV Board into a furore of activity. There was unanimous hostility to this overture by 'upstarts' from the West Country and to their low valuation. A formal rejection of the bid was sent a day later.

The two Showering brothers, Keith and Francis, had been brought up as farmers, made a success of their cider company, taken over Whiteways in 1961 and shown the world the strength of a great marketing campaign. In the early days of TV advertising they managed to convince those not rich enough to drink champagne that the miniature bottles of bubbling perry, with so little alcoholic content that it was free of excise tax, produced a similar effect, at least in terms of ambience and of those watching you drink it. Babycham became 'the drink' for ladies in pubs, 'the smart drink' for the middle and lower middle classes, and the Showering brothers made a fortune. But it was not the sort of style to appeal to W&A Gilbey, or to any of the Board of IDV.

There was though, a business logic to the bid, including such factors as Showerings having taken over Harveys of Bristol the previous year, when W&A Gilbey of Canada were agents for Harveys in Canada. Further, the vitality and good marketing of the Showerings could have been complementary to the experience and good name of IDV. But IDV were determined to remain independent of such an operation and the bid was contested.

Walter Anthony dropped all political activities to become a leader of the defence. Together with Stanley Lee he produced a host of financial information, made possible by recent arrangements to rejuvenate IDV's accounting around the world. They organised the updating of profit forecasts, which looked amazingly attractive, revised valuations and increased the dividend. It was remarkable action for a company that had tended to lack strategy and drive. Forecasts were extracted from the numerous IDV world-wide operations, while auditors and merchant banks were involved in a whirlwind of meetings. There was little time to sleep, and none for other activities, in the drive to get together a good defence document to circulate to shareholders. There was all the spirit of a war and the family was rallied to the defence. After years of nobody taking much notice of them as shareholders, suddenly they were courted and made to feel important.

IDV continued to recommend rejection, saying the offer was inadequate in relation to the potential of IDV, with expected profits of £3,200,000 for the year ending 31 May, 1967; that IDV was already starting to rationalise; and that dividends were increasing at a rate of 19% whereas Showerings increase was only 17.14%. There were acid comments from Cecil Berens, such as: 'If Showerings cared to talk to us about our business we could tell them about it, they know absolutely nothing about it now.'

IDV had formidable opponents. Showerings were confident of their aggressive approach, having won a hard but quick fight for Harveys 18 months before. They also had the support of one of the great take-over experts, Philip Shelbourne, a partner in Rothschilds which was handling Showerings' bid.

Showerings countered IDV's rejection with material such as a chart showing the change in value of an investment of £100 in Showerings and IDV, between December 1962 and June 1967: for Showerings it had increased to £307.10s, for IDV it had fallen to £60.

Showerings' bid was raised and the big institutions who were shareholders, in particular, accepted. These were lobbied for rejection by IDV, but the company knew that their best hopes lay with the family shareholders. About 100 were listed as holding between them 30-40% of the shares. Their loyalty was encouraged with such efforts as a buffet lunch, when about 70 came to hear chairman Cecil Berens make an impassioned speech for their support. Walter Anthony followed this up by writing letters and telephoning anyone he knew. There were advertisements in the newspapers to support share buying programmes and attempts to get the media on IDV's side, with sympathetic articles and TV appearances.

The fight began to get dirty, with Showerings issuing a writ for injurious falsehood on Cecil Berens and his advisors, Hambros and Kleinwort Benson, in respect to a statement on their sherry contracts (to purchase sherry, particularly Harvey's Bristol Cream) and the revision of these supply contracts being a main factor in improved profitability. Showerings claimed that none of the supply contracts had been revised.

Prospects of holding off this contested bid began to look bleak and IDV went to their main rival, Distillers Company Ltd., to talk about a link-up with them, but Distillers were not interested and it came to nothing. Then Freddie Hennessy took the step, which had been so opposed by W&A Gilbey, of talking to the breweries. He had a meeting with Watneys – IDV had started to take action.

On Thursday, 13th July there were huge purchases of IDV shares, pushing the price up to 20s 6d. It was one of the first ever Dawn Raids, later to be tightly controlled, and Showerings responded by increasing its bid by 2/- a share. The mystery purchasing stopped, but when the IDV share price fell to 18s 9d another round of buying started. The city was a hive of rumours. The press was critical. IDV took the unusual step of issuing a press announcement on Saturday, advising shareholders yet again to reject Showerings' offer and refuting the suggestion that it was responsible for the heavy buying two days before.

It stated that the substantial shareholding had been acquired by a third party not connected with IDV and that the shares had been bought for commercial reasons: to protect the third party, who had done the buying to start trading negotiations.

Showerings raised their bid on 25th July, valuing the IDV shares at 20s 5d, and at the same time their tactics became more controversial. Francis Showering, the Showering Group Managing Director, even signed a rather scathing letter on 25th July in which he referred to Cecil Berens' defence of IDV as including: 'intemperate references to our products [which] were so wide of the mark that they must be dismissed as being quite irresponsible.'

They pointed out, too, that the future estimates for IDV profits had to be queried, as in December they had not talked with such optimism to their shareholders. It was a very sudden change to be so bullish in July.

Showerings enjoyed a further boost to their bid when they won over 64-year-old Paul Dauthieu, an IDV Board Member who had sold his chain of Peter Dominic shops to the company. Sadly, he must have been an easy victim, as he was seriously ill and died soon after; but the Showering brothers went to see him in his nursing home. They convinced him of the good value of their bid and he announced his support for the offer, causing consternation at IDV and great media publicity about the split in the boardroom.

Share prices went up, but the weakening of the IDV position was soon counterbalanced. Eleven days after the Dawn Raid, on 24th July, Watney Mann came clean, announcing that it was the mystery buyer and now held 17% of the ordinary share capital of IDV. It was going to keep a neutral position: but that only lasted two weeks. By 7th August they had come down on the side of IDV.

Showerings kept fighting and, with a 26% acceptance of ordinary share capital (60% of outstanding shares, excluding holdings of IDVs supporters), by mid August they put in a third, improved bid in hope of forcing a settlement. It gave the IDV shares a cash value of 23s 1d, an increase of 92% on their value before the original offer. In the words of the Telegraph of the 16th August, they had 'moved in for the kill'.

IDV, however, were negotiating with Watney Mann. The discussions subsequently led to IDV taking over Watney Mann's wine and spirit interests, in exchange for the issue of more IDV shares. Apart from saving them from the grips of Showerings, there was much logic to the step. A partial merger with one or more breweries was what Walter Anthony had been pressing for.

On 1st September Showerings finally withdrew their bid, because of the attitude of the IDV Board and the failure to collect the support of 51% of the shareholders. It had been a three-month battle, with £41.5 million on offer from Showerings, but it had failed because the IDV Directors had the support of 40% of the original shareholders and because Watney Mann had bought that crucial 17 %.

There had been some bitter salvos from both sides in the making and rejection of three bids. The costs were high, with Showerings spending about £500,000 and then suffering a fall in their share price.

IDV were jubilant, but shaken. There were costs to them other than their defence. They absolutely had to meet demands for rationalisation to improve efficiency; but this led to a further loss of the important central feature of W&A Gilbey, loyalty, and increased the scourge that was due to the take-over mania, de-humanisation. There was a further sifting out of the older Directors, in what became known as the night of the thousand knives, with the departure of Ronnie (in the home trade, witty, good with people, but not so astute), Sir Derek (who was charming, but not energetic enough to justify keeping him in the export department) and the Honourable John Gilbey (the main promoter of Gilbeys Gin), together with Ralph Cobbold and Eddie Tatham of J & B. Corney & Barrow, as one of the comparatively unprofitable units, was sold back to its previous owners, Keith and Peter Stevens, with Keith Stevens leaving the IDV Board. Most nostalgic of all, the W&A Gilbey coach and horses were sold to Walter Anthony, for cash and at market prices.

The loss of the coaching horses was symbolic of the changing attitudes. The horses had been used for more than a century to carry goods and people. Long after being superseded by motors, they were retained because so many of the Board members held them in such attachment and because they were a good means of advertising – rather like Youngs' dray and show Shires nowadays.

The Gilbey family had supported the view that there were values more important than wholesale modernisation; yet even before the Showerings' bid, investigations were being made as to the justification for keeping the horses.

There were two opposing views. On the one hand there was the opinion that it was good public relations, with the story and tradition of the coach obtaining plenty of free newspaper coverage around the world. On the other hand, this traditional, old-world image might give the name of W&A Gilbey an old-fashioned image with the younger generation.

Views were sought from IDV companies and agents round the world. Spain, Portugal and Japan believed that the horses were a good asset for promotion and the Japanese agent's letter was illuminating:

> I agree with using the theme, since almost all Japanese, young and old, have the image that England has many good old traditional manners and customs, such as bowler hats, sticks etc. These images connecting to Gilbeys Gin is a characteristic image, but the New World wants a more 'go go image'.

The majority, however, were in favour of disbanding the horses. Once again, Walter Anthony agreed to show his support for the family traditions. He took the Gilbey coach and horses to his home near Henley-on-Thames to run them himself. He had good support, as his wife Jenifer had learnt to take the reins and became one of the few lady whips of a team of coach horses.

Of the family representatives, Jasper Grinling was showing himself to be the most able Board member. He was upgraded to become Managing Director, but sadly his wariness about becoming too involved with brewers was to prove a critical factor in the years ahead.

Watneys, in their turn, had some representatives appointed to the IDV Board. These were Simon Heneage, managing director of Brown and Pank, their wine and spirit subsidiary; and Binks Nicholson and Walter Serocold, who were respectively Finance and Executive Directors of Watney Mann.

Despite these members on the Board, IDV still kept their distance from the brewers and were never to make the trading and management connections with them that might have saved IDV from total take-over. To add to the dangerous consequences of this attitude, the person who did maintain a link, Freddie Hennessy, the man who had instigated the assistance that led to that life-saving Dawn Raid, died.

Watney Mann warranted attention, as they now owned a large part of IDV. In May 1968, after months of complicated negotiations, particularly by a financial team under Walter Anthony, Brown and Pank's wholesale wines and spirits businesses, part of Watneys, with a turnover of £26,500,000 in 1966, was exchanged for shares in IDV. This gave IDV entry to the outlets that they had been trying to acquire over the past forty years, but had had neither the cash nor the drive to do on a large enough scale. Now at last they had a large number of retail outlets, both on licence pubs and off licences and they were finally in a position to sell their goods in a competitive manner on the home front. Their goods could go back to the pubs (Watneys owned nearly 6,000) from which they had been ousted when the breweries started those far-reaching disruptions to the wine and spirit trade by venturing into it themselves. The deal rationalised production and distribution, but it also brought Watney Mann's holdings in IDV up to 37%.

IDV remained aloof from the brewers' activities and did not get involved in the next move in the take-over mania which heavily involved their backers. Watneys took on the great Grand Metropolitan Hotels Ltd. in the quest to acquire Trumans. It was a vicious battle, with Watneys trying to prevent outside interests getting into the brewery trade. There were eight bids, pushing the bidding from £34 million to £50 million. Such was the feeling of disdain in IDV that there was some actual opposition to Watney's efforts. The lack of loyalty towards Watneys was soon to backfire on them.

Watneys failed and Trumans was the first brewery to fall into the hands of an outsider. This did not end the battles, however, as the take-over momentum was gathering pace. Watney Mann had had the temerity to try and oppose Grand Metropolitan's intrusion into the brewery trade and this big conglomerate was looking for others to take over.

Sir Charles Clore, the entrepreneurial businessman who had pioneered large scale takeovers, had made an unsuccessful bid for Watneys back in 1959, but the attempt had done them a favour, stimulating them to turn their brewery industry upside down with a mass of mergers (with other like-minded firms, rather than outsiders), rationalisation and expansion into hotels, motels and wines and spirits. The end result was that Watney shareholders in 1972 had holdings worth five times the 1959 value, yet there was danger in this too. Watneys had become such an attractive company that outsiders were again looking it over. The successful intrusion into the brewery trade by property and hotel wizard Maxwell Joseph showed the possibilities. Rumours were rife that Unilever, British American Tobacco or Charles Clore might try their luck, as there had been a build-up of nominee shareholdings in Watneys and nobody had been able to identify the mystery buyers who were pushing up the price of the shares.

Watneys knew they had to strengthen their hand against such an occurrence and, true to traditional take-over defence, they decided they had to get bigger. They were worried also by IDV's attempts to solve their cash requirements by raising fresh capital from the shareholders Rights Issue, which gave Watneys two options, neither of which appealed. These were: either to make a further cash investment and subscribe, or not to subscribe and see their 37.5% holding diluted.

Negotiations with IDV could help to solve their vulnerability to a bid and their awkward position with regard to the Rights Issue. In December 1971 they began discussions with the Board. IDV no longer had the amicable link of the friendship between Freddie Hennessy and the Chairman of Watneys, Michael Webster, and they rejected the friendly offer of a merger. The IDV Board wanted to keep its independence and thought that the price was not high enough, in view of future earnings, and that it would damage IDV in its crucial sector of overseas trade, as the foreign agents opposed the merger.

Watney Mann, harassed by ever-more-persistent rumours of a bid for them, and unable to agree terms for an amicable merger, forced the pace by making a bid for IDV that valued the company at £122 million. In a letter in February 1972 to shareholders they said:

We are now totally convinced, however, that the existing partial ownership by Watney Mann of IDV is no longer in the best interests of either set of shareholders and that the two companies should merge completely in order to take the best possible advantage of the considerable opportunities for development and growth which now exist.

Its offer to the shareholders was:

a substantial increase in the market value of your investment. A significant increase in your annual income. The continuance of an equity investment, but in a group which will be more broadly based with a wide range of related activities and capable of expanding more rapidly than either company could on its own.

The IDV Board were not impressed and advised the rejection of Watney's offer. But then came the bombshell. The next largest shareholding to Watney Mann's was that of Richemont, belonging to the French Hennessy family, with 8% of the shares. They reached agreement with Watney Mann when Watneys promised to give even greater support to Hennessy Brandy through Watney outlets. This coup gave Watneys virtual success, though a last-ditch proposal was put together by Warburgs and Rothschilds, that the Rank Organisation Ltd. should buy IDV and GrandMet buy Watneys.

This initiative split the IDV Board, with chairman Cecil Berens and Managing Director Jasper Grinling favouring this new deal, but Bobbie Gold and Walter Anthony saying it was a despicable move to allow Watneys to be taken over when they had saved IDV from Showerings. On the grounds of rationalisation there was a case, too, that it was better for a wine and spirit company to have as a partner a brewery, rather than a massive conglomerate, albeit with leisure interests.

The approach by Rank failed. Watneys increased their offer and, on 11th February 1972, IDV accepted it in a letter to its shareholders. IDV was now a subsidiary of Watney Mann, which, as a consequence, became the third largest drink group in the UK. It was a company that owned considerable property – nearly 6,000 pubs and 1,000 off-licences – ran discotheques and restaurants, owned eight breweries in the UK and three in Belgium, exported beer to 40 countries and had the Coca Cola concession for the South of England and it now had IDVs world-wide business. Watneys believed themselves safe from predators.

The leaders of the resistance to the bid, Cecil Berens and Jasper Grinling, were dismissed immediately. Michael Webster, the chairman of Watneys, took over the chairmanship of IDV. Bobbie Gold and Walter Anthony were the only members of the old family retained and one Gilbey, at least, was still hanging on to his inheritance, as Walter was promised a place on the new Watney Mann board. Unfortunately, the drama continued so quickly that there was no time for this promise to be honoured.

'Where will Mr Maxwell Joseph, proud conqueror of Trumans last summer, strike next?' was the question asked in a February, 1972, *Morning Advertiser*. The same paper gave its answer on 14th March, just one month after IDV had helped to make Watney Mann a bigger company. 'So it wasn't Unilever or British American Tobacco after all – it was our old friend Maxie J.'

> Friday's dramatic, mid-morning announcement that Mr Maxwell Joseph's hungrily ambitious Grand Metropolitan Hotels has bid £355 million in shares and loan stock for Watney Mann, the Red Revolution brewing enterprise.

It was the second largest bid ever made up to that date and, if it were successful, it would boost GrandMet's market value to more than £650 million, a dramatic rise in five years from £12 ½ million. Some interesting possibilities were soon picked up by the next issue of the Sunday Times which contained the following:

> The interesting bit of the GrandMet offer document for Watneys sent out last Friday is the detailed revelations of the stock market dealings behind Max Joseph's bid. Massaging the stock market, as it is euphemistically described, is an essential back-up for the smart take-over tactician. But the ordinary shareholder is apt to be mangled if he does not know what is going on.
>
> One variation in a contested bid situation is to buy, or better to get your friends to buy, a packet of shares in your rival bidder, so that if necessary they can be dropped from a great height on the stock market to drive his shares down and all credibility from his bid. Something of the sort happened between last July and September with both GrandMet and Watney, who were slogging it out in the stock market for who could make the most expensive take-over of Truman's.
>
> Apparently once this was all over, GrandMet, the victor, and Watneys, who emerged with a £2 million plus capital profit, agreed together not to dump each others shares indiscriminately on the stock market. Watney's Michael Webster therefore discreetly liquidated his holding, without hitting the GrandMet price. But this was a fateful move, for Joseph's friends, the Rothschilds, went right on buying Watney. Even while the Truman battle was ending on September 3rd, they sold a million shares to Joseph and a bid for Watneys was on.

There was a nasty smell in the air and hints of 'warehousing'. 'Warehousing' is when persons friendly to the bidder buy shares and the bid is made in the knowledge that the bidder has guaranteed acceptance from those shareholders who 'warehoused'. Indeed, there was an extraordinary accumulation of Watney shares in the name of nominees. At the time of the first bid, National Westminster held 8.1 million shares, Rothschilds 1 million and Chase Nominees 1.3 million, a total of 26% of the shares under nominee names. Who were they representing? – the high-principled directors of the old firm of W&A Gilbey would have been shocked. To add some irony to the battlefield, all those arguments Watney Mann had used to prove they were a most rational bidder for Trumans the previous summer now backfired on them and gave GrandMet excellent ammunition for the value of their take-over of Watneys.

The Take-Over Panel[2] ordered a probe into the suspicious share dealings in March. The panel cleared Rothschilds of insider dealings and their buying of Watney Shares between June and February was approved.

The IDV Board was divided. Some, like Geoffrey Hallowes, supported GrandMet as likely to give IDV more independence, some, like Jasper Grinling's replacement as managing director, Robin Kernick, remained neutral. The two remaining family members, Robin Gold and Walter Anthony, defended their heritage in the way they thought best, by supporting Watneys. Walter Anthony put all his energies and ideas behind Watneys, despite not yet having acquired his place on the Watney Mann Board. He devised three plans. The first was to borrow money to buy Scotch Inventories Ltd., a finance company which held a lot of IDV whisky stocks. This was a way of increasing Watney Mann profits, by acquiring the financing profits, and also of increasing the balance sheet size of Watney Mann, by including in it all of IDVs whisky stocks.

The second was a radical concept. A company called Chappelfield was formed, into which wealthy supporters of Watneys could put capital, making possible large overdraft facilities and the extensive purchase of Watney shares. Over the ensuing weeks about £1 ½ million worth of shares were bought by this hastily-formed company, at great risk if the share value were to fall in the near future. It helped supporters of Watneys by acquiring Watney shares, forced up the price and restricted GrandMet's operations. Walter Anthony did a great selling job for this company, with supporters such as the Toronto Dominion Bank. On Chappelfield's Board there were directors of the stature of Stephen Sillem, ex auditor of IDV, and the two bankers, David Ewart of Guinness Mahon and John Storar of the Drayton Group. When the Grand Metropolitan take-over of Watneys was completed, these shares were sold and, made a profit for Chappelfield. It was a bold, ingenious idea.

Walter Anthony's third plan was to put into action a fall-back position, to get an American company to take over Watneys rather than GrandMet; but this idea did not get the co-operation of Watneys.

Watneys themselves made part of their defence an emotional one, with their 'Keep Watney Watneys' campaign. So effective was it at rallying support that it was soon recognised as the best-ever exercise of its kind undertaken by a potential take-over victim. Even more remarkably, it was the employees who began to take this deal from a straightforward matter of finance to questions of worker morale. Most of the 29,000 employees were so strongly against becoming part of the huge GrandMet conglomerate that they wrote to every shareholder and Member of Parliament. The letter bears reproduction as it reflects the growing insecurity of being a cog in a huge impersonal wheel and it emphasises what that whirlwind of take-overs was destroying:

the subject of this letter is your Company and our Company – Watneys.

You will probably be surprised to be addressed directly by your employees. But we hope that you will consider what we have to say and understand why we have felt moved to write to you.

First, we should explain who we are; the appointed spokesmen of the great majority of a workforce of 29,000 people. This Defence Council has been set up to give all those people a voice. Normally in a take-over situation the employees are at a loss to put their views. But feeling at Watneys is so strong that it is our duty to ourselves, our management and to you, the shareholder, to ensure that our loyalties are made known.

To put our case simply, we work for Watneys because we want to. It is a company we respect, doing well in an industry we like. Industrial relations at Watneys are progressive and good; so is Watneys' future. We have worked hard for Watney Group companies, some of us for scores of years, some families even for generations. There have been hard patches which we have helped to overcome, there have been many advances from which we have drawn pride. It has given us satisfaction to take part in building up the Watney community to its present standing. Our Company has reached a stage where it means more than ever to us to be Watney employees and we have been looking forward with confidence to sustained progress.

But suddenly this enterprise which we have done so much to help to create is threatened from the outside. We are told, to our dismay, that we may be forced to suffer a total change of employer. We do not want such a change; but it seems that our preference is irrelevant. Our management do not want such a change; and we support them to the hilt. Must we then be hostages to a system that allows all we have done to be plundered by a company that we have no respect for and which has contributed not one whit to Watneys' growth . . . that deprives us of our working identity despite the heartfelt yet well reasoned opposition of everyone, at all levels, in Watneys?

There are many shortcomings and points of friction in industrial and commercial life. Perhaps take-over battles are the worst. If anything is bound to drive a deep and unnecessary rift between the employers and the employed, it is the unchecked evil of the disputed merger. You may think, as we do, that it is foolish for national appeals to be made, on the one hand, for an end to 'the divided nation' while, on the other, the very foundations of the lives and livelihoods of thousands of men and women are allowed to be disrupted by the callous quest for size and power. . . .

There is something unacceptable to this country's tradition of natural justice when an efficient, flourishing enterprise cannot go about its business safe from the cynical raids of greedy strangers and their associates. . . .

For how much longer can the practice of buying and selling the future of loyal workforces, and the dissolution of famous Company names, be allowed to blemish the social and industrial fabric of this country?

This letter captures much of the spirit that was being destroyed by take-over mania. The small people in the company were making their protest, that they should be listened to during this extraordinary sequence of events.

One possible hitch to the take-over was removed in May, when the Department of Trade and Industry said that the bid would not be referred to the Monopolies Commission. The DTI pointed out that there would still be larger brewery groups in Allied, Bass Charrington and Whitbread.

In May, GrandMet increased their bid by £48 million to £394 million, but Michael Webster replied that the new offer was 'no great shakes' and that the document was full of a lot of nit-picking. GrandMet 'must be joking' to attempt to buy a company of Watney's size and prospects at this price.

Further support for Watneys came from an unexpected source. Whitbreads, who had sided with GrandMet the previous summer, now bought 100,000 Watney Mann shares worth £246,000, but more as a morale booster, as it could hardly influence the £390 million battle. Then, in June, they influenced the other side, selling 400,000 of their GrandMet shares to depress the price and reduce the immediate value of the offer to Watneys.

Another twist came with an announcement from Rank that they might enter the battle, although this was hardly welcome news to Watneys and Michael Webster said that a bid from Rank would be equally unwelcome. That did not stop them and, on the 25th May, Rank put in a higher bid (by £17 million) of £430 million. This led to another extraordinary development, as the notoriously autocratic, tough Rank chairman, Sir John Davis, faced an outcry and such opposition from the American division and shareholders that he was forced to withdraw the bid

This was soon followed by a higher bid from GrandMet, increasing their offer by £35 million to £435 million and making this the biggest ever take-over, but Watneys were not swayed and remained as firmly opposed to this third offer as to the first.

In June the humane touch came in again, with Group Property Executive A.R. Woodard, on behalf of the staff at Watneys, following the example of the Trade Union Defence Council by writing to the shareholders, saying:

> We believe the company's future is one of immense promise. We have no stomach for seeing the great benefits which lie in store for the company's shareholders and employees alike diverted to a conglomerate such as Grand Metropolitan Hotels.
>
> The disruptive effect of a take-over together with the lack of knowledge and understanding of the important aspects of our business exhibited by those bidding for Watneys, makes us seriously doubt whether such an environment would exist if the bid were successful. We believe, therefore, that such a result could not be in the best interests either of you, as shareholders, or the staff of Watneys.
>
> Thus, whilst fully acknowledging the right of shareholders to determine the future of their company, we feel bound to place on record to you our deep concern at the prospect of a change of management and loss of independence. As evidence of the concern of the staff, those of us who are shareholders of the company will reject the Grand Metropolitan Hotels bid and further evidence, the cost of printing this letter and the postage to some 50,000 shareholders is being borne entirely by the staff.

It was all very emotive; but human feelings were not factors in this battle; it was profits and returns that counted. On 2nd July, Maxwell Joseph made his bid unconditional and S.G. Warburg, GrandMet's merchant bankers, said that they controlled more than 50% of the shares. It was not the small shareholders who had been swayed, but Prudential Assurance, whose decision to support GrandMet a few days before had turned the tables. With such a close battle this was enough to reverse the fortunes: a week before, all had thought Watney Mann the likely winner. Michael Webster commented: 'What swung the battle in favour of Grand Metropolitan was the institutions, not the individual shareholders. The majority of them remained loyal to Watney.'

In the *Investors Chronicle* of 7th July, the total incidental costs of the biggest-ever take-over battle was estimated, including everything from stamp duty to the cost of telegrams, at well over £6 million.

Walter Anthony defended the family traditions to the end and beyond. He wanted a recount, as GrandMet only claimed 50.5% support, and he is suspicious to this day that the result of a recount of acceptances might have produced a different result – a suspicion with no proof. He tried to rally support for a minority group holding, which could have brought independence with the recession that followed this extraordinary bout of take-overs, but Watney Mann capitulated. He described their action as feeble. They had lost their fight after four months of a desperately hard contest. Nor was this all: there had been the IDV contest in the winter and Trumans the summer before. There is a limit to the energy that can be mustered in a business fight.

Walter Anthony's views echoed those of the staff and employees, but he had lost even more than them. The company, which was the material product of his family, had been swallowed up. To him, the family name was what he had lived and fought for. As he said in his preparation notes, compiled when trying to join the company in 1954 at 19 years of age: 'I am proud of the name and traditions which the family has built up and would like to play some part, however small, in carrying them on. I feel I would do better in W&A Gilbey than anywhere else, because working for it would be a vocation and not a mere job.'

When he achieved his ambition of joining the Board, his aim for W&A Gilbey was for them to survive under family control and for W&A Gilbey to grow and to be a leader in the international wine and spirit trade. He wanted the firm to be a family business, not just for the Board, but also for the staff.

After nine years with the firm the take-over mania had removed any prospect of achieving these ambitions, with the final blow being the GrandMet take-over. Walter Anthony handed in his resignation, refused compensation, and gave a farewell party in the Board Room at 1 York Gate on 31 July 1972. W&A Gilbey had fallen.

Family Postscript

With nearly a quarter of century having passed since the take-over of IDV by GrandMet, most of the main characters have retired and no member of the four founding families – Gilbey, Gold, Blyth and Grinling – remains part of this company. There is a connection, however, with those who went through the dramas of the 1960s, as the present Chairman of the whole of GrandMet is George Bull, who is Freddie Hennessy's nephew. He started his working life in Twiss & Brownings & Hallowes Ltd. and spent the rest of it with IDV and GrandMet.

Bobbie Gold left GrandMet, but stayed in the drink trade before retiring and now lives near Henley on Thames. There he helps some Gilbey cousins with their vineyard and wine businesses.

Jasper Grinling was not reappointed to the Board following the take-over by GrandMet of Watney Mann and IDV, but he continued to work for GrandMet. He is now retired and lives on his vineyard in East Anglia.

Sir Derek Gilbey died in the early 1990s and his son, Gavin, inherited the title, becoming Sir Gavin Gilbey and representative of the fifth generation. Although he lives in America, he is a great believer in the Gilbey family traditions and has done much to support them.

Marion, Lady Gilbey, Henry Walter's second wife, moved to the Isle of Man and died there in the 1980s. She went there to join her son, Walter Anthony, and his wife, Jenifer, who made the Isle of Man their home in 1974, just two years after the fall of W&A Gilbey.

Walter Anthony, despite this loss, has been able to do much to keep the name of Gilbey to the fore. Devastated by the end of the family firm, his first endeavours were to make sure the name of Gilbey was still important in the drink trade. After leaving IDV in 1972 he went back to work in the businesses of his cousin, Mark Gilbey. These businesses were Duncan Gilbey & Matheson Ltd. and Mark Gilbey & Co., a firm which specialised in helping developing countries set up distilleries producing alcoholic drinks.

In the Isle of Man Walter Anthony established Mannin Industries Ltd. as a family industrial holding company and today his son, Walter Anthony Junior serves as a Director. Forever hopeful of creating another Gilbey drink empire, Mannin Industries took a stake in Duncan Gilbey & Matheson, Walter Anthony joined the Board and then had his ambitions dashed yet again when the business was sold to the Dutch drinks firm Heineken.

Walter Anthony continued to make connections with the drink trade and Mannin Industries became shareholders in the wine and spirits off licence group, Ellis & Co. of Richmond Ltd. and he served on their Board. This became yet another small company that could not compete and the shareholders sold out to Scottish & Newcastle Breweries Group.

Drink was not his only trade and he built up interests in many activities. He joined the Board of the Isle of Man Steam Packet Company, which provides the main and usually only shipping service between the Isle of Man, the UK and the Republic of Ireland. He became Chairman of Manx Telecom in 1986, following the Manx Government granting a 20 year franchise for the Island's telephone services to British Telecom.

Mannin Industries' interests were not confined to the drink trade, either, as they helped to found and build up a successful Manx Investment Bank, Mannin International Ltd.

Walter Anthony followed his father and grandfather into an involvement in farming. This was through the family company, Gilbey Farms Ltd., at Rosehill, Henley on Thames in Oxfordshire and at Ballacallin Mooar, Marown in the Isle of Man. Like his father, he has found the profits from agriculture elusive and today most of his land is devoted to the great Gilbey interest in horses.

Those farms in Oxfordshire and Marown are the bases for equestrian activities. At Rosehill there are two cross country courses complete with water jumps and three dressage arenas and these are hired out to individuals and local clubs for events. There are also two thriving livery yards.

At Ballacallin in the Isle of Man, his family run Gilbey Grianagh Horses (GGH) Equitation Centre, with a family friend, Sheila Matthews, as partner. The Centre is the Island's leading riding school and venue of many events and clinics and there is also another business, the Grianagh Stud, which breeds riding horses and ponies. There are almost as many horses and ponies at Ballacallin as there used to be at Elsenham in Sir Walter's time. The family of Gilbey continues to be a friend of the horse.

Also at Ballacallin are a collection of some twenty horse drawn carriages, harness, uniforms and accessories and these include the original Gilbey coach and delivery vehicles, which were purchased from IDV following Showerings' bid. Both Walter Anthony and his wife, Jenifer, drive all variations of these carriages and at the Centenary Meet of the Coaching Club at Hampton Court Jenifer was the only lady driver.

Hunting is another of the family's equestrian activities, with Jenifer having been Joint Master of the South Oxfordshire Hounds and Walter Anthony, in 1972, helping Major Bill Stringer form the Windsor Forest Bloodhounds. When he moved to the Isle of Man, Walter Anthony started the Isle of Man Bloodhounds Drag Hunt, of which he is Senior Master.

Like his grandfather, Walter Anthony is very keen on showing horses and he has won prizes at shows that have previously been attended by his ancestors. These include Tring Show, to which his grandfather went when he was a clerk at the auctioneers in Tring in the late 1840s.

Like his forebears, Walter Anthony has been keen to serve, help and develop various equestrian organisations. In the Isle of Man he helped to form and has been Hon. Secretary to the Manx Horse Council. This was the Manx equivalent to the National Horse Association which his father started in 1922 and which after World War II, in 1947, became the British Horse Society of today.

In the breeding field he is helping to put into effect many of the ideas that his grandfather promoted, but could not get accepted around the turn of the century. He has done this largely through being one of the founders of the charity, the British Horse Foundation, which is helping raise the standards of British Non Thoroughbred horse breeding. Its first major achievement was to be the driving force behind the establishment of the British Horse Database, the first national register for horses and ponies in Britain.

He has directly followed his father and grandfather by twice being selected as Chairman of the London Harness Horse Parade, which is the organisation formed by the merger between the London Cart Horse and the London Van Horse Parades.

The Shire Horse Society has been one of Sir Walter's greatest memorials and Walter Anthony has been an active member of it for many years. He served on the Committee reporting on 'Heavy Horse Haulage in the 1980s' which proved conclusively that there were circumstances when heavy horses were as, or more, economic for short radius deliveries than motor vehicles. In 1996 he was appointed Chairman of the Editing Committee, which is responsible for the Stud Book and policies regarding breeding.

The family's associations with horses have certainly been upheld by Walter Anthony, but there are areas where there have been different approaches. Although

76. The demolition of W & A Gilbey Limited's gin distillery at Harlow New Town

his own direct family is close knit, with his three children being involved in various family enterprises, the great family clan has fallen apart. There has been little close contact with other members of the Gilbey family nor with the Blyth, Gold and Grinling families.

Another divergence from family traits is Walter Anthony's keen interest in politics, especially as this has been directed into being a right wing Tory of 'one nation' tradition. This interest was first realised in 1966, when he joined the Berkshire County Council, becoming Chairman of the Council's Finance Committee. A few years later he was selected as Conservative candidate for Ealing Southall, where he fought the spring election of 1974 and was defeated by the Labour candidate. After moving to the Isle of Man he stood for the lower house of the Manx Parliament, the House of Keys, and in 1982 was elected for one of the Manx sheadings (constituencies) Glenfaba. He has held various positions in the Manx Government, including being a member of the Treasury's political team.

These divergences from family trends are counterbalanced by his overriding desire to maintain the various Walter Gilbey interests and the family traditions. The Well House at Elsenham, built by his grandfather in memory of his grandmother, has been maintained by him. From the mid 1960s, he has been chairman of the King's Cottages Alms Houses at Bishop's Stortford and, together with Stanley Lee, the former Financial Controller of IDV, has modernised these houses, which were originally endowed by his grandfather.

The Gilbey Archives have been set up and housed, thanks to Walter Anthony, the Bishop's Stortford & District Local History Society and its curator, Mr Wally Wright. They are to be found in the society's small museum at the entrance to the graveyard where many of the family lie, at Bishop's Stortford Cemetery.

Admiration for the work of his ancestors has been a strong influence on Walter Anthony's life. Representative of the third generation, he has not dissipated the fortune, nor has he let slip any aspect of the Gilbey culture that was within his ability to preserve. He has led an honourable and very active life. Yet his fervent efforts have only had a small impact on the dwindling significance of the name of Gilbey and he has had to recognise that the time when the whole of Britain associated wine and horses with that famous name is slipping further and further into history. Notwithstanding, he remains ready to seize any opportunity that would reverse the trend.

Appendix
The Gilbey Archive at Bishop's Stortford

The depositing of the Sir Walter Gilbey archive at the Bishop's Stortford Local History Museum (BSLHM) presented the opportunity to sort and catalogue the many documents and photographs and to place them in conditions of storage that will ensure their long term survival.

Sir Walter held a keen interest in the history of the family name and kept a notebook on the subject. It would appear that he took the name of Tresham for his son from the third son, born in 1562, of George and Elizabeth Gylby.

Correspondence was freely exchanged between Sir Walter, family members and his many associates, but a close study of the 40 packets of letters has shown that the number available is insufficient for good continuity. Of the more interesting letters, those depicting the experiences that Sir Walter had during the Crimea War are the most descriptive and show his quickness to make the best of any situation.

Some of these letters are on display and demonstrate the practice of script overwritten at right angles on the same page. Another very interesting item from this period is a 'ledger book', which on opening was found to be a portable writing desk with several compartments, including a secret drawer. The drawer contained some Turkish coins and an engraved semi-precious stone.

The history of W&A Gilbey's business, as seen in the publications and documents, provides a particularly outstanding example of dynamic enterprise that would bring a permanent change to the pattern of wine retailing and at the same time yield a handsome profit. There was also a light heartedness between the directors, as evidenced by the spoof prospectuses for share issues of fictitious companies, such as 'The Hargrave Park Pony Company', with a director Walter Filbey and a secretary A. Knuckles.

The collection comprises some 2,500 letters, two letter files of 1000 pages each, twelve scrapbooks of press cuttings, nine ledgers, plus documents, books and catalogues. In addition to the 80 photographs, mostly from the 1930s and mainly of the family, there is a series showing the methods of working with oxen at Chateau Loudenne The archive contains 120 or more reports of visits to the vineyards of France by the directors and these take the form of a daily diary, commenting on the weather, the transport, the food, etc., even to the detail of the inconvenience of broken false teeth.

Sir Walter held collections of snuff-boxes, books, porcelain, bronzes, sporting prints, oils, china dog's heads and furniture. These items were all sold by auction and very little of Sir Walter's personal effects have survived. On display are his spectacles, a gold rimmed pipe in a case, a dress walking stick, Turkish cigarettes and visiting cards. Displays have been mounted to show W&A Gilbey's bottles and labels, a letters patent with the large wax seal of Queen Victoria and some remarkably fine examples of hand-painted artwork that was used to advertise the company's products in society magazines.

Walter Wright, Hon. Curator

Corporate Postscript

'Man must make his opportunity, as oft as find it.'

If the Gilbeys had required a motto, those words written by Francis Bacon in the 16th century, might have been apt. But on that fateful day in 1972, when their personal empire crashed, it would have seemed that there were no more opportunities to make, or find. They could not have foreseen that the firm foundations of their business – already subsumed into IDV a decade previously – would herald more opportunities than they could possibly have imagined.

After the uncertainty and upheavals of the preceding months, most employees experienced a sense of relief following the take-over. Far from being downcast at becoming victims of the largest industrial acquisition to that date, they looked forward to the prospect of a renewed spirit of enterprise. They realised that younger, fresher ideas were needed, that many of the Gilbey brands were in decline and others required a reinvigorating cash injection to breathe new life into them. There was satisfaction, too, in no longer being regarded as suppliers to some 7,000 pubs operated by Watneys. Grand Metropolitan Hotels Ltd, was perceived as a white knight, reuniting them with their international heritage and rescuing the gentlemanly wine and spirit merchants from what they, perhaps somewhat disparagingly, referred to as 'the beerage'.

Ironically, in 1972, when IDV lost its independence and W&A Gilbey suffered its demise, profits were higher than ever. 'Maxie J' soon recognised the potential of IDV and its international brands, separating them from brewing to form a semi-autonomous wines and spirits sector, with the minimum of his board's interference.

In 1972, Grand Metropolitan Hotels Ltd, with a trading profit of just under £37 million, looked very different from the company today in 1997. First established as a hotel company, it had diversified to encompass dairy produce, catering, leisure, casinos, pubs and breweries. Today having divested from hotels, leisure and some 30 different businesses, GrandMet is a multi-product, consumer brands company, specialising solely in food, and drink brands, with a trading profit in excess of £1,000 million.

Looking back at the wider scenario – beyond the boardroom dramas – 1972 saw growth, change and enthusiasm. The UK sales division moved from York Gate in London, to Harlow. 'The Home Trade', as it was called, administering wholesale and retail trades and 700 wines and spirits shops, moved to Vintner House, a new office, warehouse and distribution complex, near the huge Gilbey House production plant.

A wide range of brands was produced in Harlow, including Smirnoff Vodka, bottled around the clock to keep up with demand fuelled by a highly successful advertising campaign. One execution became an icon of the decade; young man wearing a rakishly angled hat, nonchalantly leaning against a lamp post – 'Accountancy was my life until I discovered Smirnoff,' said the message, 'The effect is shattering'. So was the effect on sales. Smirnoff was owned by US company Heublein, and distilled under a licensing agreement negotiated 20 years previously, allowing W&A Gilbey the franchise in the UK and major Commonwealth countries.

There were celebrations in 1972, marking 21 years in business for W&A Gilbey of South Africa, and 85 for Gilbeys of Australia. For Gilbeys New Zealand, a newly constructed distillery was opened, making a total of 33 nations producing Gilbey's Gin, the brand that brought international fame and fortune to the family.

Construction teams were busy in Europe too, completing a modernisation programme in Portugal, for the production of Croft Port, while over the border in Spain, builders enlarged the facilities for Croft Original, IDV's highly successful brand. Over the Atlantic, Gilbey Canada was also expanding. Barely able to keep up with US demand for its Black Velvet Canadian Whisky, the company was constructing a new distillery on 26 acres of prairie in Alberta. To the south, in the USA, Gilbey's Gin and Vodka were produced under license by National Distillers; in 1972 sales reached three million cases. American Brands were agents for a range of W&A Gilbey Scotch whiskies, which also showed good growth. But the star performer was IDV's J&B Rare, the number one Scotch in the USA. Distributed by the Paddington Corporation, a subsidiary of Liggett & Myers, the three million cases shipped that year, gained Justerini & Brooks their first Queen's Award to Industry, for export achievement.

The Gilbeys' import and export agreements were astonishingly entrepreneurial and judicious. A century ago they already had agencies established in every part of the world, including quite remote places. Large quantities of Invalid Port were shipped to Java, and in Bolivia cases bearing the Gilbey name were transported across mountain passes, on the backs of llamas. The purchase of Château Loudenne in 1875, was notable not only as their inaugural overseas acquisition, but also as the first English venture into the world of French viticulture. Within a few years they had opened several strategically positioned overseas subsidiaries, a modus operandi emulated by their competitors, in what, at that time, was an embryonic global industry.

Those activities set a pattern continued into this century. Many excellent friendships and associations were made such as that established in the 1930s with the Italian firm Cinzano, which produced Gilbey's Gin in several Latin American and European countries. Cinzano acted as agents in other parts of the world and the Gilbeys reciprocated, representing them where they lacked distributors. The relationship was to be of great consequence in the future. Another significant agreement took place in 1965 when the intrepid Gilbey export team granted a gin production license to the Palanca family, owners of the largest distillery in the Philippines.

The years following GrandMet's take-over witnessed great changes; if the Gilbeys returned today, they might have difficulty in identifying their own achievements. They would find that the production plant in Harlow, opened in 1963, had closed in 1990; its operations dispersed to sites in Scotland, France, Italy and Spain. The retail shops were sold and the warehousing and distribution facilities outsourced, enabling the UK company to focus on marketing and selling – but Gilbey Vintners sales division still retains its name.

They would, however, note that the Gilbey companies in Canada, Ireland, France, South Africa and Uruguay retain the name, and except in France, still make the gin. Other operations have been disposed of, or renamed. They would be delighted that the associations developed with Cinzano, Paddington and Heublein lasted until, ultimately, in the 1980s, they became an integral part of IDV. In the USA, American Brands produce Gilbey's Gin and Vodka under license, accounting for around 40 per cent of the brand's world sales totalling 2.5 million cases.

They would be particularly impressed with the success in the Philippines. The country's favourite sport is basketball; in the early 1980s the Palancas bought their own team – naming it the 'Gilbey Gins', creating such phenomenal brand awareness that sales have never stopped climbing. A joint venture was formed in 1988 and today the Philippines are the strongest market in the world for Gilbey's Gin, selling well over one million cases a year.

The Gilbeys would probably be amazed at the familiarity of the name in Japan and the other burgeoning markets of Asia. In Thailand, a resurrected version of their Spey Royal Whisky launched recently already has sales heading for a million cases. In India, the name's astonishing success is associated with the image of 'Britishness' and all that it implies in terms of heritage and quality. Well over two million cases of locally produced Indian whisky proudly carry the prestigious Gilbey name.

There are still many links with the name. Every year, at least six million cases of wines and spirits cross the world, each containing twelve bottles proudly displaying the highly respected 'W&A Gilbey' signature. One interesting link is Freddy Hennessy's nephew, George Bull, Chairman of GrandMet. Originally entering the business back in 1957, George Bull has lived through many of the dramas described in this book. Prior to his current position, he was appointed Chief Executive Officer of IDV in 1984, to be succeeded by John McGrath in 1992. The present incumbent, Jack Keenan, became CEO in 1996. He now heads IDV which with the acquisition of Heublein in 1987 is the largest wines and spirits company the world has seen, and, as such, the undisputed global leader. That too reflects links to the Gilbeys, who provided the bedrock for the new IDV business. Formed in 1962, its profits that year were £1.5 million; today, just 35 years later, IDV's profits have increased by £500 million.

The innovative, entrepreneurial style of the Gilbeys, the ability to turn problems into opportunities and their outward looking internationalism, have influenced the business values and aspirations of both IDV and GrandMet. Their belief in quality, customer service, strong branding and the importance attached to helping the community, are all part and parcel of the culture embedded since the earliest days.

There were negatives too, providing salutary lessons for all. In any organisation, in-fighting and disagreements eventually dissipate strength 'united we stand, divided we fall'. Valuable members of the company departed, taking their acumen and expertise straight into the arms of competitors. The caring policy that originally created so much loyalty and pride amongst both employees and the community, was initially lost when take-over mania took possession. But that, to a great extent has been recaptured; in 1996 GrandMet was voted Britain's top company in the field of community affairs.

In hindsight, perhaps the Gilbeys' most profound legacy was the part they played in building what is now a powerful, peculiarly *British* export industry, with the three major players – all British – dominating almost a quarter of the world's international spirit brands. The achievements of the Gilbeys, and the many thousands who worked for them across two centuries, brought the democracy of choice to people's desires, something we all enjoy and take for granted today.

Sitting on the terrace of Château Loudenne, the beautiful estate in Bordeaux, where the family enjoyed parties and made plans George Bull contemplates what he regards as the monument to their foresight; a symbol of heritage, authenticity, innovation and quality.

A rock in the sea of corporate change.

Ann Eastman

11/08197

As this book goes to press, the proposal to merge GrandMet and Guinness is proceeding. This presages once again massive changes including the probable demise of the names of both GrandMet and IDV. Within the newly merged organisation, the Gilbey name, at least in some form, will almost certainly survive. The legacy of the Gilbey family is therefore set to progress far into the new Millennium, continuing to bring enjoyment and smiles to the lips of millions.

Notes and References

Chapter I

1. *In the Days of my Youth*, Sir Walter Gilbey
2. *op. cit.*
3. *op. cit*
4. *op. cit*
5. *op. cit*
6. *op. cit*
7. *op. cit*
8. *op. cit*
9. *Diaries*, Sir Walter Gilbey
10. *op. cit*
11. *op. cit*
12. *op. cit*
13. *op. cit*
14. *op. cit*
15. *op. cit*
16. *op. cit*
17. *op. cit*
18. *op. cit*
19. *op. cit*
20. *op. cit*

Chapter II

1. *In the Days of my Youth*, Sir Walter Gilbey
2. *op. cit*
3. Press cuttings held at the Gilbey Archive, Bishops Stortford Cemetery
4. *ibid.*
5. *ibid.*

Chapter III

1. In the Royal Commission on Whisky, 1908-9, W&A Gilbey were described as: 'the largest distributing business in the U.K.
2. *Diaries*, Sir Walter Gilbey
3. Press cuttings held at the Gilbey Archive, Bishops Stortford Cemetery

Chapter IV

1. *In the Days of my Youth*, Sir Walter Gilbey
2. *House of Gilbey*, Ross Wilson M.A., The Wine & Spirit Trade Record
3. Letters in the Gilbey Archive, Bishops Stortford Cemetery
4. *ibid*
5. *ibid*
6. *ibid*
7. Letters in the Gilbey Archive, Bishops Stortford Cemetery
8. Letters from Sir Walter at Elsenham on 27 October 1905

Chapter V

1. Press cuttings held at the Gilbey Archive, Bishops Stortford Cemetery
2. *ibid.*
3. *ibid.*
4. *Lady's Pictoral*, 28 November 1897
5. Press cuttings held at the Gilbey Archive, Bishops Stortford Cemetery
6. *ibid.*
7. Letter in custody of Diana Gilbey
8. Letter in the Gilbey Archive, Bishops Stortford Cemetery
9. Press cuttings held at the Gilbey Archive, Bishops Stortford Cemetery. Pari Mutuel is Frances version of Britain's Tote. It holds a monopoly over betting on racehorses.
10. Press cuttings held at the Gilbey Archive, Bishops Stortford Cemetery
11. *ibid.*
12. *ibid.*

Chapter VI

1. Interview with the author
2. There are four inches to one hand
3. Press cuttings held at the Gilbey Archive, Bishops Stortford Cemetery
4. *ibid.*

5. *ibid.*
6. *ibid.*
7. *ibid.*

Chapter VII

1. Press cuttings held at the Gilbey Archive, Bishops Stortford Cemetery
2. *ibid.*
3. This was only a short 'blip' in the imports, which might or might not have been a result of the fillip of the formation of the societies. Imports soon began to rise again, although exports kept up a steady increase.
4. Press cuttings held at the Gilbey Archive, Bishops Stortford Cemetery
5. *ibid.*
6. *ibid.*
7. *ibid.*
8. *ibid.*
9. *ibid.*
10. *ibid.*
11. *ibid.*
12. *ibid.*
13. *ibid.*
14. *ibid.*
15. *The Shire Horse*, Keith Chivers
16. Press cuttings held at the Gilbey Archive, Bishops Stortford Cemetery
17. *ibid.*
18. *ibid.*
19. *ibid*

Chapter VIII

1. Sir Walter's will, executed in 1911, had evidently been prepared with the creation of a dynasty in mind. The central freehold of the Elsenham estate, some 632 acres, was entailed for future holders of the baronetcy, commencing with Henry Walter, and the residue, after legacies and bequests in trust to the four daughters totalling £50,000 for each, was then to be divided among the four sons, with the management of the remaining part of the Elsenham estate in their hands as trustees. This was subject to two important provisos. Henry Walter was given the opportunity to purchase 897 acres of the estate near Elsenham at a purchase price of £27,218 from, effectively, himself and his brothers and an option to purchase the contents of the Hall. Under the second proviso Sir Walter's ordinary shares in W&A Gilbey, those with voting rights, were left equally to Henry Walter and Arthur only. This bequest, in addition to the shares already held by them, made the two brothers the largest individual shareholders in the company. It seems Henry Walter was unwilling or unable to exercise the options given him under the will and he must, in view of his family situation, presumably not have wished to live at the Hall. As a consequence, that meant selling the contents.

Chapter IX

1. Letter from Lady Gilbey to Ronnie Gilbey, 8 April 1952
3. A panel set up to regulate corporate deals by public companies.

Index